W9-CZU-726

YALE STUDIES IN ECONOMICS : 3

YALE STUDIES IN ECONOMICS

THE REDISTRIBUTION OF INCOME

IN POSTWAR BRITAIN

A Study of the Effects of the Central Government

Fiscal Program in 1948–49

BY ALLAN MURRAY CARTTER

Assistant Professor of Economics, Duke University

New Haven: **YALE UNIVERSITY PRESS,** *1955*

London: Geoffrey Cumberlege: Oxford University Press

38680

339.2
C 328

Copyright, 1955, by Yale University Press.
Printed in the United States of America by
Vail-Ballou Press, Inc., Binghamton, N. Y.
All rights reserved. This book may not be
reproduced, in whole or in part, in any form
(except by reviewers for the public press),
without written permission from the publishers.
Library of Congress catalog card number: 54-5081

To My Wife

Preface

THE IDEA for this study began forming in my mind shortly after the Labour government took office in Britain in 1945. Since that time it has gradually evolved from a brief exploratory paper written in 1949 to a doctoral dissertation submitted to Yale University in 1952, and finally, after revision, to the present book form. I am indebted to Yale University for the opportunity to spend most of 1950 and 1951 as a Sterling Research Fellow at Cambridge University, gathering material and writing the first draft.

In rewriting the original version I have divided the book into two separate parts in an attempt to make it more compact and readable. Part I is an independent section describing the theoretical problems involved in such a statistical measure, reviewing the findings, and drawing some conclusions in regard to the postwar redistributive program. This first part is intended for the general reader.

Part II is a kind of expanded technical appendix explaining the techniques and data used in arriving at the findings summarized in Part I. The casual reader may wish to ignore Part II, although the statistical conclusions can be better evaluated if one is familiar with the sources of information and the methods adopted in the allocation of particular taxes and expenditures.

The aim of the book is solely to determine the direct income effects of postwar tax and expenditure programs on persons in Britain, grouped by size of income. The desirability of this redistributive program is not discussed, since a statistical study does not seem the proper place to attempt such judgments.

I am indebted to a number of persons for valuable advice and encouragement at various stages in the evolution of this project. Foremost among them is Lloyd G. Reynolds, who has taken a constructive interest in the study since its inception. William Fellner and James Tobin, members of the editorial committee of the Yale Studies in Economics, have also been most generous with their time in reading the manuscript, and I have benefited greatly from their suggestions on both content and style. In addition, I am grateful to Richard Ruggles and Neil Chamberlain of Yale, and Nicholas Kaldor and others at Kings' College, Cambridge, for suggestions and criticism made during the earlier writing and research stages. Duke University

vii

made time and facilities available for the final revision of the manuscript.

The aid and encouragement of my wife are mentioned last only by custom of book prefaces : they have been of immeasurable value from the first scribbled note through galley proofs and indexing.

The editors of *Economica* and *Population Studies* have kindly permitted the use of material previously published in articles by this writer. I would also like to thank the Oxford University Press for permission to use material from Tibor Barna's *The Redistribution of Income in 1937*, and Prentice-Hall for material from Kenyon E. Poole, ed., *Fiscal Policies and the American Economy*. In Chapters 7 and 8 I have adapted materials from these two sources for comparative purposes, the statistical adjustments being explained in the text. The responsibility for the use made of these adapted materials, and for any errors of fact or interpretation in the remainder of the book, rests wholly with me.

No substantial changes have been made in the manuscript since its final revision in the spring of 1953. Therefore, with the exception of a few footnotes added just before publication, I have not drawn on official data or other studies published since 1952.

Duke University   ALLAN M. CARTTER
February, 1954

Contents

Abbreviations

AER	*American Economic Review*
BOxIS	*Bulletin of the Oxford Institute of Statistics*
Cmd.	*Command Papers*
EJ	*The Economic Journal*
Eca	*Economica*
H. C.	House of Commons *Sessional Papers*
JASA	*Journal of the American Statistical Society*
JPE	*Journal of Political Economy*
JRSS	*Journal of the Royal Statistical Society*
NBER	National Bureau of Economic Research
NIESR	National Institute of Economic and Social Research
NTJ	*National Tax Journal*
OxEP	*Oxford Economic Papers*
RCIR	*Report of the Commissioners of Inland Revenue*
RES	*Review of Economic Studies*
REStat	*Review of Economics and Statistics*
TNEC	Temporary National Economic Committee

CHAPTER 1

Introduction

SECURING sufficient revenue and spending wisely have always been among the chief problems of government; and wherever governments have taxed and spent, incomes have been to some extent redistributed. In this century, however, the emphasis of government fiscal activity has been changing, and what in the past has been primarily cause is now becoming effect. For the first time on a large scale modern governments are taxing and spending for the expressed purpose of redistributing incomes. Perhaps the best example of this turnabout in the western world is the experience of Britain.

In the last few years many accounts of the innovations in Britain's economic, political, and social life have appeared in American publications. The diversity of these accounts and the lack of agreement among economists as well as journalists and practical politicians suggest that some Americans believe Britain is already in the hands of socialists (or worse), while others consider the British experiment a positive approach to a "brave new world."

The present study is concerned with the effects of taxation and expenditure programs of the British central government on persons classified by income levels. The author decided to observe the redistribution of income among groups classified by income level rather than by age, occupation, family status, or any of the numerous other possible classifications because he believed the government's efforts have been, primarily directed toward redistributing income from those with relatively high to those with relatively low incomes.

Income redistribution did not originate with Britain's postwar Labour government. In the first half of the twentieth century, predominantly a period of Conservative governments, the tax structure became increasingly progressive, and Britain developed a substantial program of social security and aid to those in poverty. In the present postwar period this has been carried considerably further. There is evident not only an increased emphasis upon redistribution, but a general expansion of governmental influence in the nation's economic affairs.

A war always strains the fiscal ability of a nation. The previously

existing tax structure must usually be greatly extended in the process
of bringing the fighting to a successful conclusion. The revenue-
raising capacity of a country is often permanently increased by such
demands, first because a premium is put on the discovery of new
sources of revenue and the improvement of old, and second because
people are more willing to accept and become partially accustomed
to heavier burdens when their homes or their countrymen are in
danger. Like a not too elastic rubber band, postwar tax revenues
seldom return to their prewar form or amount.

At war's end, the renewal of peaceful pursuits encourages a re-
appraisal of existing institutions and their roles. In the aftermath
of wars in past centuries public activities have usually increased. This
has resulted in the construction of cathedrals and public buildings
and the expansion of public services. During this century it has
chiefly taken the form of rapid extensions of social welfare programs.

The fact that central government fiscal activity is considerably
greater in postwar Britain than it was immediately before the 1939–45
war is quite obvious; one has only to look at the national income
accounts to see that the revenues and expenditures of the government
almost quadrupled in the decade 1938–48. What is not so obvious,
however, despite the claims and criticisms of the Labour government, is the extent to which income was actually redistributed in this
decade.

Many questions come to mind which cannot be answered merely
by general observation. For example, in a typical postwar year who
really gained and lost by the redistribution of income in Britain?
Did more or fewer persons gain than in the years immediately before
the war, and how much? Did the degree of redistribution change
markedly in relation to the level of national income? Was more or
less per pound sterling of tax revenue being redistributed? How
much of this was due to the Labour government's efforts? How
have the middle classes fared, from whom have come much of the
necessary leadership and political support of the postwar Labour
government? It is hoped that this study, which attempts to measure
statistically the redistribution of income through central government
finance in Britain in a typical postwar year, will succeed in answer-
ing such questions.

PREVIOUS INVESTIGATIONS

There has been increasing interest on the part of economists and
statisticians in the investigation of the weight of existing tax struc-
tures on persons of varying incomes. A fairly extensive litera-
ture exists for the experience of Britain, and since the depression of

the 1930's a number of studies have been done of the United States.

One of the earliest of the inquiries in Britain was the 1906 *Report of the Committee on Income Tax,* followed by two official studies during the first World War which brought the material up to date.[1] In the year after the war Lord Samuel, in his presidential address to the Royal Statistical Society, attempted to measure the burden of taxation on prewar and postwar incomes.[2] A comprehensive study was undertaken by the Colwyn Committee in the 1920's,[3] and a number of articles on the distribution of taxation appeared about that time in the *Journal of the Royal Statistical Society.*[4] In 1942 the National Institute of Economic and Social Research published a book comparing the burden of taxes in 1937–38 and 1940–41.[5]

Interest in measuring the burden of taxation in the United States has flourished since the beginning of the depression in the 1930's. Because of the importance of state taxes a number of these studies have been limited to an analysis of the burden of state taxation on the residents of one or a small number of states.[6] Just before the second World War three inquiries appeared, one of which was a TNEC Monograph.[7]

All of the above-mentioned studies considered the government only its role as tax collector, ignoring the effect of government expenditures. The first major attempt to combine both sides of the government account in estimating the redistribution of income in England is found in Colin Clark's *National Income and Outlay* (1937). He compared data for three sets of years in an attempt to find the direction of redistribution which could be attributed to government

1. For an enumeration of similar inquiries prior to 1900, see Robert Jones, The Nature and First Principle of Taxation (London, P. S. King, 1914) pp. 270 ff.

2. "The Taxation of the Various Classes of the People," *JRSS, 82* (1919), 143–82.

3. *Report of the Committee on National Debt and Taxation, Cmd.* 2800 (1927).

4. E.g., D. Caradog Jones, "Pre-war and Post-war Taxation," *JRSS, 90* (1927), 685–718; D. M. Sandral, "The Burden of Taxation on the Various Classes of the Community," *JRSS, 94* (1931), 83–94.

5. G. Findlay Shirras and L. Rostas, *The Burden of British Taxation.* The burden is calculated for income recipients under various family circumstances, and no estimate is made of the total tax burden by income group.

6. E.g. two official studies in New York State, *Report of the N. Y. State Commission for the Revision of the Tax Laws,* Legislative Document No. 77 (1932), 93–100; *Depression Taxes and Economy through Reform of Local Government,* Legislative Document No. 56 (1933), 21–3. See also, Harold M. Groves, *Ability to Pay and the Tax System in Dane County, Wisconsin,* University of Wisconsin, Bureau of Business and Economic Research, Bulletin No. 2 (1930) ; Mabel Newcomer, "Estimate of the Tax Burden on Different Income Classes," *Studies in Current Tax Problems* (1937), pp. 1–52.

7. Helen Tarasov, *Who Pays Taxes?* TNEC, Monograph No. 3 (1941). A revised version, comparing 1937 with 1941, was published under the title "Who Does Pay the Taxes?" *Social Research Supplement, 4* (1942), 1–48. See also, Robert B. Pettengill, "Tax Burden among Income Groups," *AER, 30* (1940), 60–71.

fiscal policy, i.e. whether or not the distribution of income net of taxes and benefits was more or less equal than the original distribution. Only two income groups were used, those above and below £250, and specific amounts of taxes and benefits for each group were not calculated.[8]

During the recent war there were two studies which attempted to allocate all taxes and government expenditures to persons grouped in a series of income ranges, one for the United States and one for the United Kingdom. In the former Charles Stauffacher made a brief survey of the 1930 decade, while the latter was a study by Tibor Barna for 1937.[9] Barna's is by far the most ambitious attempt to date and will be referred to for comparative data many times in later chapters.

Since 1945 three additional studies of income redistribution have appeared, two concerning Britain and one the United States. Dudley Seers, in *The Levelling of Incomes since 1938* (1951), has estimated the differences between pretax and posttax incomes (including transfer incomes) in Britain from 1946 to 1949 for certain income and occupational groups. Findlay Weaver has estimated income redistribution in Britain (including only divisible benefits) for three broad income classes in 1947–49.[10] The third study, made by John H. Adler, compared redistribution in the United States in 1936 and 1946–47.[11]

COMPARISON OF THE PRESENT STUDY WITH OTHERS

The present study is similar in many ways to those which have been mentioned. There are, however, some differences which should be indicated. One difference is that slightly varying methods have been used by successive authors in allocating certain taxes and benefits, and in this study some new methods have been developed which it is hoped may be useful.

A second difference is in scope. Barna, for example, included all

8. In Clark's words, "too many assumptions are involved . . . no more is attempted than to assess the incidence of taxation on the two main classes of the community" (p. 142). He classed the population as either "working class" or "well-to-do," £250 being the dividing line for 1935–36 (and corresponding real incomes for earlier years), since "the national income is divided roughly into two equal halves at the point" (*ibid.*). He assumed that all taxes on business premises, profits taxes, employers' national insurance contributions, and taxes on motor vehicles fell on the "well-to-do." All transfers and government services other than interest on the debt were assumed to fall on the "working classes."

9. Stauffacher, "The Effect of Governmental Expenditures and Tax Withdrawals upon Income Distribution, 1930–1939," *Public Policy, 2* (1941), 232–61; Barna, *The Redistribution of Incomes through Public Finance in 1937* (1945).

10. "Taxation and Redistribution in the United Kingdom," *REStat, 32* (1950), 201–13.

11. "The Fiscal System, the Distribution of Income, and Public Welfare," *Fiscal Policies and the American Economy,* ed. Kenyon E. Poole (New York, Prentice-Hall, Inc., 1951), ch. 8.

levels of government in the United Kingdom, whereas this study is limited to activities of the central government of Great Britain (Northern Ireland excluded). The purpose of excluding local government finance is to focus attention on the fiscal activities of the Labour government in a particular year. Central government activity is determined solely by the majority party in the House of Commons and presumably reflects more accurately the social policy of the governing party. Local finance is more closely bound by tradition and is limited by statute to a single source of tax revenue (local rates) and to specific local services. It is not, therefore, a malleable instrument for income redistribution.[12] Northern Ireland has been excluded because of the high degree of autonomy in local fiscal matters.

The most important difference, however, is the data used. The Stauffacher, Weaver, and Adler studies measured the extent of redistribution in a given period, using tax receipts and funds actually disbursed in that period. In the present study a slightly different approach will be adopted, since the aim is to determine the effectiveness of the Labour government's *legislated program* of a given year in redistributing incomes. At first glance there may seem little divergence between these two approaches, but there is a major difference on the one side of the government account if not on the other. Following the former—for simplicity, call it the "national accounting approach"—one would include as tax revenues current receipts from taxes charged in prior years and exclude taxes charged in the current year but not as yet collected. The importance of this can be seen by the fact, for example, that in 1948–49 70% of profits taxes owed to the government, and nearly 60% of actual receipts, were for prior years. If we use the national accounting approach the sum of taxes received in any fiscal year would probably represent not more than 80% current charges, 20% being charges from previous fiscal years. On the expenditure side of the budget there is not so noticeable a lag. About 5% of all grants available to ministries and other governmental agencies in 1948–49 were balances from prior years. Since some parts of this amount were written off as surplus during the year, not more than about 3% of 1948–49 expenditures arose from grants of prior years.[13]

This study will examine receipts and expenditures *legislated in a*

---

12. Local authority finance is probably moderately redistributive, although the determination of rate incidence is a difficult task. The benefits from local expenditures are probably not considerably greater per capita for high incomes than for low incomes, and the rate burden is probably slightly regressive. See, for example, J. R. Hicks, U. K. Hicks, and C. E. V. Leser, *The Problem of Valuation for Rating* (1944), p. 6.

13. Balances of unissued grants at the end of the fiscal year 1948–49 were much smaller, being about 1% of all grants made during the year, or £35 million.

single fiscal year (call it the "legislative approach"). That is, tax receipts will be those which have been (or are still to be) collected out of incomes subject to tax under the Finance Act of 1948. Expenditures will be those arising from grants made in the current year. In this way the results of a single year's legislative program can be more accurately observed.

In measuring the extent of income redistribution this legislative approach is felt to have a sound basis in theory as well as in practice, especially on the revenue side of the government account. When a tax is levied, it is charged against a certain income earned within a specific period. It makes little difference whether the tax is paid at the beginning or end of the year or five years later—it is a charge against that year's income. Certainly in accounting procedures a rational business firm or individual would deduct the tax—or a provision for the future payment of the tax—from income when it was earned. In a similar way, accruals of income to a business firm would be counted as income in the year in which they accrued. This being so, when measuring the effects of government operations on the economic status of private individuals the relevant measure is individual income in a specific year, allowing for accruals of income and tax liabilities. The national accounting approach might better measure the effect on people's bank accounts, money receipts, and disbursements, but the legislative approach appears to measure more accurately the effect on their annual net incomes.

One common limitation of all such studies of income redistribution is that the level of total income is taken as given and is assumed to be unaffected by the extent or direction of redistribution. Although this may in fact be the case with a particular program of redistribution, it is not necessarily so. It is probable that a substantial redistribution of income does have some effect on the existing and future level of the national income, but since it is not at all clear in postwar Britain in which direction this effect may lie, central government finance is assumed to have had a neutral effect on the size of total income.

Plan of the Book

This book is divided into two parts, Part I being an analysis of the redistribution of income in 1948–49 and Part II being an outsize technical appendix discussing in detail the allocation of particular taxes and expenditures. The first chapter of Part I is particularly important to both sections, for it defines the problem and presents the theoretical tools which will be used in allocating taxes and benefits to income groups. Such a statistical study must be based on a number of assumptions regarding the determination of incidence, and the validity of these assumptions is in turn a limiting factor in evaluating the statistical findings.

In Chapters 3–5 the statistical findings (from Part II) are summarized briefly, and the remaining five chapters of Part I are an analysis of these findings. The changes in income and wealth inequality are discussed, and the redistributive program in 1948–49 is compared with prewar Britain and with prewar and postwar experience in the United States.

In Part II, after a presentation of basic population, income, and wealth data, four chapters are devoted to a detailed discussion of the allocation of particular types of taxes and two chapters to the allocation of transfer incomes and other divisible benefits.

It was hoped that this division of the material into two parts would make it easier for the casual reader to get an indication of what has happened, while at the same time there would be sufficient explanation of the methods and basic data used to satisfy the student and researcher in the field.

PART ONE

CHAPTER 2

The Theory and Method of Measuring the Redistribution of Income

THE SOURCE and destination of government tax revenues and expenditures can be viewed in two different ways. If one were to observe the flow of funds through the government account with an accountant's eye, tax receipts would be recorded in relation to their legal sources, and expenditures in relation to the persons or organizations to whom the Exchequer actually disbursed funds. In this manner a large share of personal income taxes would appear to be paid by corporations, customs duties would be a tax only on the importer, excise duties would bear on the manufacturer or seller of a commodity, etc. Similarly, expenditures other than direct transfers to the private sector would appear to benefit government employees and the firms from whom the government purchased goods and services.

From the taxpayers' view, however, all taxes appear to be borne by people in some capacity, e.g. as wage or salary earners, shareholders, consumers, etc. Similarly, all expenditures are intended to benefit persons either directly or indirectly, being directed toward protecting them from thieves and their homes from fire, educating their children, providing medical services, defending their country, providing communal services, etc. This second view might be called the "benefit" approach, as contrasted with the accountant's "legal" approach.[1]

This second view of the government taxing and spending process will be used here in estimating the redistributive effects of government fiscal policy. In this sense the government redistributes income by paying cash benefits to, or providing services for, members of the community in a certain pattern, in turn raising funds through the taxing process which bears upon members of the community in a different pattern.

Since the patterns of both taxing and spending are not decided upon individually through a price system but are determined by collective decisions, one cannot value the gains and losses subjectively. It is

1. The "legal" approach is similar to Stauffacher's "pure monetary" and Adler's "money flow" concepts. See Stauffacher, p. 236; Adler, pp. 360-1.

impossible to tell whether, on balance, all persons or groups of persons are better or worse off as a result of government fiscal operations. We have no means of determining whether persons acting individually would have desired to purchase the same quantity or pattern of services in the absence of both taxes and government expenditures. The only guides available are the actual amounts given over to the government in taxes and the amounts spent by the government on various goods and services. But while the amount paid in taxes by taxpayers and the receipt of taxes by the government are identical and have a common denominator in pounds, shillings, and pence, on the other side of the budget this is not true. The government spends funds and, except in the case of income transfers, people in turn are the recipients of state-sponsored services. The only way to reduce the expenditure side of the government account to common terms is to value government services at their factor cost, so that we may say that the government spends, for example, £170 million on education and the nation's state-educated children receive £170 million worth of services. Actually these services may be "worth," in terms of subjective satisfactions, more or less than the factor cost of providing them, but there is no other rational manner of placing a monetary value on them. In Stauffacher's words, "The benefit approach is . . . primarily concerned with . . . charging the 'cost' of certain services provided by the government to the group(s) which they are intended to benefit." [2] Presumably a democratic government will carry on only those services which the electorate feels provide subjective benefits at least equal to their factor cost; that is to say only if they provide benefits which appear as great as, or greater than, those obtainable from any alternative use of the funds either publicly or privately. This may be a somewhat naive interpretation of political democracy in action, but as a rough approximation it at least provides a rationale for factor-cost valuation of government services.

If government services are valued at factor cost, the task of determining the redistribution of income is made possible, and the government account may be used as an indication of total income losses (taxes) and total income gains (benefits from government transfers and expenditures on goods and services). When one includes the surplus or deficit [3] the government account always balances, so that by definition the sum of taxes is equal to the sum of benefits. It should be pointed out, however, that this implicitly assumes that the government is neutral toward the level of national

2. P. 236.
3. See p. 49 below for a discussion of the surplus or deficit as a positive or negative benefit.

income.[4] Public finance is here viewed as a diversion of resources from private to public use which does not affect the prices of resources or the value of their output. The national income and its original distribution are taken as given, and the redistribution of income is observed merely as a program for altering the initial distribution of income. In later chapters the validity of these assumptions concerning both the size and original distribution of income will be questioned.

Figure I

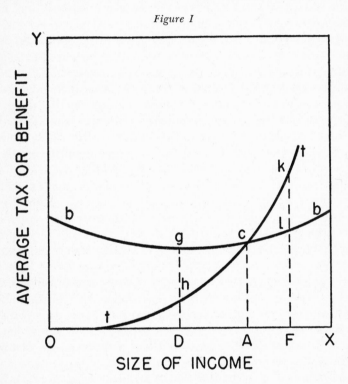

SIZE OF INCOME

The redistribution of income among income groups can be measured by observing the difference between the amount any group contributes in the form of tax revenues to the government and the amount the government in turn spends in the interests of that group. Given a generally progressive system of taxation and an expenditure program which attempts to channel a large share of the state's transfer payments or services to the benefit of the lower income groups,

4. This statement should not be confused with a system of "neutral finance" where each person pays taxes equal to his share in the receipt of government services. Cf. Frederic C. Benham, "Notes on the Pure Theory of Public Finance," *Eca*, n.s., *1* (1934), 436 ff.

there is some level of income at which a taxpayer with an average-sized family just breaks even. Diagrammatically this could be represented similarly to the businessman's breakeven chart, persons with incomes above the breakeven point in this case being net losers and persons below this income level being net gainers in the redistributive process. In Figure I this is indicated by the crossing of the average tax line (*tt*) and average benefit line (*bb*) at point *C*. Persons with incomes less than *OA* would be gainers by the amounts represented by the distance between the two lines; e.g. the average person with an income equal to *OD* would gain an amount equal to *gh*. Those with incomes greater than *OA* would be losers; e.g. taxes exceed benefits by *kl* for an income of *OF*. The statistical problem of attempting to measure the extent of income redistribution lies in finding the average breakeven income and determining the aggregate income gains and losses for persons with incomes below and above this income.

INCIDENCE OF TAXES AND BENEFITS

Whenever a tax is imposed upon one or more members of a community, a series of economic adjustments to that tax is made throughout the community which affect the income positions of many persons not directly subjected to the tax. The total adverse income effects of practically every tax can be expected to be considerably greater than the amount of the original tax, because of the interdependence of personal incomes. For example, a tax of one pound on the income of X will reduce his net income by a pound, and since X, as a result of this income reduction, will probably curtail his expenditures (probably by something less than a pound) the tax will also cause the incomes of those dependent upon his expenditures to be reduced, and so on as the effects dissipate themselves. In Keynesian terms this is the multipler effect of an autonomous change in income, the ratio of the rate of change in total income to the original change (the tax) being determined by marginal propensities to consume.

The traditional treatment of tax incidence found in most works on public finance, however, divides the total adverse income effects of taxation into two classifications. "Incidence" proper, i.e. the direct income effect of a tax (the one pound reduction in X's income), is distinguished from the "effects" of a tax, i.e. the indirect income effects resulting from the expenditure adjustments caused by the incidence of the tax (the reduced income of X's wine merchant arising from X's curtailment of expenditures). This distinction may be useful analytically, but it sometimes results in misunderstandings. For instance, if, as is fairly common, incidence is defined as "the ulti-

mate resting place" or the "final burden" of a tax,[5] it is very misleading. Under such a definition when a one-pound tax is levied, the first
pound of income loss which cannot be compensated for (i.e. shifted)
is called "the final burden," while remaining income losses take on a
mysterious transcendental nature. The distinction between "incidence" and "effects" is purely arbitrary, existing only in economists'
minds.

There is, however, another sense in which the distinction between incidence and effects is meaningful. Even though both are
integral parts of the stream of income adjustments following in the
wake of a tax (or government expenditure), the direct income effects
are usually observable, measurable, and predictable, whereas the indirect effects are not equally susceptible to appraisal. The direct income effects of a tax or expenditure can usually be traced to a specific
person or group of persons, while the indirect effects are so dispersed
and haphazard that this is seldom possible. In this sense incidence
might be defined as the deliberate or foreseeable effects of a tax (expenditure) on individuals, while the "effects," insofar as particular
persons lose or gain, can be said to be largely accidental.

Since the accidental effects of government taxes and expenditures
are not easily measurable, a statistical study of income redistribution
is necessarily limited to the direct income effects of taxes and expenditures. If we were concerned merely with one side of the government account, omitting the indirect effects would be a serious over-
sight. When we are dealing with taxes and expenditures together,
however, the indirect effects, unlike the direct, tend to compensate
each other. For example, if one pound is taken away from X in taxes
and one pound is given to his neighbor Y in, say, the form of a cash
payment from the government, the net indirect effects will probably
be small, since Y will probably expand his expenditures by about the
amount X contracts his. Their patterns of consumption may be dis-
similar, so that some readjustment in the kinds of goods available is
necessitated by this redistribution of income, but the indirect effects
will not substantially affect the relative distribution of income in
the community. It can be said, therefore, that the direct effects of taxes
and expenditures are primarily distributional, whereas the indirect
effects are related primarily to the level of incomes. Whether or not
the national level of income will change as a result of government
fiscal policy will depend upon the over-all balance of the income-

5. Cf. Otto von Mering, *The Shifting and Incidence of Taxation* (Philadelphia,
the Blakiston Co., 1942), pp. 1–5; William R. Green, *The Theory and Practice of
Modern Taxation* (New York, Commerce Clearing House, 1938), p. 32; H. A.
Silverman, *Taxation, Its Incidence and Effects* (London, Macmillan, 1931), pp. 89 ff.

increasing effects of expenditures and the income-decreasing effects of taxes. Contrasting just the direct income effects, however, should indicate the relative changes in the distribution of income caused by public finance (or at least the intentional changes in distribution).[6]

We have attempted to define incidence as the direct income effect, or deliberate effect, of a tax or expenditure. Before the discussion of particular taxes and expenditures, something further needs to be said about the general locale of incidence and the shifting of taxes or benefits. Incidence will be said to have shifted whenever one consciously and successfully takes some action to compensate for the reduction in net income occasioned by the tax (or when similar action is taken which negates the increase in net income occasioned by an expenditure). The term "consciously" should not be taken to mean, however, that the burden which is being shifted is always recognized as a tax.[7] An increase in the excise duties on cigarette lighters, for example, would be seen by the local tobacconist only as an increase in the cost of lighters, cause unknown. However, if, as a result of this cost increase, he raises his prices correspondingly, it can be said that he is consciously attempting to shift the tax burden forward to the consumer.

Tax shifting is a common phenomenon, but in many cases the person assessed is not in a position to shift the burden to a second party. Since no single assumption concerning incidence and shifting

6. A good description of the theoretical problems involved in determining the adjustments occasioned by the imposition of taxes is presented in Richard A. Musgrave and others, "The Distribution of Tax Payments by Income Groups: A Case Study for 1948," *NTJ, 4* (1951), 1–53. The problem of measuring the burden of tax payments by income groups is seen as an attempt to compare the distribution of income in two equilibria, before and after taxes. These writers take to task "most authors employing the time-honored distinction between 'incidence' and 'effects'" (p. 6), pointing out that "what counts is how income positions are changed on balance by the entire tax adjustment" (*ibid.*). They conclude that "if there is any meaningful way in which the end results of the tax adjustments may be divided, it appears to be between changes in the *level* of income before tax, and the changes in the *distribution* of income net of tax" (*ibid.*). After a sophisticated discussion of theoretical problems, they adopt the same time-honored methods of allocating taxes, and conclude, in words sounding like those they have just finished criticizing, that their study "trace[s] the absolute tax yield under the given revenue structure to its resting place by income brackets" (p. 9). In their study, however, as in the present one, an attempt has been made to "lay our cards on the table and give the reader an opportunity to familiarize himself with the underlying . . . procedures and assumptions" (p. 10).

7. Von Mering has taken the view, in criticizing Mayer, that "it is irrelevant whether or not the shifting is intentional," but by intentional he means "conscious of any connection between the change in price and the imposition of the tax" (p. 4). Whether the tax is recognized as such, or seen merely as addition to cost, seems of little importance. For the tax to be shifted it is necessary merely that someone be conscious of the effects of the tax, for otherwise it would be absorbed rather than shifted.

is satisfactory for all taxes and expenditures, it will be necessary to make a number of separate classifications in choosing assumptions for the allocation of taxes and expenditures to income groups.

In the case of direct taxes on personal income and wealth, the traditional assumption that incidence is on the legal payer of the tax seems to be valid. Most people do not have the opportunity to shift directly the burden of the income tax to others, although this may be possible to some extent for those who provide direct consumer services. It is sometimes argued that wage earners may attempt to shift the tax forward to their employers through trade union demands for compensating wage increases. In general, however, it seems unlikely that trade unions are successful in getting wage increases (which they would not otherwise have gotten) to compensate for a tax increase; in reverse it is even more unlikely that a decrease in taxes would make trade unions amenable to a wage decrease or would greatly temper their demands for future increases. In the limiting case (which some persons think may become the general case) of an inflationary period, where wage demands are based largely on cost-of-living arguments, the chances that an increased tax on wage income could be (at least temporarily) shifted to employers may be considerably greater, but even here it is difficult to determine whether the tax itself occasions the wage demand. If the alternative to an increase of taxes on wage incomes were a larger government deficit (or smaller surplus), it could equally well be argued that the alternative would mean higher cost of living and a similar demand for wage increases even in the absence of the additional tax.[8] Despite these possible qualifications, the general unshiftability of personal income taxes appears to be a quite realistic assumption.

Direct taxes on wealth, in the form of death duties, are usually assumed to fall on the deceased. Death duties are an unavoidable tax for owners of estates, and presumably these estate owners make different decisions during their lifetimes on investments, insurance, gifts, etc. than they would in the absence of such a tax. In this sense death duties can be thought of as a deferred annual capital tax.[9] Here,

8. Except for an increase in national insurance contributions, there was no general increase in direct tax rates on wage incomes in Britain from 1941 to 1948. Also, wages remain relatively controlled after the war, so the discussion above is for Britain largely academic. The 10% increase in income taxes in the U. S. following the outbreak of the Korean war, however, may have affected wage demands.

9. Death duties have been described as an annual capital tax rather than an annual tax on capitalized income, because we are interested in determining who contributes the tax revenues received by the government. If the concept of the tax on capitalized income is used, one runs into the difficulty that total taxes on income may conceivably be greater than 100%. For example, the marginal rate of tax on personal income

as with direct taxes on personal income, it seems a reasonable assumption that direct taxes on capital are not shifted to others.

If we turn to taxes on profits, it becomes more difficult to make any single generalization concerning incidence. Economic theory tells us that under perfect conditions profits taxes cannot be shifted by the owners of a company to others. This would be true as long as entrepreneurs actually maximized their profits, because with a flat-rate tax on profits the price and output conditions which maximized total pretax profits would be identical to that which maximized total posttax profits. If the market were also perfectly competitive, there would be no profits in the long run (at least none for the marginal firm), so that the profits tax would have no direct effect on price or output. With imperfect world conditions, however, it seems quite possible that the owners of business concerns may be able to shift at least part of the tax burden either forward to consumers or backward to other agents of production. In almost every case where this actually happens it is due to the fact that business firms do not really maximize short-run profits so precisely as economists sometimes infer. Profits taxes may be partially shifted forward in the form of higher prices if businessmen commonly figure an allowance for profits taxes in estimating their per unit costs, or if the tax discourages restraint when producers could charge more and increase gross profits, or if profits taxes retard long-run business expansion. Profits taxes may also be partially shifted backward to wages if a firm's wage plan is partly based on profit sharing or if a smaller net profit strengthens management's hand or resolve in refusing wage increases. In addition, profits as defined for tax purposes are seldom pure profits in the economist's sense, so that some portion of a profits tax may be properly considered as a cost of production. Apart from (or in addition to) any conscious attempts to shift the burden of a profits tax, it is also possible that further repercussions will directly arise from a reduction in the supply of commodities occasioned by the im-

---

(income tax and surtax combined) reached 97.5% at an income of £20,000 in 1948–49. If this income arose entirely from capital, it is probable that death duties expressed as an annual rate on income would exceed 2½%. It would be absurd, however, to say that combined annual taxes on *income* were greater than 100%, for one would then be better off with a smaller income than with a larger one. As long as taxes on income and taxes on wealth are each separately less than 100%, there must always be a positive income left after taxes; hence when combined they cannot total 100% or more. If death duties are expressed as a tax on capital, rather than capitalized income, this problem does not arise. What is really being said here is that the "burden" of death duties on the future income stream from capital is less than the actual loss of future gross income due to death duties; a 50% reduction in the size of one's estate does not represent a full 50% reduction in one's future income stream under a progressive income tax structure. This means that in effect the government is paying part of every tax by a future loss in receipts from other taxes.

position of the tax, although this would not be included in the incidence of taxes as defined above.[10]

What conclusions regarding taxes on business profits can one reach from the choice of conflicting possibilities? The assumption that this tax falls only on profits is quite certainly not 100% valid, but it is probably more valid than any other single assumption. The study of United States tax payments by income group in 1948 referred to above [11] used six different assumptions, accepting as the "standard case" the assumption that one-third of the profits tax fell on consumers, one-eighth on wage earners, and the remainder, roughly 55%, on profits. For the present study the assumption of 100% incidence on profits will be used, not merely because it is simpler, but because it is felt that the final results will be more nearly accurate for the year under survey. In Britain, unlike the United States in the same period, wage and price controls considerably reduced the possibility of forward and backward shifting. In addition, whatever small proportion of the tax was actually shifted is felt to have been roughly balanced by a similarly small proportion of consumption taxes shifted in the opposite direction, i.e. from consumers to profits.[12] To the extent that the Musgrave "standard assumption" may be more correct than the one chosen here, the distribution of profits taxes given in Chapter 4 understates the incidence of profits taxes on incomes below £500 and overstates the tax on incomes above £1,000.[13]

As for customs and excise taxes, economists seem to be in general agreement that their incidence is primarily on the consumer, although here, too, there is a degree of uncertainty. In the long run, given time enough for industries to adjust to such taxes, the prices of taxed articles will tend to rise by about the amount of the tax as long as the industry is a "constant cost" one (i.e. if the entrance of new firms or exit of old ones does not raise or lower the basic cost structure of the industry). Some particular industries may not come within

10. An attempt to pass a portion of the tax forward to consumers would be a reduction in supply, but if a similar portion were shifted to wages, this would be a reduction in per unit (and marginal) costs. These two forces might therefore counteract each other, leaving supply relatively unchanged.

11. Musgrave. See above, p. 16, n. 6.

12. Musgrave, p. 20, assumes 100% incidence of customs and excise taxes on consumers. See below, n. 13.

13. The author has calculated the profits tax on the Musgrave "standard assumption," the results being almost identical for the £500–1,000 range with the assumption used here. Since, as will be seen in Ch. 6, the redistributive breakeven point falls within this income range, the choice of assumptions makes no difference in determining who gained or lost through income redistribution in 1948–49. The estimated amount of redistribution, however, differs by about 6% under the two assumptions. If the reader prefers the alternative assumption, he may deduct about £78 million from the estimated aggregate net redistribution of income in Ch. 6.

this category, but it can be assumed on balance to be true for industry as a whole. In the short run, however, only if perfect competition exists within product markets can the price of goods to consumers be assumed to rise by the full amount of the tax. However, even under less than perfect competition, in the short run the price of taxed articles will probably be greater than the price in the absence of a tax by the full amount of the tax *at the new adjusted output.* This

Figure II

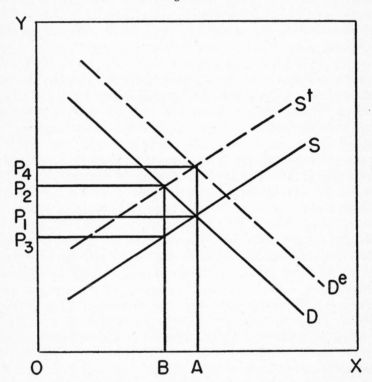

can best be illustrated by a diagram of price determination. If, in Figure II, *D* is the demand curve, *S* the supply curve in the absence of the tax, and S^t supply including the tax, then the tax will raise prices from P^1 to P^2. (This diagram can be viewed as representing a single firm or an industry under imperfect competition in the short run, or an industry under any degree of competition in the long run if increasing costs exist.) The increase in price is less than the full amount of the tax, the tax also causing the output to decrease from *OA* to *OB*. At the new price, however, consumers are paying an amount (equal to the full tax per unit) greater than would be necessary, in the absence of the tax, to encourage producers to maintain the new output OB. That is, P^3 would be sufficient to bring forth OB output, the difference between P^2 and P^3 being the amount of the tax per unit.

In one sense, therefore, consumers always pay the full amount of the tax on any particular output (assuming no changes in elasticity of supply or demand), although in comparison with conditions in the absence of a tax it could also be concluded that the tax is shared by consumers with entrepreneurs through lower profits and with wage earners through diminished employment.

If we were only concerned with the incidence of taxes we could stop at this point, but when one considers the possibility of a compensating expenditure by government the case for 100% incidence on the consumer improves. If, for example, the government placed an excise tax on a single industry and used the entire proceeds to purchase part of the output of that industry, it is likely that demand would increase sufficiently to offset the increase in supply prices occasioned by the tax. In such a case the final output would be about the same as before the tax. This is indicated in Figure II by the demand curve D^e, the resulting output being the original OA, and the new price P^4. The difference between P^1 and P^4 is equal to the amount of the tax, and there is no loss to the producer or wage earner.

It can be concluded, after weighing these possibilities, that a tax without a corresponding expenditure probably tends to raise prices by less than the exact amount of the tax, the actual difference between pretax and posttax prices depending upon relative supply and demand elasticities, degrees of monopoly, the effect of lower profits and wages on consumer effective demand, the stage of production where the tax is levied, and sellers' mark-up policies, etc. Such a tax with a compensating government expenditure is more likely, on balance, to raise prices by about the amount of the tax per unit. The price and output adjustments arising from a general excise tax, however, cannot be assumed the same for every industry, some prices increasing more, some less, than the tax per unit of sales.

It seems most reasonable to assume, therefore, that consumption taxes are wholly shifted to the consumer. This choice is further supported by two limiting cases not mentioned above. In the first, over half of the imports subject to customs duty are bought by Britain in a world market where she represents a small share of the total demand. The supply of these goods within the relevant limits can be assumed as almost perfectly elastic. This would mean, as for constant cost industries above, that prices would be raised by about the full amount of the tax. In the second case, the largest share of goods on which excise taxes are charged were, in 1948–49, still under rationing, and black (or "grey") markets existed. Within relevant ranges the demand for these items was almost perfectly inelastic. Regardless of supply elasticities the tax would tend to increase prices again by the full amount. One hundred per cent incidence on consumers, therefore, seems a close approximation to actual fact. If some small portion is actually shifted to profits rather than to consumers, in the allocation of taxes in Chapter 4 this tends to be counterbalanced by any small portions of the profits tax which are shifted in the reverse direction, from profits to consumers.

The only tax category remaining to be discussed is employee and employer contributions to national insurance. In this case it will be assumed that the tax falls entirely on wages, since even the employers' contribution must be considered as part of the per man wage cost by the employing firm. To account for this, as pointed out in the succeeding chapter, the employers' contribution will be included as part of the income of insured persons, even though it is not represented in their actual wage checks.

The incidence of benefits needs little explanation, for benefits can be broken down into categories matching the division of taxes, and their incidence can be assumed to parallel that of taxes.[14] Thus, transfer incomes and particular services provided for specific persons can be assumed, like direct taxes on personal incomes, to be unshiftable. Subsidy payments can similarly be considered to be the counterpart of excise taxes, the benefits assumed to be wholly shifted to consumers. In some few instances where subsidy payments are made by the government to keep submarginal producers in operation, this assumption may not be valid, but by far the largest part of subsidies are actually paid with the intention of reducing prices to consumers. The remaining government expenditures (which are classified as "indivisible," since they are not intended to benefit specific persons) are assumed unshiftable. Whatever benefit a person may receive from the existence of an orderly governed society is assumed to be not amenable to transference to another.

In reviewing the assumptions concerning the incidence of taxes and benefits which will be used throughout this study, two general classifications can be made:

a) Direct taxes on income and wealth, direct benefits in the form of government transfers of income to persons, and specific services performed for persons will be assumed unshiftable. Incidence will be assumed to be on the person who actually pays the tax or who actually receives the benefit.

14. See pp. 152–4 below for a detailed classification of expenditures.

b) Indirect taxes on goods and services and subsidy payments by government to producers will be assumed wholly shifted to the final consumer. Incidence will be assumed not on the actual payer of the tax or receiver of the subsidy, but on the consumer of the taxed or subsidized article.

Having been told that incidence is an arbitrary measure and that the assumptions on which the statistical findings will rest may be considerably less than 100% valid, the reader is perhaps wondering how useful the resulting estimate of income redistribution may be. When he reads Part II and finds there additional assumptions concerning the allocation of particular taxes and expenditures to income groups, he may be even more dubious. There is, however, a brighter side to the picture. Even though theoreticians, and especially economists, have learned to be suspicious of anything which involves numerous assumptions—because the assumptions involved in describing, say, the actions of a perfectly competitive market, take one successively further away from reality—in a statistical study of the present type two assumptions may actually be better than one, for imperfections in one assumption may be at least partially offset by imperfections in another. This has been suggested above in the allocation of profits and consumption taxes, and it could be equally true that imperfections in the allocation of the sum of taxes to income groups are, by the use of parallel assumptions, canceled on the allocation of the sum of benefits.

There is also another sense in which the danger of imperfect assumptions may be minimized. If we were concerned with the functional distribution of income, that is, allocating taxes and benefits to wages, profits, rents, etc., an assumption which was only 90% correct would be 10% wrong. However, since we are certain that all taxes *ultimately fall on people* in one way or another, when concerned with the personal distribution of income an apparent 10% error may be in fact considerably less. To use a hypothetical example, in allocating employers' national insurance contributions to income groups on the assumption of incidence on wage incomes, 40% is found to fall on the £250–500 income group. If this assumption is invalid and this tax is really shifted entirely to consumers, then we find that about 39% of the tax still falls on the £250–500 income group. This fact minimizes the degree of error, although the danger of misstatement of taxes is particularly great on the very highest and lowest income groups.

In outlining the methods to be used in this study to allocate taxes and benefits, it should be obvious that the statistical findings will be no better than the theoretical foundations on which they rest. The allocations have been made as accurate as possible, based on the assumptions mentioned above and on the existing data. Nothing can be claimed, however, in the way of mathematical precision, and it may be wisest to judge the estimated redistributive gains and losses as indications of relative benefit or loss rather than absolute amounts. As will be pointed out in a later chapter, even with widely varying assumptions the conclusions seem to point to a particular level of income (or a narrow range of income) as the redistributive break-even point, so that the findings may be more correct in determining *who* has gained and lost than *how much*.

A further cautionary note should be added. This study is not intended as a gauge of equity or real welfare, although it is concerned with some of the most important things on which they are based. It is hoped that it may be useful, however, in focusing attention on the over-all programs of taxation and spending. Too often one is tempted to judge a particular tax or expenditure program in vacuo. In this respect it is useful to recall Marshall's comment on taxes:

All onerous taxes and rates must be judged in equity as a whole. Almost every onerous tax taken by itself presses with undue weight on some class or other; but this is of no moment so long as the inequalities of each are compensated by those of others, and variations in the several parts synchronize. If that difficult condition is satisfied, the system may be equitable, though any one part of it regarded alone would be inequitable.[15]

Only by analyzing the burden of the aggregate tax program—and the same may be said of expenditure programs—can the relative merits of various taxes at the margin be adequately weighed.

Before leaving the discussion of methodology, the manner in which the redistribution of income will be estimated can be stated in more precise terms. The aim is to measure the degree to which the incomes of economic units grouped by size of income were affected by the revenue-raising and spending activities of the central government of Great Britain in 1948–49. The "economic unit" is the economic family *as defined for tax purposes*. Under this definition any married couple, or single person over 16, with an income exceeding £120, or such persons with incomes below £120 if not claimed as dependents by other tax families, is a basic family unit. Children and adults at least partially dependent upon others, with incomes of less than £120, are classified as dependents in these tax families.[16]

The term "income" when used in reference to family units refers to actual money and income-in-kind received from outside the fam-

15. "Memorandum on the Classification and Incidence of Imperial and Local Taxes" (1897), *Official Papers of Alfred Marshall* (London, Macmillan, 1926), p. 337. Cf. his *Principles of Economics* (8th ed. New York, 1948), p. 802.
16. See p. 28 below for a further discussion of the composition of these economic units.

ily,[17] and may include payments for factor services plus payments received from the government without the performance of any productive service (i.e. transfer incomes). Funds, goods, or services received from other sources are not included as income—e.g. intrafamily payments, gifts, capital gains, lottery winnings, etc. Income is further classified in the following chapter by type of receipt.[18]

The redistribution of income will be estimated by allocating taxes and benefits to income groups, so that the original income received by each group can be compared to its final income net of taxes and benefits (which will be called "consumer income"). The difference between the original income and consumer income for any group (or alternatively, between the total taxes and total benefits of that group) will be referred to as the redistributive gain or loss. Summing up the gains and losses of all income groups is not meaningful, since it results in a solitary zero (i.e. redistributive gains by low income groups equal losses by high income groups). Therefore, when the term "aggregate net redistribution" is used, it is taken to mean the sum of all gains, or alternatively the sum of all losses. For example, if it was found that one pound was redistributed from high to low income groups, the sum of gains and losses would be zero, but the aggregate net redistribution would be one pound.

SUMMARY

This chapter has sought to make explicit the basic assumptions of incidence. It has been assumed that all direct taxes are really paid by the legal payer of the tax and that all indirect taxes are shifted to consumers. Similarly, government expenditures in the form of specific services or transfer incomes have been assumed to benefit the receivers of those services or incomes by the factor cost to government of providing them. Expenditures on subsidies are assumed to be shifted forward to benefit consumers, while the remaining indivisible expenditures are assumed untransferable.

Since a study of this nature lies within the realm which Keynes described as "the black arts of inductive economics" and is dependent upon "the shifting sands of economic statistics," it can make no claims to precise accuracy. Given the same basic data, another would no doubt have handled some of it differently and have obtained different results on particular aspects of the measure of redistribution, although it is hoped that his final results would not have differed substantially.

17. In some cases where there is a family business, income-in-kind originating within the family is counted as income. The most important example of this is the value of produce consumed by small farmers, where members of the family are also farm laborers.

18. See p. 32.

CHAPTER 3

The Distribution of Income and Wealth, and the Government Account

BEFORE an attempt is made to allocate taxes and expenditures, it is necessary to group the population by income and wealth classes and to investigate the nature of the government account in 1948–49. This basic data will be presented briefly in the present chapter. The way in which the distribution of income and wealth has been estimated and a more detailed breakdown of the government account can be found in Chapter 11 (Part II).

POPULATION

The population of Great Britain in December, 1948, was approximately 48,890,800. Of this number 52.8% were female and 47.2% were male. By age group the population was divided as follows:

Under 16	11,537,000	23.6%
16–65	32,078,800	65.6%
Over 65	5,275,000	10.8%

The total working population was estimated at 23,185,000, 69.3% being male;[1] about 3½% of this number were in the armed forces, and 1½% were unemployed at the end of 1948, leaving a civilian population actually at work of 22 million.

The Inland Revenue report for 1948–49 classified tax returns by income range. It also, for the first time since 1939, classified returns by family classification.[2] From these data, allowing for the exclusion of Northern Ireland,[3] the distribution of persons by income tax family above the exemption limit can be estimated. Table 1 shows this distribution. There are 45,092,800 persons, or 92.2% of the population, in income groups above the income tax exemption limit

1. *Report of the Ministry of Labour and National Service, 1948–49, Cmd.* 8017 (1950), p. 47.
2. See *RCIR, 1949, Cmd.* 8052 (1950), tables 85, 86.
3. No. Ireland incomes above £135 were 1.8% of the total number in the U. K. In Table 1 the number of persons in each income group has been reduced proportionately.

TABLE I

Classification of Income (before Tax) by Family Circumstances, Great Britain, 1948–49

Income Range (In Pounds)	No. of Incomes	No. of Wives	No. of Families With: 1 Child	2 Children	3 Children	4 Children	Total Children	No. of Dependents	Total No. of Persons
	1	2	3	4	5	6	7	8	9
Under 135	(2,793)	(462)	(238)	(38)	(12)	(5)	(370)	(173)	(3,798)
135–250	8,943.0	2,953.0	1,279.0	525.0	233.0	117.0	3,496.0	1,303.0	16,695.0
250–500	8,417.0	5,136.0	1,864.0	840.0	419.0	202.0	5,609.0	1,636.0	20,798.0
500–750	1,658.0	1,092.0	323.0	170.0	89.0	45.0	1,110.0	278.0	4,138.0
750–1,000	583.0	414.0	111.0	65.0	34.0	17.0	411.0	88.0	1,496.0
1,000–2,000	532.0	403.0	107.0	65.0	33.0	16.5	402.0	77.0	1,414.0
2,000–3,000	110.7	86.0	20.0	13.0	6.6	3.0	77.8	16.2	290.7
3,000–5,000	63.5	50.0	11.4	6.9	3.8	1.9	44.2	9.1	166.8
5,000–10,000	30.1	23.2	3.6	2.0	1.2	.6	13.6	3.8	70.7
10,000–20,000	8.4	6.4	.9	.5	.2	—	2.5	1.2	18.5
20,000 and above	2.3	1.7	.2	.2	.1	—	.9	.2	5.1
	23,141.0	10,627.3	3,958.1	1,725.6	831.9	408.0	11,537.0	3,585.5	48,890.8

(£135). The remaining 3¾ million persons in families not liable to income tax are also shown in the table in parentheses on the first line, "Under £135." The method by which the composition of this group has been estimated is explained in Chapter 11.

Column 1 of Table 1 lists the number of persons filing returns with the Inland Revenue. Husband and wife, if filing a joint return, are counted as a single income.[4] Column 2 shows the number of wives in each income group, that is, the number of married persons filing returns. Of those filing tax returns just 50% were married persons.

Columns 3 to 6 show the number of families with different numbers of children. The Inland Revenue has estimated this distribution primarily from the prewar income census, adjusted for postwar conditions by the sampling of recent returns. There were some families claiming more than four children as dependents, but the number was so small that the Inland Revenue, rather than making a separate classification, included them as families of four. For the work in later chapters it is only necessary to know the total number of children and the number of families who have more than one child; hence these Inland Revenue figures are sufficient.

Column 8 of Table 1 lists the number of other adult dependents claimed for tax purposes. Most of these dependents were close relatives of the income recipients, but some few were housekeepers.

In column 9 the total number of persons in each income group is given, and it is seen that the bulk of the population (about 77%) was grouped in the two income ranges between the incomes of £135 and £500.

From a statistical point of view it would be desirable if these groups could be further broken down into narrower income ranges, but unfortunately the sources of published data are not adequate for this.

Who are the people making up the various income groups in Table 1? Without attempting to attach name tags to specific income classifications, it may be useful to indicate generally the types most commonly found in four broad income classifications.

Above £2,000 was a group of relatively well-to-do persons comprising about 1½% of the population in 1948–49. For the most part they were high-salaried executives, successful professional people, and persons living largely on income from capital. The average person in this group possessed capital worth about £40,000, although income from investments accounted for only 40% of his total income.

Between £500 and £2,000 was a very heterogeneous group making

4. Separate returns could be filed if either husband or wife made application during the first six months of the calendar year, but the total amount of the tax was not reduced by separate returns.

up roughly 15% of the population. Included in this group were many independent tradesmen, civil servants, people in professional occupations, most white-collar salary earners, and some leisured persons. The average person in this group possessed about £3,700 accumulated savings, and 85% of his income was earned.

Most of the adult, fully employed, wage earners came within the income limits of £200 to £500. The average industrial wage in 1948–49 was approximately £320, and it is probable that about 75% of industrial wage earners received between £250 and £400. Extending the limits to £200 and £500 would require the inclusion of most highly skilled workmen, foremen, clerical workers, sales clerks, many tradesmen, and most agricultural laborers. About 65% of the population fell within this income range in 1948–49, and over 90% of income for this group was earned.

The remaining 18% of the population, with incomes not exceeding £200, are difficult to classify. This group consisted largely of young or unskilled workers, others unemployed for a substantial part of the year, transient (largely agricultural) laborers, Britain's gypsy population, a majority of enlisted personnel in the armed forces, and many retired persons and others living on small accumulations of capital.[5] Some of the persons in the last two categories and a number of young workers still living at home perhaps should not really be classed as having low incomes, but about three-fourths of the approximately 9 million persons in this group depended solely upon their incomes for support. It is indicated in Table 1, however, that the average-sized income family for persons under the tax exemption limit (£135) was 1.35, and only 1.87 in the £135–250 range. The majority of persons in this lowest income group, therefore, were single persons rather than family supporters.[6]

This division of persons into four broad income classes is at best a generalization, but it may serve to indicate the kinds of persons found in these ranges. It will be seen in later chapters that the dividing line between those who lost and those who gained by the redistribution of income was at such a level that nearly all wage earners registered net gains, while all well-to-do persons and a majority of those in the middle £500–2,000 group were net losers in 1948–49.

One point should be emphasized, however, in speaking of income classifications: the income levels in Table 1, which will be used

5. Persons living on gifts from family or friends who had slightly more than £120 personal income would also be included in this group, as would others living on the proceeds of casual or windfall receipts, legacies, maturities of insurance policies, etc., which were tax exempt.

6. In Chapter 11 a more detailed estimate is made of the family classification of persons in the lowest income group. See pp. 127–30, below.

throughout, are determined by *income subject to tax*. It will be seen later in this chapter that total personal incomes for some groups average more than the upper income limit of the grade in which they are placed. For example, a man who earned £225 in employment during the year but who received in addition £25 unemployment compensation, £50 from a war disablement pension, and possibly additional amounts for sickness benefit, wife's maternal care, etc. might have a total personal income above £300. However, he would still be placed in the £135–250 income group because his taxable income was only £225. Since there is no accurate method of determining the distribution of income by size classification other than by using income tax data, this nomenclature has been retained. As an alternative the income grades in Table 1 could have been labeled, A, B, C, etc., but it was felt that this would be even more confusing than classification by tax liability. The incomes used in describing the low income, wage-earning, middle income, and well-to-do groups have been incomes as defined for tax purposes.

DISTRIBUTION OF INCOME

The national income of Great Britain for the fiscal year April 6, 1948, to April 5, 1949, was £9,855 million. National income by distributive shares is shown in Table 2.[7]

TABLE 2

Composite National Income, 1948–49

ITEM	(IN MILLION POUNDS)
Wages	3,996
Salaries	2,177
Pay and allowances of the armed forces	244
Employers' national insurance contribution	171
Professional earnings	159
Income from farming	274
Profits of sole traders and partnerships	782
Trading profits of companies and public enterprises	1,512
Other public income	78
Rent of land and buildings	462
National income	9,855

The national income is a useful aggregate for social accounting purposes, but there are two other basic classifications of income which

7. The National income shown in Table 2 is a composite figure representing income which was subject to tax under the Finance Act of 1948. Professional earnings and profits, which are taxed in the year following the period earned, are 1947–48 figures. For a full description of the way in which Table 1 was constructed, see Ch. 11 below.

will be most valuable here. One is total income received by persons in return for productive services (e.g. in the form of wages and salaries, rents, interest, and profits), and the other is total income received from all sources, whether technically productive or not. Both of these classifications differ from national income, as will be shown below. It will also be useful to distinguish between income actually received in cash (or in kind) and income which can be credited to persons on the basis of ownership claims even though it is not actually received. Income which is actually received will be referred to here as *personal income,* and personal income plus income which can be imputed to persons although not actually received will be called *private income.* This imputed income will be designated *nonpersonal income.* When these three terms are used, they will refer to total income received (directly or by imputation), whether in return for productive services or not.

The first of the two classifications mentioned above, income from productive services, will be called *factor income.* This in turn can be broken down into *personal factor income* and *private factor income,* the difference between these two being *nonpersonal income* (e.g. undistributed company profits).

Before illustrating the relationship of these aggregates to national income, two additional items should be defined. *Public income* is taken to mean the net profit of charitable organizations and trading profits of government enterprises, and *transfers* refers to government payments to private persons without a corresponding service being performed (e.g. payments for social insurance benefits, postwar tax credits, family allowances, etc.).

With these items defined, the following equivalents can be illustrated: [8]

Private income = national income + transfers + interest on national debt — public income.

Private factor income = national income + interest on national debt — public income.

Personal income = national income + transfers + interest on national debt — public income — nonpersonal income.

Personal factor income = national income + interest on national debt — public income — nonpersonal income.

8. It should be pointed out that interest on the national debt is often classed as a transfer in social accounting but here it is included as factor income. From the point of view of public finance loans to the government are not necessarily "productive" (e.g. if such loans go to cover a deficit) but from the point of view of an individual faced with a variety of investment choices, interest on government securities is a definite payment received for the contribution of a productive resource, regardless of the use which government makes of the funds.

More simply, the four main aggregates can be related directly to one another:

Private income = transfers + private factor income
Private factor income = nonpersonal income + personal factor income
Personal factor income = transfers + personal income
Personal income = private income — nonpersonal income

In Table 3 the distributions of these four major income aggregates are given by income grades. The manner in which they have been determined is explained in detail in Chapter 11.

TABLE 3

Distribution of Income in Great Britain, 1948–49
(In Million Pounds)

Income Range (In Pounds)	Personal Factor Income	Personal Income	Private Factor Income	Private Income
Under 135	333.4	493.7	362.3	522.6
135–250	1,916.2	2,239.6	2,077.4	2,400.8
250–500	3,195.7	3,390.6	3,446.6	3,641.5
500–750	1,113.8	1,134.3	1,251.2	1,271.7
750–1,000	564.1	571.8	638.1	645.8
1,000–2,000	780.3	787.0	947.9	954.6
2,000–3,000	295.6	297.2	409.9	411.5
3,000–5,000	265.4	266.3	397.9	398.8
5,000–10,000	216.4	216.8	362.2	362.6
10,000–20,000	121.7	121.8	223.7	223.8
20,000 and above	88.1	88.1	216.9	216.9
Totals	8,890.7	9,607.2	10,334.1	11,050.6

DISTRIBUTION OF WEALTH

The total value of capital in private hands in 1948–49 is estimated to have been approximately £29,900 million.[9] This figure has been estimated by using the "estate method," that is, using the number and value of estates becoming liable to death duties in any year as a random sample of living persons owning capital. The method, and the Inland Revenue data used for the estimate, are explained more fully in Chapter 11.

9. Private capital is the net monetary value of all personal goods plus claims against business and government. Total private capital exceeds the value of the nation's physical assets by the inclusion of the value of insurance policies, the government debt, etc.

In Table 4 the distribution of private capital by size of holding is given. To allocate taxes on capital to income groups, however, it is also necessary to know the distribution of private capital among income groups.

TABLE 4

Distribution of Private Capital, by Size of Holding

SIZE OF HOLDING (IN THOUSAND POUNDS)	NUMBER OF HOLDINGS	CAPITAL VALUE (IN MILLION POUNDS)
Under .1	19,632,655	883
.1–.5	6,571,430	1,928
.5–1	1,877,000	1,551
1–2	1,203,700	1,481
2–5	1,184,900	4,126
5–10	510,240	3,854
10–15	188,850	2,448
15–20	96,290	1,745
20–25	53,205	1,260
25–50	98,090	3,504
50–100	38,610	2,725
100–200	12,706	1,750
200–300	3,184	754
300–500	1,735	653
500 and above	1,193	1,245
	31,473,798	29,907

To find this distribution a new method has been developed, based on recent information published in the Inland Revenue reports. The method is outlined in the latter part of Chapter 11,[10] but the results are summarized in Table 5, giving capital holdings by income group.[11]

CENTRAL GOVERNMENT ACCOUNT

Now that population, income, and wealth have been classified by income groups and before turning to the allocation of taxes and benefits, a brief picture of the over-all government account in 1948–49 should be given. This account will differ from the usual government

10. See also the author's "A New Method of Relating British Capital Ownership and Estate Duty Liability to Income Groups," *Eca, 20* (1953), 247–58.

11. The estimate of capital in Table 4 is based on death duty statistics of a four-year period, 1946–50. It was felt that the death duty data for a single year might be atypical of the postwar period, giving a mistaken impression of the amount and relative distribution of private capital. Similarly, capital has been allocated to income groups in Table 5 on the basis of information concerning investment incomes of a two-year period, 1947–49, to lessen, as far as possible, distortion which might arise from any unusual returns of a single year.

account, as given in the national income White Papers, in two respects. First, the account of the national insurance funds will be combined with the regular central government account because even though technically the former is an extrabudgetary account, its operation will be considered here as part of the central government's fiscal program for redistributing income. Second, the income side of the government account will consist of the total expected yield of taxes imposed under the Finance Act of 1948, rather than actual receipts in the fiscal year, and expenditures will be the sum of grants issued during the fiscal year plus the amount by which surplus balances at the end of the fiscal year exceeded those at the beginning of the year. After these two adjustments the government account will indicate the fiscal operations of the central government arising from legislation of a single year, 1948–49.

TABLE 5

Distribution of Private Capital, by Income Groups

INCOME RANGE (IN POUNDS)	TOTAL PRIVATE CAPITAL (IN MILLION POUNDS)
Under 135	523
135–250	2,420
250–500	8,197
500–750	4,877
750–1,000	1,978
1,000–2,000	3,493
2,000–3,000	1,780
3,000–5,000	2,096
5,000–10,000	2,012
10,000–20,000	1,217
20,000 and above	1,314
Total private capital	29,907

In Table 6 the central government combined account is summarized. On the receipts side of the account, revenues are indicated by their general sources, and on the other side, expenditures are classified by the manner in which they will be allocated to income groups. A more detailed breakdown of taxes and expenditures is given in Chapter 11, below.

About 40% of government expenditures are divisible, that is they can be allocated to particular income groups with a fairly high degree of accuracy. These are transfers (payments made to private persons without a corresponding service being performed) and other divisible expenditures (on health, housing, education, subsidies on consumer goods, etc.). Indivisible expenditures are for the general operations of government, including national defense. Debt charges and the combined surpluses have been included as indivisible items, this classification being explained more fully in Chapter 5, below.

TABLE 6

Combined Government Account, 1948–49
(In Million Pounds)

REVENUES		EXPENDITURES	
Direct Taxes on Income		Transfers to Private Accounts	
Income tax	1,317.1	Transfer incomes	665.0
Surtax	126.9	Other Divisible Expenditures	
Profits tax	274.4	Goods and services	549.6
Direct Taxes on Capital		Subsidies	460.3
Death duties	180.9	Indivisible Items	
Special contribution	112.2	Goods and services †	1,323.3
Indirect Taxes		Interest on debt ‡	500.0
Customs and excise *	1,513.3	Surplus	574.9
Other indirect taxes *	170.3		
Other Taxes		Total expenditure	4,073.1
National insurance			
contribution	378.0		
Total revenue	4,073.1		

* About £50 million of revenues which are technically Customs and Excise duties have been classified as other indirect taxes. See Chapter 14 for an enumeration of this amount.

† £24 million government income from property has been deducted from indivisible goods and services, the figure listed in Table 6 being net expenditures on these indivisible items.

‡ Total debt charges were almost £520 million, but the excess over £500 million was met from receipts under various acts, e.g. Local Authority Loan Act (1945), Housing Act (1944), Coal Industry Nationalization Act (1946), etc. See *Finance Accounts of the United Kingdom for the Financial Year 1948–49, H. C.* 189 (1949), pp. 30–1.

SUMMARY

In this chapter the population has been arranged by tax families in a series of income grades, and the distribution of income and capital in 1948–49 has been estimated. It should be emphasized again that throughout the rest of this study the labeling of income groups is by income assessed to income tax. Thus, especially in the lower income ranges, the total income, personal and nonpersonal, of some individuals in each of the income groups may actually exceed the upper limit of the particular range in which they have been placed. For example, the average private income of persons in the £135–250 grade is about £270, although the average income subject to tax was only £200. The difference is accounted for by imputed nonpersonal income (undistributed corporate profits) and tax-exempt incomes (chiefly transfers), received by the £135–250 group.

In the latter part of this chapter the government revenue and expenditure account has been presented. Further statistical details concerning population, income, wealth, and the government account are given in Part II, Chapter 11.

The necessary basic data has now been summarized. The next two chapters will estimate the allocation of taxes and expenditures in 1948–49 by income group. The statistical findings will be summarized in Chapter 6.

CHAPTER 4

The Distribution of Taxes

TAX LIABILITIES imposed under the Finance Act of 1948 totaled £4,073 million. These liabilities can be classified by the manner in which they bear on persons, i.e. direct taxes on income, direct taxes on capital, and indirect taxes. Each of these major classifications will be discussed separately, the over-all distribution of taxes being summarized in Table 12 at the end of the chapter.

DIRECT TAXES ON INCOME

Direct taxes on income in 1948–49 yielded approximately £2,100 million, or about 51½% of total government tax revenue. There were four major types of direct taxes on income: income tax, surtax, profits tax, and national insurance contributions. The last of these was a compulsory insurance premium, but it will be simplest to include it here.

The British income tax is a standard rate of tax (9s. on the pound, or 45%, in 1948–49), which is made progressive in the lower income ranges by reduced rates and the operation of certain reliefs and allowances, and in the upper income ranges (above £2,000) by a progressive surtax. The income tax is charged on all private income, including withheld corporate profits, while the surtax is limited to personal income actually received.[1]

The effective rate of tax on personal income, i.e. the average rate of income tax and surtax combined, is progressive through all ranges of income, approaching a maximum marginal effective rate of 19s. 6d. (97.5%). Figure III, on semilog scales, shows the marginal and average rate of tax on personal income for married persons without children, assuming 100% earned income. The Inland Revenue has estimated that there were 20.4 million individuals with incomes above the exemption limit (£135) in 1948–49, 5.9 million being relieved from tax due to reliefs and allowances.[2]

---

1. Certain types of organizations were exempt from the income tax, or paid only at reduced rates. (See p. 160 below for further discussion.) The income tax is charged on current income, while the surtax is charged on income earned in the previous fiscal year. (See p. 158.)
2. *Cmd.* 8052, table 22.

In columns 3 and 4 of Table 7, the estimated distribution of income tax and surtax on personal incomes is shown, the total yields being £932.6 million and £126.9 million respectively. In columns 1 and 2 of Table 8, these amounts are shown as percentages of personal income for each income group.

Figure III. Marginal and average rates of income tax and surtax combined, 1948–49.

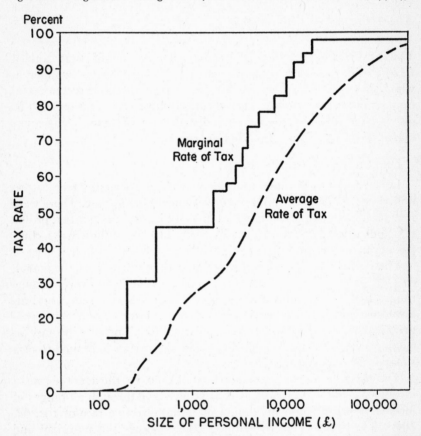

Before July 5, 1948, contributions to national insurance were compulsory only for employed persons earning not more than £420, under the unemployment, national health insurance, and contributory pensions schemes. Contributions for the first quarter of the 1948–49 fiscal year, therefore, have been allocated on the basis of the number of income earners in the three lowest income groups. After July 5 the new national insurance acts went into effect, making insurance compulsory for all employed, self-employed, and unoccupied persons (with the exception of full-time housewives). Contributions for the last

three quarters of the fiscal year have therefore been allocated in proportion to the number of income earners in each income group. Although contributions were slightly higher for self-employed and unoccupied persons, who presumably were chiefly in the upper income
groups, more wives of persons in the lower income grades can be
assumed to have made contributions. The average contribution per
tax family, therefore, has been assumed equal for all income ranges.
The estimated distribution of national insurance contributions is
shown in column 5 of Table 7 in pounds, and in column 3 of Table 8
as a percentage of personal income.[3]

TABLE 7

*Distribution of Direct Taxes on Personal Income,
and Determination of Disposable Income
(In Million Pounds)*

INCOME RANGE (IN POUNDS)	No. OF INCOMES 1	PER- SONAL INCOME 2	IN- COME TAX 3	SURTAX 4	NATION- AL INSUR- ANCE CON- TRIBUTION 5	TOTAL TAXES 6	DIS- POSABLE INCOME 7
Under 135	2,793.0	493.7	—	—	29.0	29.0	464.7
135–250	8,943.0	2,239.6	29.64	—	151.0	180.64	2,058.96
250–500	8,417.0	3,390.6	147.52	—	148.0	295.52	3,095.08
500–750	1,658.0	1,134.3	124.43	—	29.0	153.43	980.87
750–1,000	583.0	571.8	105.74	—	10.4	116.14	455.66
1,000–2,000	532.0	787.0	185.95	—	8.0	193.95	593.05
2,000–3,000	110.7	297.2	86.05	6.58	1.6	94.23	202.97
3,000–5,000	63.5	266.3	87.94	18.20	.6	106.74	159.56
5,000–10,000	30.1	216.8	81.33	33.36	.3	114.99	101.81
10,000–20,000	8.4	121.8	47.36	32.58	.1	80.04	41.76
20,000 and above	2.3	88.1	36.64	36.20	—	72.84	15.26
	23,141.0	9,607.2	932.60	126.92	378.0	1,437.52	8,169.68

Adding together income taxes on personal income, surtaxes, and
national insurance contributions, we have a total of £1,437.5 million
unavoidable taxes on personal income as shown in column 6 of Table 7.
Column 7 indicates disposable income remaining after the deduction
of the sum of unavoidable taxes from personal income for each income
group. In Table 8, column 5, disposable income is also shown as a percentage of personal income for each income group. Even though the

3. In the White Paper *National Income and Expenditure of the United Kingdom,
1946 to 1950,* Cmd. 8203 (1951) employers' national insurance contributions were
for the first time treated as part of the national income and therefore as a direct tax
on income. In this study the employers' contribution is assumed to be part of the wage
income of employed persons, included in personal income in Ch. 3. The total contribution of both employees and employers is therefore deducted here as a direct tax on
personal income. See also p. 159, below.

national insurance contribution was regressive, income and surtaxes were sufficiently progressive to make the combined effect of these un-avoidable taxes progressive through all income grades, ranging from 5.9% for the lowest income group to 82.8% for incomes above £20,000. The average disposable income was 85% of original personal income, and all income groups above £750 lost a larger percentage of their incomes than the average loss in unavoidable personal taxes.

TABLE 8

Direct Taxes on Personal Income and Disposable Income as Percentages of Total Personal Income
(In Percentages)

INCOME RANGE (IN POUNDS)	INCOME TAX	SURTAX	NATIONAL INSURANCE CONTRIBUTION	ALL TAXES	DISPOSABLE INCOME AS PERCENTAGE OF PERSONAL INCOME
	1	2	3	4	5
Under 135	—	—	5.87	5.87	94.13
135–250	1.33	—	6.74	8.07	91.93
250–500	4.35	—	4.37	8.72	91.28
500–750	10.97	—	2.57	13.54	86.46
750–1,000	18.49	—	1.82	20.31	79.69
1,000–2,000	23.62	—	1.02	24.64	75.44
2,000–3,000	28.95	2.90	.53	32.38	67.62
3,000–5,000	33.06	6.84	.22	40.12	59.88
5,000–10,000	37.49	15.39	.14	53.02	46.98
10,000–20,000	38.86	26.76	.08	65.70	34.30
20,000 and above	41.70	41.09	—	82.79	17.21
Average	9.71	1.32	3.94	14.97	85.03

In addition to income tax on personal income, an estimated £384.5 million in income tax was charged on the undistributed profits of corporations and on the incomes of insurance companies and societies.[4] This amount can be imputed to persons on the basis of their possession of shares, insurance policies, and interests in societies. Indices showing the relative distribution of corporate holdings, insurance policies, etc. are developed in Chapter 12, and on the basis of these this portion

4. Societies listed in the "Registrar's Field" (i.e. chartered as mutual aid societies) are either exempt from income tax completely (e.g. friendly societies, trade unions, cooperatives), or pay at reduced rates on the assumption that the members of these societies are in low income groups where they would normally be subject to tax at less than the standard rate. Income tax on the income of building, collection, and industrial assurance societies and miscellaneous clubs and organizations has been estimated at an average rate of 25%. See also p. 160, below.

of the income tax charged on nonpersonal incomes has been allocated to income groups as shown in column 2 of Table 9.

The remaining direct tax on income was the profits tax charged on corporations, which yielded £274.4 million in 1948–49. Profits below £2,000 were exempt, and profits between £2,000 and £12,000 were charged at reduced rates. The standard rates on profits exceeding this latter figure were 25% on distributed profits and 10% on undistributed profits. The profits tax liability is allocated to income groups in column 3 of Table 9 on the basis of the ownership of corporate shares.[5]

TABLE 9

Distribution of Direct Taxes on Private Income
(In Million Pounds)

INCOME RANGE (IN POUNDS)	DIRECT TAXES ON PERSONAL INCOME	INCOME TAX ON NONPERSONAL INCOME	PROFITS TAX	TOTAL DIRECT TAXES	DIRECT TAXES AS PERCENTAGE OF PRIVATE INCOME
	1	2	3	4	5
Under 135	29.00	4.50	1.19	34.69	6.6
135–250	180.64	20.05	4.09	204.78	9.0
250–500	295.52	55.69	29.88	381.09	10.5
500–750	153.43	38.46	26.87	218.76	16.6
750–1,000	116.14	21.01	15.89	153.04	24.1
1,000–2,000	193.95	51.62	39.75	285.32	28.5
2,000–3,000	94.23	35.49	28.32	158.04	38.8
3,000–5,000	106.74	40.92	32.63	180.29	44.6
5,000–10,000	114.99	45.29	36.73	197.01	57.1
10,000–20,000	80.04	31.65	25.76	137.45	63.6
20,000 and above	72.84	39.82	33.29	145.95	73.0
Totals	1,437.52	384.50	274.40	2,096.42	(19.0)

Table 9 summarizes the distribution of all direct taxes on income, the total of these taxes being £2,096 million as indicated in column 4. In column 5 direct taxes on income are represented as percentages of private income for each income group. The combined direct income taxes were progressive, ranging from 6.6% for the lowest income group to 73% for the highest.

DIRECT TAXES ON CAPITAL

There were two major taxes based on capital ownership in 1948–49: death duties charged on estates falling in,[6] and the special contribution, which was, in effect, a nonrecurring capital levy.

5. See p. 161 for a full description of the estimated yield of the profits tax and the method by which it has been allocated.
6. The term "falling in" refers to estates coming under the purview of the Inland Revenue at the death of estate owners.

The total yield of death duties on estates falling in 1948–49 is estimated at £181 million, £156 million arising from estate duty and £25 million from minor duties (e.g. legacy and succession duties). Death duties are allocated to income groups in column 1 of Table 10, by the same method which was used in estimating the distribution of capital.[7]

The special contribution was a special tax imposed in 1948–49 on persons with gross incomes above £2,000 who had investment incomes exceeding £250. Although it was technically a progressive tax on investment incomes it can be considered as a capital levy.[8] The distribution of the special contribution is indicated in column 2 of Table 10.

TABLE 10

Distribution of Death Duties and the Special Contribution
(In Million Pounds)

INCOME RANGE (IN POUNDS)	DEATH DUTIES	SPECIAL CONTRIBUTION	TOTAL CAPITAL TAXES	AS PERCENTAGE OF CAPITAL HOLDINGS
	1	2	3	4
Under 135	.37	.	.37	.07
135–250	1.78	.	1.78	.07
250–500	9.64	.	9.64	.12
500–750	12.14	.	12.14	.25
750–1,000	6.79	.	6.79	.34
1,000–2,000	20.75	.	20.75	.59
2,000–3,000	14.59	15.95	30.54	1.71
3,000–5,000	21.98	20.30	42.28	2.01
5,000–10,000	28.73	29.12	57.85	2.89
10,000–20,000	25.43	23.85	49.28	4.04
20,000 and above	38.70	23.01	61.71	4.68
Totals	180.90	112.23	293.13	(.98)

Capital taxes were progressive, yielding an amount in 1948–49 equal to about 1% of total private capital.[9]

7. See p. 32 above. The allocation of death duties is explained in more detail in Chapter 13.
8. If considered as a tax on income, it raises the maximum marginal rate of tax on income to 147.5%. The rates began at 10% for investment incomes of £250, rising to 50% for investment incomes of £5,000 or greater. If the yield on capital is assumed to be approximately 4%, the special contribution as a capital tax had an effective maximum rate of 2%. See Chapter 14 for further discussion of this tax.
9. See p. 34 above for an estimate of private capital holdings by income group.

INDIRECT TAXES

Indirect taxes accounted for £1,684 million in revenue in 1948–49, 90% of this amount arising from Customs and Excise duties. Customs and Excise duties are allocated to income groups in column 1 of Table 11 on the basis of estimates of consumer expenditures given in Chapter 14. Other indirect taxes are also discussed in Chapter 14, their distribution being summarized in column 2 of Table 11. Since

TABLE 11

Distribution of Indirect Taxes
(In Million Pounds)

INCOME RANGE (IN POUNDS)	CUSTOMS AND EXCISE 1	OTHER IN-DIRECT TAXES 2	TOTAL IN-DIRECT TAXES 3	AS PERCENT-AGE OF DISPOS-ABLE INCOME 4
Under 135	91.75	1.59	93.34	20.1
135–250	409.84	7.51	417.35	20.2
250–500	592.82	16.04	608.86	19.7
500–750	168.79	12.57	181.36	18.5
750–1,000	72.24	7.95	80.19	17.6
1,000–2,000	95.32	14.02	109.43	18.4
2,000–3,000	32.62	5.46	38.08	18.8
3,000–5,000	25.78	5.65	31.43	19.6
5,000–10,000	14.18	4.92	19.10	18.7
10,000–20,000	5.82	3.19	9.01	21.5
20,000 and above	1.98	3.72	5.70	37.3
Miscellaneous *	2.12	4.13	6.25	
Unallocable *		83.56	83.56	
Totals	1,513.26	170.31	1,683.57	(20.6)

these taxes were paid primarily out of personal disposable incomes, in column 4 of Table 11 indirect taxes are expressed as a percentage of disposable income for each income group. Indirect taxes can be seen to be moderately regressive up to an income of about £1,000,

* "Miscellaneous" refers to taxes falling on government, foreign visitors, and exports. The full amount of taxes falling on these three groups could not be estimated accurately, but for certain duties it was felt that some allowance should be made. Customs and Excise duties have been assumed to fall on the consumer, so that only about £2 million fell into the miscellaneous category as taxes paid by foreign visitors. For other indirect taxes it has been assumed that the purchaser of goods from industry absorbs the cost of the tax on materials used in production; so about £2½ million has been allocated to government and £1¾ million to exports; £83½ million has been classed as unallocable (i.e. absorbed by industry). See pp. 169 ff. below for a fuller description of the assumptions and methods used in allocating indirect taxes.

becoming progressive above that level. The large percentage for the highest income group is due primarily to dissaving, i.e. to consumption expenditures being greater than disposable incomes.

SUMMARY: THE DISTRIBUTION OF ALL TAXES

Now that the distribution of taxes in each tax classification has been estimated, the results can be combined to indicate the distribution of the total tax burden by income groups. In Table 12 this is done, column 4 showing the distribution of the sum of taxes. In column 5 taxes are shown as a percentage of private income for each income group.

TABLE 12

Distribution of All Taxes
(In Million Pounds)

INCOME RANGE (IN POUNDS)	DIRECT TAXES ON INCOME 1	CAPITAL 2	INDIRECT TAXES 3	TOTAL TAXES 4	TAXES AS PERCENTAGE OF PRIVATE INCOME 5
Under 135	34.69	.37	93.34	128.40	24.5
135–250	204.78	1.78	417.35	623.91	25.8
250–500	381.09	9.64	608.86	999.59	27.5
500–750	218.76	12.14	181.36	412.26	32.7
750–1,000	153.04	6.79	80.19	240.02	37.7
1,000–2,000	285.32	20.75	109.34	415.41	41.6
2,000–3,000	158.04	30.54	38.08	226.66	55.7(51.8) *
3,000–5,000	180.29	42.28	31.43	254.00	62.9(57.9) *
5,000–10,000	197.01	57.85	19.10	273.96	79.9(71.4) *
10,000–20,000	137.45	49.28	9.01	195.74	90.6(79.6) *
20,000 and above	145.95	61.71	5.70	213.36	106.6(95.1) *
Miscellaneous			6.25	6.25	
Unallocable			83.56	83.56	
Totals	2,096.42	293.13	1,683.57	4,073.12	36.9(35.9) *

* Figures in parentheses exclude the special contribution, which was not a permanent part of the tax program.

The over-all tax program was progressive through all income grades, total tax liabilities ranging from 24.5% of private income for the lowest income group up to 106.6% for the highest income group if the special contribution is included, or 95.1% if this nonrecurring tax is excluded. It should be pointed out, however, that death duties are included here as an annual capital tax. The average person with a wholly earned private income exceeding £20,000 paid only about 78% of his income in taxes.[10]

Indirect taxes took the largest percentage of income in the lowest income groups, accounting for over 60% of all taxes paid by persons with incomes below £750. Above £750, taxes on income and capital were most important, indirect taxes accounting for only 5% of taxes paid by the three highest income groups.

Further description of the way in which the allocation of various taxes has been determined is given in Chapters 12–14 in Part II.

Now that the distribution of taxes has been estimated for 1948–49, the distribution of benefits arising from government expenditures needs to be determined. In Chapter 5 these benefits are allocated to income groups, and in Chapter 6 the statistical findings concerning the extent of income redistribution in 1948–49 are summarized.

10. The percentages for the highest income groups in column 5 of Table 12 may also be somewhat misleading, in that capital appreciation has not been included as part of private income. Appreciation in the value of capital assets has approximated 2½% annually since the recent war, so that the average person in the £20,000 and above group had a capital gain (perhaps unrealized) of £10,000–15,000 in 1948–49. If this is added to private income and total taxes are then indicated as a percentage of income, the percentages become roughly 93%, including the special contribution, and 81% excluding it. See pp, 103 ff. for further discussion of the importance of capital appreciation in the postwar years.

CHAPTER 5

The Distribution of Benefits

BENEFITS arising from government expenditures have been divided into three categories: (1) transfers, (2) other divisible expenditures, and (3) indivisible expenditures.[1] Transfers are defined here as income payments made to persons by the central government without the performance of any reciprocal service. They include, therefore, all social security and related payments made by the state where the receipt of such income is determined by particular circumstances other than productive contributions. Other divisible expenditures include expenditures on housing, health, and education, and subsidies on consumer goods etc., which can be allocated to income groups with a fair degree of accuracy. Indivisible expenditures include all expenditures on general governmental operations, defense, colonial programs, maintenance of law and justice, etc. Indivisible expenditures deserve their title not only because it is impossible to allocate accurately to income groups the actual benefits received from these expenditures, but also because indivisible expenditures are not intended to benefit particular income groups in specific amounts.

The allocation of benefits under each of these three classifications will be summarized in this chapter. A more detailed description of particular programs and methods of allocation can be found in Chapters 15–17 in Part II.

DISTRIBUTION OF TRANSFERS

Transfer incomes paid to private persons by the state totaled £665 million in 1948–49, social security and related payments accounting for more than 75% of this amount.

The new national insurance acts took effect in July, 1948, extending the coverage of social insurance and raising the benefits rates for many programs. Total benefit payments by the national insurance fund were approximately £84 million in the first quarter of the fiscal year under the old schemes and £263 million during the remaining three quarters of the fiscal year under the new national insurance acts. In addition, during the fiscal year there were noncontributory pen-

1. See p. 35, above.

sions and national assistance benefits of £67 million, old age tobacco coupons valued at £8¾ million, family allowance payments amounting to almost £60 million, and transfers-in-kind of milk and welfare foods amounting to £35½ million. The allocation of these sums is indicated in columns 1–4 of Table 13. The social security programs have been grouped together under the headings of pensions (including contributory and noncontributory old-age, widows, orphans, and guardians benefits), health [2] (national health insurance, sickness and maternity, and industrial injuries benefits), unemployment, and miscellaneous (family allowances and expenditures on milk and welfare foods). The individual programs are discussed in more detail, and the methods of allocation explained, in Chapter 15.

Transfers not classed as social security benefits cost the state £151 million in 1948–49. In this category, war pensions were most expensive, amounting to £86 million; armed forces leave pay cost £21 million; postwar tax credits, £19 million; scholarships and educational allowances, £14½ million; and training allowances, £10 million. The combined allocation of these amounts is shown in column 6 of Table 13, more information concerning these items being given in Chapter 15.

TABLE 13

Distribution of Transfers
(In Million Pounds)

INCOME RANGE (IN POUNDS)	PEN- SIONS 1	SOCIAL SECURITY			TOTAL SOCIAL SECURITY 5	OTHER TRANS- FERS 6	TOTAL TRANS- FERS 7
		HEALTH 2	UNEM- PLOYMENT 3	MISCEL- LANEOUS 4			
Under 135	86.90	7.24	11.29	4.32	109.75	27.63	137.38
135–250	195.65	29.78	5.93	30.49	261.85	53.53	315.38
250–500	50.11	27.19	2.96	44.26	124.52	51.94	176.46
500–750	.05	1.22	—	9.19	10.46	8.41	18.87
750–1,000	.01	.39	—	3.20	3.60	3.77	7.37
1,000–2,000	—	.35	—	2.98	3.33	3.21	6.54
2,000–3,000	—	.07	—	.38	.45	1.14	1.59
3,000–5,000	—	.04	—	.11	.15	.72	.87
5,000–10,000	—	.02	—	.02	.04	.39	.43
10,000–20,000	—	—	—	—	—	.08	.08
20,000 and above	—	—	—	—	—	.02	.02
Totals	332.72	66.30	20.18	94.95	514.15	150.84	664.99

OTHER DIVISIBLE BENEFITS

Other divisible benefits totaled £1,010 million in 1948–49. The major types of expenditure in this category were government sub-

2. The cost of the national health service is not included; the service is being treated under sec. *Other Divisible Benefits,* below.

sidies of £471 million; the cost of the national health service, which
for the last three-quarters of the fiscal year was £254 million; expenditures on education of £172 million; housing expenditures of
£70 million; and miscellaneous expenditures of £45 million.[3]

The estimated allocation of these expenditure classifications is
summarized in Table 14. A more detailed division and an explanation
of methods used in estimating their allocation is given in Chapter 16.

TABLE 14

Distribution of Other Divisible Benefits
(In Million Pounds)

INCOME RANGE (IN POUNDS)	SUB-SIDIES 1	EDU-CATION 2	NATIONAL HEALTH SERVICE 3	HOUS-ING 4	MISCEL-LANEOUS 5	TOTAL 6
Under 135	29.13	5.84	16.05	11.14	8.16	70.32
135–250	142.25	55.59	83.22	34.10	14.46	329.62
250–500	185.82	90.24	112.68	24.36	11.80	424.90
500–750	40.44	17.84	23.47	—	3.77	85.52
750–1,000	16.55	2.06	8.33	—	1.68	28.62
1,000–2,000	16.24	—	7.26	—	2.27	25.77
2,000–3,000	3.82	—	1.57	—	.69	6.08
3,000–5,000	2.58	—	.84	—	.46	3.88
5,000–10,000	1.26	—	.36	—	.29	1.91
10,000–20,000	.43	—	.05	—	.12	.60
20,000 and above	.15	—	.01	—	.04	.20
Miscellaneous *	9.50	—	—	—	—	9.50
Unallocable *	22.93	—	—	—	—	22.93
Totals	471.10	171.57	253.84	69.60	43.74	1,009.85

* See note to Table 11, p. 43, above.

INDIVISIBLE EXPENDITURES

In contrast to transfers and other divisible benefits there is no
ready manner of determining which particular persons benefit or
are intended to benefit from the services the cost of which has been
classified as indivisible. The choice must be made, however, of
whether to include these items in the measure of redistribution.
Excluding them would give an incomplete picture, and if an equivalent portion of total tax revenues were omitted, it would in any case
be tantamount to making an assumption concerning their allocation.
On the other hand, including them on the basis of any single as-

3. For a further enumeration of other divisible expenditures, see pp. 152–4.

sumption as to who really benefits from the presence of law and order, the existence of a standing army, the operations of a government audit bureau, etc. may result in conclusions which some persons feel to be incorrect. A compromise course has been adopted here: indivisible expenditures will be allocated on the basis of three quite different assumptions. The reader may choose which of these, if any, he will accept.

Before listing these assumptions, it should be mentioned that indivisible expenditures in 1948–49 included civil expenditures for general governmental operations of £620 million, expenditures on the armed forces of £727 million, interest on the national debt of £500 million, and the combined surpluses on current account and of the extrabudgetary (national insurance) funds of £575 million.

At first thought it may seem a dubious classification to include interest on the debt and the surplus as indivisible benefits; there are, however, two ways in which they may be thought of as benefits. From one point of view they are general governmental expenses representing the cost of certain benefits which are being paid for in installments. In this sense the real benefits which these sums represent are that the German invasion threat is no longer present and Britons can again lead peaceful civilian lives. From another point of view, since current expenditures could have been financed without resort to such high taxation, all persons as consumers have benefited from the absence of additional inflationary pressure which would have existed had there been no surplus in 1948–49 or had tax revenues been insufficient to meet debt charges.

Debt charges and the surplus could equally well be deducted from the revenue side of the government account instead of being added to the expenditure side. In the case of interest charges this would approximate business accounting procedures, interest being considered a cost deducted from gross income before the determination of net profit. Deducting interest and the surplus from government revenues would result in what might be called net expendable revenue, both sides of the government account then being reduced by £1,275 million.

In practical terms, so long as interest and the surplus are allocated to income groups in the same manner as other indivisible expenditures, it does not matter which side of the government account includes these items. The final estimate of income gains and losses resulting from redistribution is unaffected by this choice. This being true, debt charges and the surplus are included as indivisible expenditures here chiefly for statistical simplification, so that a single allocation will suffice for all indivisible items.

Three basic assumptions will be made concerning the possible benefits accruing from indivisible expenditures.

1. It will be assumed that benefits are equal per capita for every
income group. A very broad and literal interpretation of democracy
is implied by this assumption, benefits being assumed identical for
young and old, Labourite and Tory, rich and poor.

2. It will be assumed that benefits are proportional to net private
income. Net private income has been chosen as a middle-of-the-road
assumption, because it represents the total private command over
goods and services net of all unavoidable taxes.

3. It will be assumed that indivisible benefits are proportional to
the sum of taxes paid by each person or group. This implies that the
current total tax burden on each income group represents the willing
sacrifice (if only temporarily) of persons in that group for the sake
of continuing the present economic, social, and political system. This
is an extreme assumption, but the opposite extreme is represented in
assumption 1.

Net indivisible expenditures in 1948–49 totaled £2,337 million,
consisting of the following:

	(IN MILLION POUNDS)
Indivisible civil expenditures	620.07
Armed service expenditures	697.53
Net Revenue Department expenditures	29.71
Interest on the debt *	500.00
National fund surplus	144.04
Surplus on current account	430.93
Total indivisible expenditures	2,422.28
Adjustments:	
Plus: unallocable divisible expenditures †	+22.93
Less: unallocable taxes ‡	−83.56
Government income from property §	−24.00
Net indivisible expenditures	2,337.65

* See p. 154 n.
† See Table 96, p. 229.
‡ See Table 84, p. 204.
§ See p. 154.

To avoid making a number of separate classifications, £23 million
found unallocable in the preceding section has been added and £84
million unallocable taxes and government income from property has
been deducted, to arrive at net indivisible expenditures.

In Table 15, the allocation of these net indivisible expenditures is shown under each of the three assumptions outlined above.

TABLE 15

Allocation of Indivisible Expenditures

INCOME RANGE (IN POUNDS)	ASSUMPTION 1 (MILLION POUNDS)	(PER-CENTAGE)	ASSUMPTION 2 (MILLION POUNDS)	(PER-CENTAGE)	ASSUMPTION 3 (MILLION POUNDS)	(PER-CENTAGE)
Under 135	181.70	7.77	126.02	5.39	67.08	2.87
135–250	797.98	34.15	573.12	24.53	320.23	13.71
250–500	994.15	42.52	859.36	36.77	545.64	23.34
500–750	198.05	8.47	247.12	10.57	242.75	10.38
750–1,000	71.61	3.06	124.61	5.33	147.10	6.29
1,000–2,000	67.78	2.90	182.36	7.80	280.36	11.99
2,000–3,000	14.02	.60	68.25	2.92	142.62	6.10
3,000–5,000	7.94	.34	62.15	2.66	167.36	7.16
5,000–10,000	3.29	.14	46.51	1.99	169.69	7.26
10,000–20,000	.89	.04	25.95	1.11	123.21	5.27
20,000 and above	.24	.01	22.20	.95	131.61	5.63
	2,337.65	100.00	2,337.65	100.00	2,337.65	100.00

SUMMARY: DISTRIBUTION OF BENEFITS

Table 16 summarizes the distribution of benefits by income groups. Columns 6 to 8 show the distribution of total benefits under each of the three assumptions concerning the allocation of indivisible expenditures. In Table 17 benefits are shown as percentages of private factor income for each income grade.

TABLE 16

Summary Allocation of Benefits, by Income Group
(In Million Pounds)

INCOME RANGE (IN POUNDS)	TRANSFERS 1	BENEFITS 2	INDIVISIBLE BENEFITS ASSUMP. 1 3	ASSUMP. 2 4	ASSUMP. 3 5	TOTAL BENEFITS ASSUMP. 1 6	ASSUMP. 2 7	ASSUMP. 3 8
Under 135	137.38	70.32	181.70	126.02	67.08	389.40	333.72	274.78
135–250	315.38	329.62	797.98	573.12	320.23	1,442.98	1,218.12	965.23
250–500	176.46	424.90	994.15	859.36	545.64	1,595.51	1,460.72	1,147.00
500–750	18.87	85.52	198.05	247.12	242.75	302.44	351.51	347.14
750–1,000	7.37	28.62	71.61	124.61	147.10	107.60	160.60	183.09
1,000–2,000	6.54	25.77	67.78	182.36	280.36	100.09	214.67	312.67
2,000–3,000	1.59	6.08	14.02	68.25	142.62	21.69	75.92	150.29
3,000–5,000	.87	3.88	7.94	62.15	167.36	12.69	66.90	172.11
5,000–10,000	.43	1.91	3.29	46.51	169.69	5.63	48.85	172.03
10,000–20,000	.08	.60	.89	25.95	123.21	1.57	26.63	123.89
20,000 and above	.02	.20	.24	22.20	131.61	.46	22.42	131.83
Miscellaneous *		9.50				9.50	9.50	9.50
Totals	644.99	986.92	2,337.65	2,337.65	2,337.65	3,989.56	3,989.56	3,989.56

* See note to Table 11, p. 43.

Now that both sides of the government account have been exam-
ined and the allocation of taxes and benefits estimated, the extent of
income redistribution through central government finance in 1948–49

TABLE 17

Benefits Arising from All Divisible and Indivisible Expenditures
as a Percentage of Private Factor Income, by Income Group

	INDIVISIBLE BENEFITS ALLOCATED ON BASIS OF		
INCOME RANGE (IN POUNDS)	ASSUMPTION I (PERCENTAGE)	ASSUMPTION 2 (PERCENTAGE)	ASSUMPTION 3 (PERCENTAGE)
Under 135	107.5	92.2	75.8
135–250	69.4	58.7	46.5
250–500	46.2	42.4	33.2
500–750	24.2	28.2	27.8
750–1,000	16.9	25.2	28.7
1,000–2,000	10.6	22.6	33.0
2,000–3,000	5.3	19.0	36.6
3,000–5,000	3.2	16.7	43.1
5,000–10,000	1.6	13.5	47.5
10,000–20,000	.8	11.9	55.3
20,000 and above	.2	10.3	60.8
Average	38.5	38.5	38.5

can be determined. This will be done in Chapter 6, and the two succeeding chapters will compare these findings with prewar Britain and
with income redistribution in the United States.

CHAPTER 6

The Redistribution of Income in 1948–49

IN BRINGING both sides of the government account together again we have returned to the position of Chapter 3, where the government account was first analyzed. Now, however, something is known about the distribution of the pieces, and we can draw on Chapters 4 and 5, which summarized the distribution of taxes and expenditures, to determine the actual extent of income redistribution in 1948–49.

In the first part of this chapter the view will be limited to those items which may be classed as relatively certain, that is, excluding benefits arising from indivisible expenditures. In the second part indivisible benefits will be included under each of the assumptions concerning their allocation made in Chapter 5, and the aggregate net redistribution will be determined.

COMPARISON OF THE DISTRIBUTION OF TAXES AND DIVISIBLE BENEFITS

From a study of Table 18 below one thing appears certain. No matter what conclusions one may reach concerning the allocation of indivisible expenditures, at least the two lowest income groups registered absolute gains totaling approximately £100 million. Glancing back to Table 13 in the last chapter, one may see that the lowest income group actually received £9 million more in transfer incomes alone than it paid in taxes. Without including almost 60% of the expenditure side of the government account (i.e. indivisible expenditures), the two lowest income groups, comprising 51% of all income recipients and including 41% of the population, showed net gains.[1]

To show more clearly the relationship of these divisible expendi-

1. This does not necessarily mean that 51% of income recipients actually made net gains. The £135–250 showed an aggregate gain of £21 million, but it is likely that an average income of about £225 was the breakeven point, probably a third of the persons in this group being net losers. It is unfortunate that the available tax data is presented in such broad income ranges that 75% of the population is grouped within two income ranges (between £135 and 500). Narrower income grades would show that only those persons with incomes of less than about £225 were really net gainers.

tures to tax payments, Table 19 gives divisible expenditures as a percentage of all taxes for each income group.

TABLE 18

Comparison of the Distribution of Taxes and All
Divisible Expenditures
(In Million Pounds)

INCOME RANGE (IN POUNDS)	ALL TAXES	DIVISIBLE EXPENDITURES	NET GAIN OR LOSS
Under 135	128.40	207.70	+79.30
135–250	623.91	645.00	+21.09
250–500	999.59	601.36	−398.23
500–750	412.26	104.39	−307.87
750–1,000	240.02	35.99	−204.03
1,000–2,000	415.41	32.31	−383.10
2,000–3,000	226.66	7.67	−218.99
3,000–5,000	254.00	4.75	−249.25
5,000–10,000	273.96	2.34	−271.62
10,000–20,000	195.74	.68	−195.06
20,000 and above	213.36	.22	−213.14
Total	3,983.31	1,642.41	−2,340.90

The lowest group received in divisible expenditures—we might call them the "tangible benefits"—62% more than they paid in taxes. The £135–250 group slightly more than broke even, getting 103.4%.

TABLE 19

Divisible Expenditures as a Percentage of Taxes,
by Income Ranges

INCOME RANGE (IN POUNDS)	DIVISIBLE EXPENDITURES AS PERCENTAGE OF TAXES (PERCENTAGE)
Under 135	161.8
135–250	103.4
250–500	60.1
500–750	25.3
750–1,000	15.0
1,000–2,000	7.9
2,000–3,000	3.4
3,000–5,000	1.9
5,000–10,000	.8
10,000–20,000	.3
20,000 and above	.1
Average	41.2

The £250–500 group got back more than the average of the whole population. Above that range the returns diminished rapidly. By the time one reached an income of £3,000 the tangible benefits were negligible. It is obvious that there was a marked redistributive effect in 1948–49, in the pattern of taxing and spending.

Table 20, in the second column, shows the average amount per tax family spent by the government in the form of divisible expenditures. Tax liabilities rose at a steady rate, almost doubling from one group to the next. Even the lowest incomes paid a considerable sum in taxes, although they were exempt from the major direct taxes on personal income. Average benefits declined until the £1,000–2,000 group was reached, rising again beyond that point. This resulted from the scissors effect produced by transfers and other divisible benefits, the former declining as incomes rose, and the latter rising slightly per capita.

TABLE 20

Average Taxes and Benefits from Divisible Expenditures per Tax Family and Per Person
(In Pounds)

	PER TAX FAMILY		PER PERSON	
INCOME RANGE	AVERAGE TAX	AVERAGE DIVIS-IBLE BENEFIT	AVERAGE TAX	AVERAGE DIVIS-IBLE BENEFIT
	1 *	2	3 *	4
Under 135	46.0	74.8	33.8	54.7
135–250	69.7	72.2	37.4	38.6
250–500	118.0	71.4	48.1	28.9
500–750	248.0	62.9	99.7	26.7
750–1,000	412.0	61.7	160.0	24.0
1,000–2,000	800.0	60.7	295.0	22.8
2,000–3,000	2,000.0	69.2	778.0	26.6
3,000–5,000	4,000.0	74.8	1,500.0	28.2
5,000–10,000	9,100.0	77.7	3,900.0	32.8
10,000–20,000	23,300.0	80.9	10,600.0	35.8
20,000 and above	92,700.0	95.7	41,800.0	42.0
Average	172.1	71.0	81.5	33.5

* Figures between £100–1,000 have been rounded off to the nearest pound, those above £1,000 to the nearest one hundred pounds.

Average taxes and divisible benefits per person are also shown in Table 20. This, in one sense, is a better comparison, because to a large extent taxes and benefits depended directly on the number of dependents in the average tax family.

The distribution of benefits per taxpayer declined only slightly over the three lowest income groups, but the per person measure indicates that this is because of the differences in family size. The average benefit per person declined quite rapidly within this range, but because the average tax family was about twice as large in the £250–500 group as in the "under £135" group, this decline is partly concealed in column 2. Benefits, looked at in either way, increased again above £2,000, but the increase in benefits was negligible viewed in the perspective of the comparative increase in taxes.

TABLE 21

Net Private Income after Taxes and Divisible Benefits
(Average Private Factor Income for Each Income
Range: 100)

INCOME RANGE (IN POUNDS)	DIVISIBLE BENEFITS	TAXES	NET PRIVATE INCOME
Under 135	57.4	35.5	121.9
135–250	31.1	30.0	101.1
250–500	17.5	28.9	88.6
500–750	8.4	33.0	75.4
750–1,000	5.7	37.6	68.1
1,000–2,000	3.2	43.8	59.4
2,000–3,000	1.9	55.3(51.4) *	46.6(50.5) *
3,000–5,000	1.2	63.8(58.8)	37.4(42.4)
5,000–10,000	.7	75.7(67.3)	25.0(33.4)
10,000–20,000	.3	87.4(75.4)	12.9(23.9)
20,000 and above	.1	98.3(87.0)	1.8(13.1)
Average	15.9	38.6(37.4)	77.3(78.5)

* Figures in parentheses exclude the special contribution, a temporary, nonrecurring tax.

Another way of looking at the effect of taxes and divisible benefits is to observe them as percentages of original income. In Table 21 the average private factor income for each group is represented by the index number 100. In column 1 the average divisible benefit for each group is shown as a percentage of original income; and in column 2 the average tax liability is shown as a percentage of that income. Factor income has been used because it excludes both taxes and transfer incomes, representing the original income of persons before any changes arose from the direct redistributive effects of government activities. Columns 1 and 2 are partially interdependent, because some of the taxes paid by persons were not wholly on factor incomes but on benefits themselves (e.g. transfer incomes). The apparent decline in taxes as a percentage of income over the first three income groups arises because the receipt of transfer incomes allowed the consumption of the lowest income groups to be considerably greater than their factor incomes. Thus, consumption taxes were accentuated as percentages of factor incomes. Benefits, in column 1, declined steadily through all income ranges. Net private incomes after taxes and benefits were greater than original earned factor incomes only for the two lowest groups. In the upper brackets net incomes were a much smaller percentage of original factor income, almost reaching zero if one were to include the 1948–49 capital levy (the special contribution).

Since indivisible expenditures have not as yet been included, the net redistribution of incomes in pounds, shillings, and pence is not very meaningful at this stage. If we include only divisible benefits, income gains accrued only to the two lowest income groups (of £100 million), while all other groups were net losers (of £2,441 million). The redistributive tendency in these figures, however, is quite evident. In Table 22 the percentage is given of total taxes paid and divisible benefits received, by each income group.

TABLE 22

*Percentage of Total Taxes Paid and Divisible Benefits
Received by Income Groups*

INCOME RANGE (IN POUNDS)	PERCENTAGE OF TOTAL TAXES (CUMULATIVE)		PERCENTAGE OF TOTAL DIVISIBLE BENEFITS (CUMULATIVE)	
Under 135	3.3	3.3	12.6	12.6
135–250	15.7	19.0	39.0	51.6
250–500	25.0	44.0	37.0	88.6
500–750	10.3	54.3	6.3	94.9
750–1,000	6.0	60.3	2.2	97.1
1,000–2,000	10.4	70.7	2.0	99.1
2,000–3,000	5.7	76.4	.5	99.6
3,000–5,000	6.4	82.8	.3	99.9
5,000–10,000	6.9	89.7	.1	100.0
10,000–20,000	4.9	94.6	—	100.0
20,000 and above	5.4	100.0	—	100.0
	100.0		100.0	

The two lowest income groups paid 19% of the taxes and received 51.6% of the divisible benefits. Persons with incomes below £500 paid 44% of all taxes while receiving 88.6% of these benefits. Needless to add, persons above £750 paid almost half of all taxes and were the recipients of only 3% of the divisible benefits. If all other ex-penditures were allocated in similar proportions, the aggregate net redistribution would clearly be considerable, with an income level somewhere in the neighborhood of £500 being the dividing line be-tween gains and losses.

AGGREGATE NET REDISTRIBUTION OF INCOME

The distribution of indivisible benefits needs to be added to divisible benefits to determine the aggregate net redistribution of income. Using the allocation of indivisible benefits under the three assump-tions as outlined in Chapter 5,[2] Table 23 compares the distribution of total benefits with the distribution of total taxes. Columns 2–4 give the distribution of total benefits, and columns 5–7 indicate the re-distributive gain or loss for each income group.

The miscellaneous item at the bottom of Table 23 is a balancing item, including government agencies and foreigners, and may not be indicative of actual net gains or losses for these groups.[3]

The totals for columns 5–7 at the bottom of Table 23, indicate the aggregate net redistribution of income. Under the assumption of equal per capita benefits from indivisible expenditures, the aggre-gate net redistribution of income is £1,679 million. Under the assump-tion of indivisible benefits proportional to total tax contributions the aggregate net redistribution is only £638 million. Under the median assumption of benefits proportional to net private income, redis-tribution reaches £1,264 million. Assumptions 1 and 3 represent the extremes, so that it can be concluded that not less than £638 million and not more than £1,679 million was redistributed, the actual amount being somewhere in between. For the purpose of comparison with prior years the median assumption of £1,264 million redistributed will be used in succeeding chapters.

2. See pp. 50–1, above.

3. In Chs. 4 and 5 attention was concentrated on the allocation of taxes and benefits to persons, but where the government or foreigners obviously paid taxes or received benefits these were included. It should be noted, however, that these sums are limited to indirect taxes and benefits. Taxes paid to governments abroad by British residents, and some minor direct tax receipts of the British government from nonresidents, have been excluded. See also p. 43 n., above.

TABLE 23

Comparison of the Distribution of All Taxes and All Expenditures, and the Aggregate Redistributive Gains and Losses for Each Income Group

(In Million Pounds)

Income Range (In Pounds)	Distribution of Taxes 1	Distribution of Total Expenditures			Aggregate Redistributive Gains or Losses		
		Assump. 1 2	Assump. 2 3	Assump. 3 4	Assump. 1 5	Assump. 2 6	Assump. 3 7
Under 135	128.40	389.40	333.72	274.78	+261.00	+205.32	+146.38
135–250	623.91	1,442.98	1,218.12	965.23	+819.07	+594.21	+341.32
250–500	999.59	1,595.51	1,460.72	1,147.00	+595.92	+461.13	+147.41
500–750	412.26	302.44	351.51	347.14	−109.82	−60.75	−65.12
750–1,000	240.02	107.60	160.60	183.09	−132.42	−79.42	−56.93
1,000–2,000	415.41	100.09	214.67	312.67	−315.32	−200.74	−102.74
2,000–3,000	226.66	21.69	75.92	150.29	−204.97	−150.74	−76.37
3,000–5,000	254.00	12.69	66.90	172.11	−241.31	−187.10	−81.89
5,000–10,000	273.96	5.63	48.85	172.03	−268.33	−225.11	−101.93
10,000–20,000	195.74	1.57	26.63	123.89	−194.17	−169.11	−71.85
20,000 and above	213.36	.46	22.42	131.83	−212.90	−190.94	−81.53
Totals	3,983.31	3,980.06	3,980.06	3,980.06	+1,675.99 −1,679.24	+1,260.66 −1,263.91	+635.11 −638.36
Miscellaneous	6.25	9.50	9.50	9.50	+3.25	+3.25	+3.25
	3,989.56	3,989.56	3,989.56	3,989.56	±1,679.24	±1,263.91	±638.36

If the aggregate redistributive gains or losses for each income group are divided by the number of tax families in each group, the average gain or loss can be seen, as in Table 24. For incomes below £750 the choice of assumption in allocating indivisible benefits does not make more than about £50 difference, but for the very high incomes the difference between assumptions is very marked.

TABLE 24

Average Redistributive Gains and Losses per Tax Family, by Income Group

INCOME RANGE (IN POUNDS)	REDISTRIBUTIVE GAINS OR LOSSES (IN POUNDS)		
	ASSUMPTION 1	ASSUMPTION 2	ASSUMPTION 3
	1	2	3
Under 135	+93.9	+74.0	+53.0
135–250	+93.5	+66.4	+38.2
250–500	+70.8	+54.7	+17.5
500–750	−66.2	−36.6	−39.2
750–1,000	−227	−136	−97.6
1,000–2,000	−593	−377	−193
2,000–3,000	−1,846	−1,358	−688
3,000–5,000	−3,800	−2,945	−1,290
5,000–10,000	−8,915	−7,480	−3,385
10,000–20,000	−23,115	−20,130	−8,555
20,000 and above	−92,500	−83,000	−35,400

It is interesting, viewing both Tables 23 and 24, that the choice of assumption concerning indivisible benefits does not have much effect on the dividing line between groups registering redistributive gains and losses. Under all three assumptions the £250–500 group registered gains, and the £500–750 group losses. The similarity of the redistributive breakeven points on the income scale can perhaps be more clearly seen in Figure IV. Although with a series of narrower income grades one could determine more accurately the average income at which he just broke even, from the curves in Figure IV it would appear that the income where the redistributive effect was just neutral was approximately £550–600 under assumption 1, and about £600–650 under assumption 2 or 3. It should be remembered also that here we are speaking of taxable income (before the deduction of any reliefs and allowances), whereas total personal income for persons in the £500–750 range averaged about £85 greater than their taxable incomes. The breakeven point, in terms of the average total personal income, was therefore slightly over £600 under the first assumption, and about £700 under assumption 2 or 3.

The redistributive effect of the government's tax and expenditure programs can be shown better perhaps by indicating the difference between private factor income and private consumer income (i.e. income after the addition of all benefits and the subtraction of all taxes). Table 25 gives consumer income as a percentage of private factor income for each income group under each of the assumptions concerning the allocation of indivisible benefits. It is the counterpart of Table 21 above, except that in Table 25 all benefits are included.

Figure IV. Average redistributive gains and losses by size of income under three alternative allocations of indivisible expenditures.

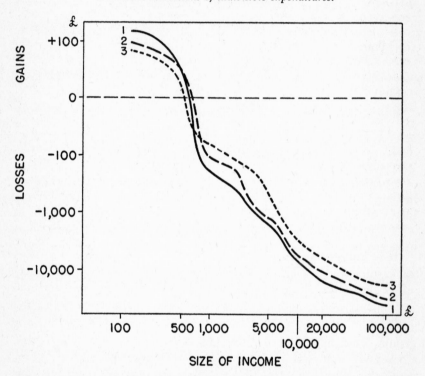

In purely money terms (valuing government services at factor cost) Table 25 shows that the lowest income group was between 40% and 72% better off as a result of the government's fiscal program. Using the median assumption (2), consumer income as a percentage of original private factor income ranged from 156.7% for the lowest income group down to 12% for the highest income group. If one excluded the special contribution, consumer incomes for persons above £2,000 were not reduced quite so substantially, as shown in parentheses in Table 25.

TABLE 25

Consumer Income as a Percentage of Private Factor Income, by Income Group

INCOME RANGE (IN POUNDS)	ASSUMPTION 1	ASSUMPTION 2	ASSUMPTION 3
Under 135	172.1	156.7	140.4
135–250	139.4	128.6	116.4
250–500	117.2	113.4	104.3
500–750	91.2	95.2	94.8
750–1,000	79.3	87.6	91.1
1,000–2,000	66.8	78.8	89.2
2,000–3,000	50.0(53.9) *	63.2(67.1) *	81.4(85.3) *
3,000–5,000	39.7(44.7)	53.2(58.2)	79.5(84.5)
5,000–10,000	25.9(34.7)	37.8(46.6)	71.8(80.6)
10,000–20,000	13.3(24.3)	24.5(35.5)	67.9(78.9)
20,000 and above	1.9(12.7)	12.0(22.8)	62.4(73.2)

* Figures in parentheses exclude the special contribution, a special, nonrecurring tax.

SUMMARY OF THE REDISTRIBUTION OF INCOMES

Additional ways of illustrating the extent of the redistribution of incomes could be given, but there will be a further analysis in the following chapter, comparing British income redistribution in 1948–49 with a prewar year. In this chapter the extent of redistribution has been estimated at between £638 million and £1,679 million. If one uses the median assumption in allocating indivisible benefits, assuming them to be proportional to private income net of all unavoidable taxes, redistribution is estimated at £1,264 million for 1948–49.

Under each of the three assumptions allocating indivisible benefits, aggregate income gains were registered for the three lowest income groups, i.e. for groups with taxable incomes not exceeding £500. Conversely, aggregate redistributive losses were estimated for all income groups above £500. The breakeven point, or the income at which the average taxpayer contributed in taxes exactly the amount which the government spent in his behalf, fell somewhere between about £550 and £650 of taxable personal income, or between approximately £635 and £735 of total personal income. (In terms of private income, including imputed undistributed profits, the breakeven point was between £700 and £800.)

Excluding indivisible benefits, the lowest income group received benefits of about £29 more per tax family than it paid in taxes. The

£135–250 group slightly better than broke even, and higher income groups lost in direct proportion to their total incomes.

The statistical conclusions indicate quite clearly that there was a substantial degree of income redistribution in 1948–49. As pointed out in Chapter 2, the exact amount in pounds is subject to a considerable degree of error. Regardless of precise amounts, the figures are certainly indicative of a major shift of income away from high income groups toward the three lowest income groups. The figures themselves, however, are not very meaningful unless compared with another year or another country. In the next two chapters, therefore, comparisons will be made with prewar Britain and with the United States.

CHAPTER 7

The Redistribution of Income in Great Britain in 1937 and 1948–49

THE STATISTICAL findings summarized in the last chapter will be more meaningful if they can be compared with an earlier year in Great Britain. In this chapter Tibor Barna's *Redistribution of Incomes through Public Finance in 1937* will be adapted for the purpose of comparing the prewar and postwar redistribution.

PREWAR AND POSTWAR INCOME REDISTRIBUTION

Barna's study of the redistribution of income was briefly discussed in the introductory chapter, when it was pointed out that there were a number of differences in the scope and method of his study as compared with the present one.[1] A few adjustments can be made, however, to permit comparable statistical conclusions. In the discussion and tables which follow, Barna's findings have been adjusted in the following manner. Taxes collected by local authorities and expenditures financed out of local funds have been deducted. Expenditures by local authorities out of specific grants issued from the central government, however, are still included. Barna deducted interest on the national debt from tax receipts to determine net (expendable) revenue; here, interest on the debt has been added to indivisible benefits. For comparative purposes it has seemed most reasonable to use the assumption of proportionality to net private income in allocating indivisible expenditures. This assumption differs somewhat from Barna's median assumption, so that the adjusted total of indivisible expenditures for 1937 has been reallocated on the basis of assumption 2 used above in Chapter 5. No attempt has been made to deduct taxes and expenditures concerning Northern Ireland in the 1937 data. Taxes and expenditures are therefore probably about 1%–3% greater than would have been the case if Great Britain alone had been considered.

In Table 26 the distribution of taxes and expenditures for the two sets of years are presented. In order to make the comparison more realistic, in pairing off income grades the 1937 ranges have been

1. See pp. 4–5, above.

doubled in 1948–49 so that, for example, the 1937 £125–250 range is directly compared with the 1948–49 £250–500 range. In this manner the same real income levels for the two years are more nearly comparable. The national price index in 1948–49 (1938 = 100) was about 187–90, and Seers has estimated that the working class cost of living index in 1948–49 was about 176–80 and that of the middle class 199–201.[2]

TABLE 26

Redistribution of Income in 1937 and 1948–49
(In Million Pounds)

INCOME RANGE (IN THOUSAND POUNDS)		DISTRIBUTION OF TAXES		DISTRIBUTION OF BENEFITS		AGGREGATE REDISTRIBUTIVE GAINS AND LOSSES	
1937	1948–49	1937	1948–49	1937	1948–49	1937	1948–49
		1	2	3	4	5	6
<.125	<.250	173.9	752.3	447.9	1,551.8	+274.0	+799.5
.125–.25	.25–.5	180.0	999.6	281.4	1,460.7	+101.4	+461.1
.25–.5	.5–1.	88.5	652.3	99.2	512.1	+10.7	−140.2
.5–1.	1–2.	82.5	415.5	42.6	214.7	−39.9	−200.8
1–2.	2–5.	82.0	480.6	30.2	142.8	−51.8	−337.8
2–10.	5–20.	186.0	469.7	39.1	75.5	−146.9	−394.2
>10.	>20.	157.4	213.3	9.9	22.4	−147.5	−190.9
Totals		950.3	3,983.3	950.3	3,980.0	±386.1	+1,260.6 −1,263.9

The aggregate net redistribution in 1937 was about £386 million, and approximately £1,260 million in 1948–49. As percentages of the national income, the redistribution was 8.8% in 1937 and 13.1% in 1948–49. Thus, in 1948–49 income redistribution was considerably greater both absolutely and relative to total income. This increase in redistribution, however, was primarily due to the great expansion of the size of the government account. The effective rate of redistribution, i.e. the amount redistributed per pound of tax revenue, declined from 40.6% in 1937 to only 31.8% in 1948–49. As will be emphasized in a later chapter,[3] this decrease came about because a larger number of the postwar welfare programs were designed to afford roughly equal per capita, rather than strictly redistributive, benefits.

The comparison of redistributive gains and losses by income group for these two years can be seen more clearly if the average gain or loss is determined. Table 26 does not indicate the number of persons in each income range in the two years, and there has obviously been a rather marked shift in the distribution of income over the decade. In

2. *Levelling of Incomes*, p. 21.
3. See p. 122, below.

Table 27 the number of persons and the average redistributive gain
or loss per person in each income class is given.[4]

TABLE 27

Average Redistributive Gains and Losses per Capita,
by Income Range; 1937 and 1948–49

INCOME RANGE (IN THOUSAND POUNDS)		NO. OF PERSONS (IN MILLIONS)		AGGREGATE REDISTRIBUTION (IN MILLION POUNDS)		REDISTRIBUTIVE GAIN OR LOSS PER CAPITA (IN POUNDS)	
1937	1948–49	1937	1948–49	1937	1948–49	1937	1948–49
1		2		3		5	6
<.125	<.25	21.80	20.50	+274.0	+799.5	+12.6	+39.0
.125–.25	.25–.5	18.75	20.80	+101.4	+461.1	+5.4	+22.2
.25–.5	.5–1.	4.82	5.63	+10.7	−140.2	+2.2	−24.9
.5–1.	1–2.	1.21	1.41	−39.9	−200.8	−33.0	−142.5
1–2.	2–5.	.45	.46	−51.8	−337.8	−115.	−735
2–10.	5–20.	.26	.09	−146.9	−394.2	−565	−4,380
>10.	>20.	.02	.005	−147.5	−190.9	−7,375	−37,450
Totals		47.30	48.89	±386.1	+1,260.6 −1,263.9		

The aggregate net redistribution in 1948–49 was about 3.3 times
greater in pounds than in 1937. In the prewar year both gains to low
income groups and losses to high income groups were considerably
smaller than in 1948–49. The groupings in Tables 26 and 27 do not
show very accurately what the breakeven income level was, but a
closer inspection of the figures in Barna and in Chapters 4 and 5 above
indicate that this income level was approximately £400–425 in 1937
and £600–650 in 1948–49.[5] If these ranges are roughly correct, then
net gainers included about 42–43 million persons in 1937 and 43–44
million in 1948–49. In both years, therefore, about 85–90% of the
population were in income groups which gained, and the other 10–
15% in groups which lost.

If the same money income levels in the two years are compared, it
is interesting to note that if one had the same income in both years,
up to an income of about £1,000 one was better off in money terms in
1948–49 than in 1937. That is to say, in 1948–49 the low income
gainers gained more and the lower middle income losers lost less than
before the war. This can be seen in Table 27, comparing the average
gain or loss for the same money income levels of the two years in

4. Barna did not estimate the number of income families in the lowest income
group; so a per capita measure is used here. In Ch. 3 the number of incomes below
£135 was estimated, but only 8% of the population were in this lowest income group
in 1948–49, as against 45% in 1937.

5. These are in terms of taxable income. See p. 61, above.

columns 5 and 6. For example, the average gain for the £250–500 income range was £2.2 in 1937 and £22.2 in 1948–49; the average loss for the £500–1000 range was £33 in 1937 and only £24.9 in 1948–49. Even in the £1000–2000 grade the average private consumer income in 1948–49 was only 2% less than in 1937. This would seem to imply that in purely money terms few persons with incomes not exceeding £2,000 were any worse off in the postwar years, and most were considerably better off. It should be emphasized, however, that this comparison has been made in terms of private income, not personal income. Nonpersonal income in the form of undistributed profits was a much larger percentage of private income in the postwar year. Above £10,000, for example, in 1937 only 20% of private income was in the form of withheld profits, while in 1948–49 this had risen to almost 50%. Thus, in a sense, persons in the highest income groups escaped heavier taxation in 1948–49 by letting a larger share of company profits accrue.[6]

The effect of redistribution on personal incomes can best be seen by comparing personal factor and disposable incomes for the two years. In Table 28 disposable incomes for the roughly equivalent real income ranges are shown as percentages of original personal factor incomes (i.e. before deducting direct taxes on income or adding transfer incomes received from the government).

TABLE 28

Disposable Income as a Percentage of Personal Factor Income,
1937 and 1948–49

INCOME RANGE (IN THOUSAND POUNDS)		DISPOSABLE INCOMES AS PERCENTAGES OF PERSONAL FACTOR INCOMES	
1937	1948–49	1937	1948–49
<.125	<.25	117.4	112.2
.125–.25	.25–.5	101.1	96.8
.25–.5	.5–1.	96.9	85.6
.5–1.	1–2.	85.5	76.0
2–2.	2–5.	76.0	64.7
2–10.	5–20.	59.7	42.5
>10.	>20.	27.1	17.3

Here it appears that low income families with roughly the same *real* incomes in the two years were about equally well off, while middle and high incomes were considerably worse off in 1948–49 than in

6. This was a profitable move if the value of shares in the securities market reflected additions to company reserves. An extra pound of profits devoted to dividend payments netted the man with an income of £20,000 only 4½d. after profits and income taxes (i.e. 1.87% on the pound). On the other hand, a pound left in the company as

1937.[7] If we compare the same money income grades, we find the percentages for incomes between £250 and £5,000 were almost identical for the two years, lower money incomes being favored in the postwar year and higher incomes being substantially better off in 1937.

The impact of direct personal taxes in the two years can be most dramatically contrasted by showing the personal income necessary in each year to obtain a given disposable income. In the following example the taxpayer is assumed to be a single person with income wholly earned. To net, after income and surtax, the incomes in column 1, a man's personal income must have been approximately the amounts shown in columns 2 and 3 for 1937 and 1948–49.

Net Personal Income	Necessary Gross Personal Income	
	1937	1948–49
500	570	640
1,000	1,203	1,450
5,000	7,790	47,500
10,000	19,000	247,500
25,000	60,000	847,000
100,000	278,000	3,847,000

All of the net incomes shown above were within the range of possibility in 1937, but by 1948–49 it had become virtually impossible for anyone to net more than about £10,000.[8] This is not to say, however, that it was impossible for anyone in 1948–49 to have spent £10,000 or more without being any worse off, since gifts and windfall or capital gains were not subject to tax.

In comparing tax rates and returns for 1937 and 1948–49, one might well ask how much of the increase in tax revenues was due to the increase in the money level of the national income and its initial distribution and how much was due to the changing tax structure itself. It is impossible to estimate accurately what tax revenues would have been like in one year with the tax rates of another year. However, using the average tax per person in each income group in one

undistributed profits added about 10s. 6d. to free reserves after profits and income tax (i.e. 52.5% on the pound). If the market value of shares reflected as much as $\frac{1}{25}$th of additions to reserves, one could sell enough shares to retain the money value of capital intact, and gain from this abstinence. There was also the hope that taxes on income would some day be reduced, making it possible to net more on each pound of profits received in future dividends.

7. If the working class cost of living in 1948 was 90% above 1938, then the two lowest income groups in Table 28 were almost exactly equally well off in these two years. This is taking into account, however, only direct taxes and cash benefits.

8. In 1937 there were 99 persons with income before tax greater than £100,000. By 1948–49 this number had dropped to 48. See surtax assessments, *RCIR, 1939, Cmd.* 6099 (1940) and *RCIR, 1950, Cmd.* 8103 (1951).

year and multiplying by the number of persons in that income group in the other year, some indication of the effect of changing income and tax patterns can be gleaned. In Table 29 the effective rate of all taxes for the average person in each income group in 1937 and 1948–49 has been applied to the income data of the opposite year.

TABLE 29

Effect of the Change in the Level and Distribution of the National Income on Tax Yields, 1937 and 1948–49
(In Million Pounds)

INCOME RANGE (IN POUNDS)	1948–49 EFFECTIVE TAX RATE ON INCOME DATA OF		1937 EFFECTIVE TAX RATE ON INCOME DATA OF	
	1937	1948–49	1937	1948–49
	1	2	3	4
Under 135 *	746.6	128.4	161.4	28.1
135–250	705.4	623.9	168.2	149.8
250–500	227.2	999.6	92.5	399.4
500–1,000	142.5	652.3	79.9	390.4
1,000–2,000	135.7	415.5	80.5	252.3
2,000–10,000	374.0	754.6	186.7	380.5
10,000 and above	407.9	409.0	152.7	152.7
	2,739.3	3,983.3	921.9	1,753.2

* £125 in 1937.

Column 1 shows roughly how much tax revenue might have been raised in 1937 if the 1948–49 schedule of tax rates had been in effect.[9] This amount, £2,739 million, is almost exactly three times the total amount which was actually collected in taxes in 1937, as shown in column 3. Column 4 indicates the amount that might have been collected in 1948–49 if the 1937 schedule of tax rates had still been in effect. In this case tax yields in 1948–49 would have been only about 40% as great as they actually were, as shown in column 2. When we compare the same year under different tax rates, the change in the effective rates appears to have made a great difference in the tax yield. The changing distribution of income does not appear to have had so important an effect on tax revenues, although there has been a very noticeable shift in the income groups from whom the largest absolute yields were obtained. It might be safely concluded

9. This is obviously a very imperfect measure, subject to numerous theoretical objections. If 1948 tax rates had been in effect in 1937 the entire pattern of consumer behavior would probably have been different, and one suspects that the initial distribution of income would have differed substantially. But even though people would have acted differently, the total amount of tax revenues given in columns 1 and 4 of Table 29 can be used as a very rough index of the effect of the changing distribution of income on tax yields.

that the largest portion of the increase in tax revenues over the decade has been due to the change in tax rates, and a considerably smaller portion due to the change in the level and distribution of the national income.

One cannot analyze expenditures in quite the same manner, because few expenditures automatically varied with changes in income. About the only expenditures which were closely related to income variations were those transfers related to unemployment and public assistance. Central government expenditures on unemployment benefits and noncontributory pensions totaled £136 million in 1937, while 1948–49 expenditures on these items, plus the newly organized national assistance, totaled only £95 million. If the 1948–49 rates of benefit had been in effect in 1937 it is likely that the sum of these transfers would have been six or seven times greater than were actual payments in 1937. On the other hand, 1937 regulations, if they had been applied to income and employment conditions in 1948–49, would probably have resulted in expenditures only about one-fifth as great as actual expenditures in 1948–49. In this case it can only be concluded that the tendency to reduce the sum of these transfers because of fewer eligible persons (e.g. fewer unemployed and poverty stricken elderly persons) was greater than the tendency for these payments to increase because of the higher rates of benefit.

Another type of change between 1937 and 1948–49 was in the relative importance of particular kinds of taxes and expenditures. The different sources of revenue in the two years are shown in Table 30 as percentages of total tax revenue (excluding national insurance contributions).

The most noticeable change was in the proportion of direct taxes on income to total taxes, 46.4% of all taxes arising from this source in 1948–49 as against 39.1% in 1937. This increase was entirely due to the profits tax, income tax and surtax accounting for 39.1% in 1937 and 39% in 1948–49. It is interesting to see that the surtax was relatively less important in providing revenue in 1948–49 than in 1937. This was partly because surtax rates did not increase greatly in the decade, the effective rate of tax being increased by the raising of the standard rate of income tax (from 25% to 45%). Also, the number and amount of incomes assessed to surtax increased by only about 75%, while the number of persons assessed for income tax increased from 3.7 million in 1937 to 14.5 million in 1948–49, even though the exemption limit was £10 higher in the postwar year.

Taxes on capital were smaller relative to the sum of taxes in 1948–49, despite the presence of the special contribution. If this tax were excluded as a nonrecurring tax—i.e. not a part of the permanent tax program—taxes on capital would be an even smaller percentage of the tax yield for 1948–49. In pounds, death duties did not quite double, while the sum of all tax revenues increased 4½ times.

TABLE 30

Types of Tax as Percentages of Total Tax Yields,
1937 and 1948–49

	PERCENTAGES	
	1937	1948–49
Income tax	32.5	35.6
Surtax	6.6	3.4
Profits tax (national defense contribution)		7.4
Direct taxes on income	39.1	46.4
Death duties	11.3	4.8
Special Contribution	—	3.0
Direct taxes on capital	11.3	7.8
Total direct taxes	50.4	54.2
Customs and excise	40.5	40.9
Stamp duties	3.2	1.5
Other indirect taxes	5.9	3.4
Total indirect taxes	49.6	45.8
Total	100.0	100.0

On the expenditure side of the budget the changes are summarized in Table 31, which shows the general division by type of expenditure for the combined central government and national insurance fund accounts. Since the large surplus in 1948–49 tends to inflate indivisible expenditures, columns 3 and 4 indicate the division of current expenditures, excluding the surplus on current account and that of the extrabudgetary funds. The combined surpluses totaled £575 million in 1948–49, as against only £85 million in 1937.[10]

Transfer incomes were a much smaller percentage of total expenditure in 1948–49, although if one were to include the cost of the national health service as a transfer-in-kind (as the cost of medical benefits are classified for 1937), transfers would be about 8 percentage points greater and other divisible expenditure reduced accordingly. Indivisible expenditures declined slightly despite the large increases in military expenditures and debt charges. If one were to divide expenditures further, separating subsidies from other divisible expenditures, subsidy payments to industry and agriculture would

10. See Table 10, above p. 42, for 1948–49; and Barna, p. 45, for 1937.

be approximately 3.9% in 1937 and about 13.4% in 1948–49. Thus the sum of transfers to private persons plus transfers to the business sector (subsidies) would be about equal for the two years.

TABLE 31

Types of Expenditure as Percentages of Total Expenditures of the Central Government and Extrabudgetary Funds, 1937 and 1948–49

TYPE OF EXPENDITURE	INCLUDING SURPLUSES		EXCLUDING SURPLUSES	
	1937	1948–49	1937	1948–49
Indivisible expenditures	59.2%	58.8%	55.1%	52.1%
Other divisible expenditures	15.8%	24.9%	17.4%	28.9%
Transfers	25.0%	16.3%	27.5%	19.0%
	100.0%	100.0%	100.0%	100.0%

INEQUALITY OF PREWAR AND POSTWAR INCOMES

The statistical findings of the previous chapter indicated that there was a considerable redistribution of income through public finance in 1948–49. The extent to which incomes were partially leveled, however, was given in terms of pounds. This estimate and the comparison with 1937 indicated the absolute amounts which had been shifted, rather than the resulting degree of income equality achieved. It may be more useful—especially for the purposes of the next chapter, where the British experience will be compared with that of the United States—to attempt to indicate the changing pattern of income inequality.

The degree of inequality can be expressed by various mathematical indices,[11] but an index will be used here which incorporates the concept of the aggregate net redistribution of income as defined and used in previous chapters. Inequality will be measured by the percentage of income which would have to be shifted from high to low income groups in order to achieve an equal distribution of income per capita. The use of such a device will permit the estimated redistribution in 1937 and 1948–49 to be contrasted with the theoretical redistribution necessary to bring about perfect equality. It hardly needs saying that this does not imply that perfect equality is a desirable norm; perfect equality merely serves as a useful yardstick to measure the effectiveness of a program which has been publicly declared to have the diminishing of income inequalities as one major goal.

11. See, for example, Dwight B. Yntema, "Measures of the Inequality in the Personal Distribution of Wealth or Income," *JASA, 28* (1933), 423–33; and Hugh Dalton, "The Measurement of the Inequality of Incomes," *EJ, 30* (1920), 348–61.

For measuring inequality in this manner the extremes are zero for perfect equality and one for perfect inequality.[12] It should also be noted that this type of index weighs the amounts of income above and below the mean, emphasizing dispersion rather than skewness in the distribution curve. This is not a disadvantage as long as that which is being measured is kept in mind, and such an index has distinct advantages in simplicity and in its applications.

Applying this measure of income inequality to pretax incomes for a number of years, we have an indication of how far the redistributive process would have had to go to level incomes exactly. Table 32 indicates that in 1880 about 42% of personal factor income would have had to be redistributed in order to achieve an equalitarian distribution. This percentage declined to 27% in 1937, and reached 24% in 1948–49. The percentage of private factor income redistribution necessary to achieve equality has slightly diminished, from 29% in 1937 to 27% in 1948–49.

TABLE 32

Inequality of Pretax Incomes *

YEAR	PRIVATE FACTOR INCOME	PERSONAL FACTOR INCOME
1880	—	.42
1913	—	.40
1928	—	.38
1937	.29	.27
1948–1949	.27	.24

* For the years prior to 1948–49 the following estimates of income distribution have been used in estimating the degree of inequality: for 1880 and 1913, Arthur L. Bowley, *The Change in the Distribution of the National Income, 1880–1913* (1920), pp. 16–7; for 1928, Clark, p. 76; for 1937, Barna, pp. 31–41. The estimates for the pre1937 years are only approximations, because the available income data is imperfect.

The diminishing degree of inequality in the distribution of initial incomes, before taxes or benefits, can also be represented diagrammatically. In Figures V and VI private and personal factor income distributions are shown as Lorenz curves for 1937 and 1948–49. The slightly diminished area under the curve for the more recent year indicates movement in the direction of greater equality.

Turning to posttax incomes in Table 33, one may observe the inequality of personal and private incomes after the deduction of taxes. In the left hand column net private income inequality is shown

12. The upper limit is actually a fraction less than one. For example, perfect inequality would be present in a population of 100 if one person had all the income and the other 99 had none. In this case 99% of the total income would have to be redistributed to establish perfect equality, and the index would record inequality as .99.

to have diminished from about .21 in 1937 to .15 in 1948–49. The degree of inequality of disposable income has similarly declined, from .23 to .16.

Figure V. Distribution of personal factor income, 1937 and 1948–49.

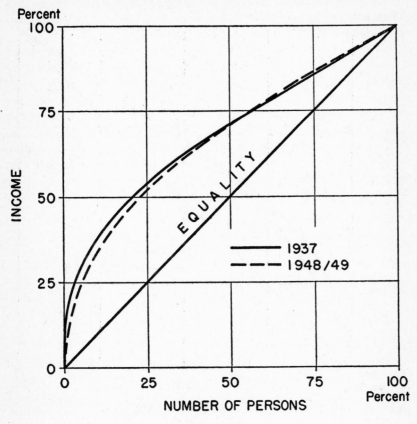

TABLE 33

Inequality of Posttax Incomes *

YEAR	NET PRIVATE INCOME	DISPOSABLE INCOME
1880	—	.41
1913	—	.38
1928	—	.30
1937	.21	.23
1948–49	.15	.16

* See note to Table 32, above.

Tables 32 and 33 indicate two interesting things. One is that the distributions of both personal and private factor incomes were slightly more equal in 1948–49 than in 1937, even though one might have anticipated the reverse trend considering the relatively greater degree of prosperity in 1948–49. The difference in inequality, however,

Figure VI. Distribution of private factor income, 1937 and 1948–49.

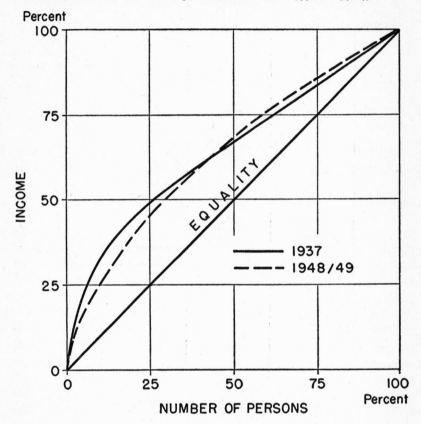

appears slightly less for private incomes, probably because of the larger percentage of undistributed corporate profits in the postwar year. The second interesting point is that up to 1937 the diminishing degree of inequality of disposable income appears to be primarily the result of the changing distribution of personal factor income, whereas the decline in disposable income inequality from 1937 to 1948 is seen to be almost entirely due to the redistributive effects of direct taxes and transfers.

Table 34 compares the inequality of income after taxes and benefits with original income inequality, indicating the net redistribution. The first line shows the reduction of inequality of personal incomes caused by all unavoidable taxes and all divisible benefits, and the second line indicates the reduction in the inequality of private incomes by all taxes and all benefits.

TABLE 34

Reduction of Income Inequality through the Redistribution of Income

	INEQUALITY OF FACTOR INCOME DISTRIBUTION		INEQUALITY AFTER TAXES AND BENEFITS		NET REDISTRIBUTION	
	1937	1948-49	1937	1948-49	1937	1948-49
Personal income	.27	.24	.17	.13(.14) *	.10	.11(.10) *
Private income	.29	.26	.20	.15(.16)	.09	.11(.10)

* Parenthetical figures exclude the special contribution.

The figures in Table 34 show not only that the initial distribution of income was slightly less unequal in 1948-49 than in 1937, but also that the redistribution of income was relatively greater in the more recent year, especially when one includes the special contribution. The resulting inequality of income was such that in 1948-49 the redistribution of another 13% of personal income would have resulted in a precise leveling of personal incomes per capita, and the redistribution of another 15% of private income would have brought about perfect consumer income equality.

In the last few pages perfect equality has been used as a yardstick to measure the effectiveness of the redistribution of income. Most persons who favor greater income equality, however, do not think of precise equality per capita as a desirable norm.[13] They think, instead, of diminishing the gap between the highest and lowest incomes while retaining smaller absolute differential rewards and incentives. In place of perfect equality, therefore, it may be interesting to substitute a narrow range of incomes around the average income as a yardstick. Let it be assumed in the next few paragraphs that the equalitarian's concept of an ideal distribution is one in which the following is true: the highest income is not more than ten times greater than the lowest income, and the lowest income is not less than half the average income.[14] Thus the upper and lower limits

13. A possible exception was the late G. B. Shaw, who differed from most other Fabians by often proclaiming this "Babouvist heresy." See, e.g., *Everybody's Political What's What* (London, Constable, 1944), p. 56.

14. The range could equally well be in the ratio of 5:1, 25:1, etc. This is only a general way of expressing a possible theoretical goal. Practically, this type of goal would be almost impossible to achieve short of legislating the amount of income one could legally receive. In practice the range of posttax incomes is reduced by a steeply rising marginal tax rate on high incomes and welfare payments to the lowest incomes.

of such a semiequalitarian range would be .5x and 5x, x being the average income.

The average private factor income per income recipient was just under £200 in 1937 and about £445 in 1948–49; the hypothetical income ranges would therefore be approximately £100–1,000 and £225–2,250 respectively for the two years.

Since by definition aggregate consumers' income (after all taxes and benefits) is the same as aggregate private factor income, these ranges can also be applied to final consumers' income to see the effectiveness of the redistributive process in bringing more persons within these assumed "ideal" ranges.

TABLE 35

Percentage of Income Recipients and Total Income below, within, and above an Assumed "Ideal" Range of Incomes, 1937 and 1948–49

	PERCENTAGE OF INCOME RECIPIENTS			PERCENTAGE OF TOTAL INCOME		
	BELOW MIN.	WITHIN RANGE	ABOVE MAX.	BELOW MIN.	WITHIN RANGE	ABOVE MAX.
Private factor income						
1937	33 *	65.7	1.3	15 *	64	21
1948–49	37	62.1	.9	16	70	14
Consumer income						
1937	22 *	77.2	.8	10 *	72	18
1948–49	12	87.4	.6	5.5	89.1	5.4

* The lower limit of this assumed range in 1937 was less than the income tax exemption limit; so the number and amount of incomes below £110 in 1937 is subject to a considerable margin of error.

In Table 35 it is seen that a slightly larger percentage of income recipients were within the hypothetical range in 1937 than in 1948–49, although a larger percentage of total income fell within the range in the latter year. After the redistribution of income, however, a

No precise range could be achieved, however, without a guaranteed minimum income and a 100% marginal tax rate above the maximum, a combination which, given such a narrow hypothetical range, would be most unsatisfactory from the point of view of incentives. In postwar Britain, social security programs have almost guaranteed a minimum of about £65, and there were less than 100 persons with posttax incomes greater than £6,000 in 1948–49, so that it might be said there were almost minimum and maximum incomes enforced by government; but this range was more in the nature of 100:1. However, even if a narrow range of incomes is an impractical way of expressing an equalitarian goal, it may still be useful as a measure of inequality and has been suggested as an aim of social policy in Britain. See, e.g., Francis Williams, *Socialist Britain* (1949), p. 113.

considerably larger number and amount of incomes fell within this range in 1948-49 than in 1937. By 1948-49 about 87% of income recipients, with 89% of the nation's income, had incomes not less than half nor more than 5 times the average consumer income. Redistribution reduced the number of persons outside this range by a third in 1937, and by two-thirds in 1948-49.

SUMMARY, PREWAR AND POSTWAR REDISTRIBUTION

The estimated redistribution of income in 1948-49 has been compared with a similar estimate for 1937, and redistribution appears to have been greater in postwar Britain in absolute terms and relative to the national income but slightly less per pound of tax revenue raised. Allocating indivisible benefits for both years in proportion to the distribution of net private income, the redistribution has been estimated at £386 million, or 8.8% of the national income, in 1937, and at £1,260 million, or 13.1% of national income, in 1948-49. Although the precise amounts estimated here are subject to a considerable margin of error, the figures should be roughly indicative of the relative importance of the redistributive programs for the two years.

The dividing line between persons who, net of taxes and benefits, were losers and gainers through this redistributive process was slightly over £400 in 1937 and about £650 in 1948-49 (personal income). In both years, therefore, about 85%-90% of the population are estimated to have gained, although in the postwar year those who gained, gained more, and those who lost, lost more.[15]

In measuring income inequality one sees that the original distribution of income was slightly less unequal in the postwar year, and the redistribution of income was more effective in reducing inequality of consumer income in 1948-49 than in 1937. The distribution of consumer income in 1948-49 was such that only about 12% of income recipients received less than half the average income and less than 1% had incomes more than 5 times the average income.

In the following chapter the findings of this chapter will be compared with the prewar and postwar experience of the United States.

15. It is interesting to note that if indivisible expenditures are excluded for both years, only persons with income not exceeding about £225 were gainers in either year. If indivisible benefits are not valued as such, this would indicate that fewer persons benefited in 1948-49. This is also implied in Table 28 above, in the comparison of personal factor incomes and disposable incomes.

CHAPTER 8

Income Redistribution in Great Britain and the United States

THE LAST chapter indicated that the government in Britain is doing substantially more in the way of redistributing incomes in the post-war period than it did in the late 1930's. Is this true to the same extent in other Western countries? It would be useful to compare the findings for Britain with those for a number of other countries, but the only one for which somewhat comparable data is available is the United States. In *Fiscal Policies and the American Economy* Adler has made a less detailed but adequate estimate for the United States in 1938–39 and 1946–47.[1] Although a number of adjustments must be made in order to compare the two sets of data, such a comparison will be useful.

REDISTRIBUTION OF INCOME IN THE UNITED STATES, 1938–39 AND 1946–47

When one sets out to adapt the American data, a conceptual problem arises which was not a difficulty when two different years in the same country were being compared: the central governments of Britain and the United States do not perform identical functions in their fiscal operations. For example, in raising funds British local governments have only the single source of local rates, whereas American state governments have the power to tax incomes and estates, and both state and municipal governments can impose sales and excise taxes. (The central governments of both countries make grants-in-aid to lower governmental units, but this is not technically a source of revenue.) In terms of expenditures, the British central government finances the largest share of expenditures on education, housing, and assistance to those in need. In the United States, on the other hand, education is almost wholly financed by state and local governments, most public housing projects are locally owned, and unemployment compensation is determined and administered by the states. Because of these differences in function, central government

1. Pp. 359–421. See also the appendix, "The Statistical Allocation of Taxes and Expenditures in 1938–39 and 1946–47," by E. R. Schlesinger.

revenues and expenditures in the two countries are not strictly comparable.

In adjusting the United States data, therefore, it has seemed reasonable to attempt to include in the measure of redistribution that part of state and local fiscal activity which corresponds to central government fiscal operations in Great Britain. To accomplish this, local property taxes and poll taxes have been subtracted from the distribution of United States tax revenues, as given by Adler. On the expenditure side of the combined accounts, an equivalent amount has been deducted, consisting of expenditures which correspond to the purely local British expenditures. Thus, all expenditures on police and fire protection and local administration have been deducted, plus one-half of local expenditures on roads and housing. An additional amount, equal to the difference between the sum of these expenditures and the receipt of local property taxes, has been deducted from local expenditures on education. After these adjustments, the data on distribution of United States taxes and expenditures are in their inclusiveness more nearly comparable to those for Great Britain.

The remaining adjustments are of an accounting nature. Adler did not make a similar classification of indivisible expenditures, so that expenditures on national defense, foreign aid, and miscellaneous expenditures, plus debt charges and the surplus, have been included in this category and in the tables below have been distributed in proportion to net private income. This makes the distribution of indivisible benefits comparable for the two countries.[2]

What Adler calls "personal income" differs from that used in the preceding chapters by the inclusion of amounts equal to gross corporate profits and estate and gift taxes. These items have been deducted to give a distribution of personal income similar to that for Great Britain.

It should also be mentioned that the definition of "consumer unit," used in the American study, differs somewhat from the "tax family" used for Great Britain. Single blood relations (or near relatives living with parents or relatives) who had incomes above the tax exemption limit are classified in the United States data as part of larger consumer units if half their incomes were pooled toward joint expenditures. If, however, contributions were less than half of income and total income was above the tax exemption limit, such a single person is automatically considered a separate consumer unit.[3] In the

2. I.e. assumption 2 is used for both countries. See pp. 48–50, above.

3. See definition of the consumer unit used in the 1948 Federal Reserve Bulletin, *Survey of Consumer Finances,* p. 1, n., adopted by Adler. See also, National Resources Committee, *Consumer Expenditures in the United States* (1939), pp. 98–9.

British data any single adult with an income above the tax exemption limit was classified as a separate tax family, regardless of the possibility of income pooling. The number of single persons actually pooling their income with that of a larger unit was probably rather small in the United States, so that the difference between United States "consumer units" and British "tax families" should not be great.[4] The pooling of some incomes in the United States distribution of income will tend to reduce somewhat the number of units in the lowest income ranges and to raise slightly the redistributive breakeven point, but the effect on the aggregate net redistribution of income should be relatively minor.

After the adjustment of the United States data as outlined above, the distribution of income, taxes, and benefits for the United States in 1938–39 and 1946–47 is summarized in Table 36. The distributions as given by Adler are presented in the same seven money income ranges for the two years; so it was not possible, as with the British data, to make the comparison by pairing off income grades for the two years which represented roughly the same real incomes.

To the left of the dividing line in Table 36 the redistribution of personal incomes by unavoidable taxes and income transfers is indicated, columns 2 and 5 showing personal factor incomes and disposable incomes. In both 1938–39 and 1946–47 the three lowest income groups gained more in transfer incomes than they lost in direct taxes. The postwar increase in transfers and direct taxes is also evident from the totals for the two years. While incomes did not quite

---

4. The size of the average consumer unit in the U. S. in 1946–47 was approximately 2.8 persons, and the average tax family in Britain in 1948–49 was 2.1 persons. The difference appears to be almost entirely the result of real differences in family sizes rather than an indication of considerable pooling of incomes. The marriage rate in the U. S., e.g., is much higher, and people tend to marry much younger. Thus the percentage of persons over 16 who were married in 1948 was only 50% in Great Britain, and 80% in the U. S. The percentage of those who were (or had been) married in the 45–54 age group was 86.9% in Britain and 92.1% in the U. S., and for the 20–24 age group it was 32% and 59% respectively. Also, the U. S. population contains a larger percentage of young persons, and the average schooling period is about three years longer. For example, persons aged 0–19 represented only 28.7% of the population in Britain, but 34.4% in the U. S. The percentage of persons aged 14–18 engaged in fulltime education was 75.5% in the U.S., and only 13.4% in Britain. These factors account for most of the difference in the average size of the family unit. If the proportion of young and old in the population were the same in Britain as in the U. S., and if 75% of children aged 14–18 remained in school in Britain, and if 80% of British adults were married, the average-sized tax family would then be almost identical to the average size consumer unit in the U. S. It would appear, therefore, that the pooling of income by adults with incomes above the income tax exemption limit in the United States is statistically insignificant in the postwar period. The U. S. consumer unit and the British tax family appear to be at least roughly comparable, each representing an economic unit in most cases living on a single income (or joint income if husband and wife have separate incomes).

TABLE 36*

Distribution of Income, Taxes, and Benefits in the United States, 1938–39 and 1946–47
(In Billion Dollars)

1938–39 Income Range (In Dollars)	No. of Consumer Units (In Millions)	Personal Factor Income	Transfers	Direct Personal Taxes	Disposable Income	Private Income	All Taxes	All Benefits	Consumer Income	Net Gain or Loss
	1	2	3	4	5	6	7	8	9	10
Under 1,000	16.80	9.73	1.61	.09	11.25	11.62	1.22	4.53	14.93	+3.31
1,000–2,000	15.41	22.17	.74	.16	22.75	23.46	2.65	3.07	23.88	+.42
2,000–3,000	4.80	12.14	.11	.07	12.18	12.48	1.41	.98	12.05	−.43
3,000–4,000	1.65	5.35	—	.05	5.30	5.59	.65	.35	5.29	−.30
4,000–5,000	.64	2.67	—	.03	2.64	2.73	.36	.21	2.58	−.15
5,000–7,500	.46	2.52	—	.04	2.48	2.67	.41	.21	2.47	−.21
7,500 and above	.50	11.29	—	1.09	10.20	11.50	3.06	.41	8.85	−2.65
	40.26	65.87	2.46	1.53	66.80	70.05	9.76	9.76	70.05	±3.73
1946–47										
Under 1,000	8.1	3.03	2.57	.10	5.50	3.17	.91	4.34	6.60	+3.43
1,000–2,000	11.1	17.85	2.84	.83	19.86	18.40	2.71	7.01	22.70	+4.30
2,000–3,000	11.3	30.06	2.73	1.97	30.82	30.87	5.11	8.73	34.49	+3.62
3,000–4,000	8.3	31.94	1.95	2.24	31.65	32.83	5.42	7.81	35.22	+2.39
4,000–5,000	4.8	21.81	.88	2.24	20.45	22.43	4.80	4.61	22.24	−.19
5,000–7,500	4.4	30.25	—	2.98	27.27	31.68	6.80	4.84	29.72	−1.96
7,500 and above	2.4	50.96	—	9.17	41.79	56.77	18.41	6.82	45.18	−11.59
	50.4	185.90	10.97	19.53	177.34	196.15	44.16	44.16	196.15	±13.74

* Adapted from Adler, in *Fiscal Policies and the American Economy*, ch. 8.

triple, transfers increased to more than four times their amount in
1938–39, and direct taxes in the postwar year yielded almost thirteen
times as much revenue.

In the right half of Table 36 the aggregate net redistribution is
shown, columns 6 and 9 indicating original private factor income and
final consumers' income respectively. The aggregate net redistribution (the totals shown in column 10) in 1938–39 is estimated at
$3.73 billion, and $13.74 billion in 1946–47. In the earlier year only
the first two income groups were net gainers, the dividing line between income gains or losses being in the neighborhood of $2,000. In
1946–47 the four lowest income groups registered net gains, and the
dividing line between net gains or losses had risen to about $4,500.

The aggregate net redistribution of income amounted to 5.4% of
national income in 1938–39 and had climbed to about 7.5% in
1946–47. These percentages are considerably less than those found
for Great Britain, where 1937 redistribution was estimated at 8.8%,
and 13.1% in 1948–49. However, the fiscal program of the United
States, as far as it went, tended to have almost equal redistributive
effects, the smaller percentage of the national income redistributed
being largely explained by the relatively smaller government taxation and expenditure programs. In 1938–39, for example, United
States tax revenues were 14.3% of national income, as against 21.8%
in Great Britain in 1937. In the postwar year United States tax
yields were only 24.1% of income, while they had reached 41.3%
in Great Britain. Before the war the average redistribution was about
38% of each tax dollar in the United States, and 41% of each tax
pound in Britain. In the postwar years it was 31% in the United
States and 32% in Britain. The effectiveness of each tax dollar
(pound) was therefore about the same for the two countries, but the
entire fiscal program was smaller in the United States relative to
national income.

INCOME INEQUALITY IN THE UNITED STATES AND GREAT BRITAIN

It is difficult to compare two countries in monetary terms, especially where the currency unit is not the same. The effects of public
finance on the distribution of income can perhaps best be indicated
by applying the measures of income inequality used in the previous
chapter. In Chapter 7 income inequality was measured by the percentage of income which would have had to be redistributed in order
to achieve a perfectly equal distribution of income per capita.[5] By

5. See pp. 73–4.

application of this measure to the United States data Table 37 compares the extent of income inequality in Britain and the United States.

TABLE 37

Income Inequality in Great Britain and the United States

	GREAT BRITAIN	UNITED STATES	GREAT BRITAIN	UNITED STATES
	1937	1938–39	1948–49	1946–47
1. Personal factor income	.27	.30	.24	.29
2. Disposable income	.23	.28	.16	.25
3. Private factor income	.29	.31	.26	.31
4. Consumers' income	.20	.26	.15(.16) *	.24
5. Net redistribution (3 minus 4)	.09	.05	.11(.10) *	.07

* Bracketed figures exclude the special contribution.

Looking first at the relationship of factor incomes, it is interesting to notice that there was a greater difference between the two countries in the postwar years than before the war. Over the decade the inequality of factor incomes declined considerably in Britain, while it remained almost stationary in the United States.[6] One might have anticipated that inequality would have been greater in the relatively more prosperous postwar years, since inequality tends to vary di-

6. Since this chapter was written, Simon Kuznets' *Shares of Upper Income Groups in Income and Savings* (1953) has been published, throwing further light on the changing pattern of income distribution in the U. S. Professor Kuznets finds that since 1936 the income share of the upper 5% of the U. S. population has declined markedly. This decline does not show up clearly in Table 37, partly because approximately the upper 25% of income recipients is being used here (i.e. persons whose incomes were above the mean income) and also because Kuznets used per capita incomes rather than income per family unit. The measure of inequality used below on pp. 90–1, however, does indicate a decline in the share of upper income groups similar to that given by Kuznets. If we were to recast the British data so as to obtain a per capita measure of upper income shares, the approximate percentage shares of the top 5% of persons in personal and disposable incomes would be as follows:

	Gt. B.	U. S.	Gt. B.	U. S.
	1937–38	1937	1948–49	1946
Personal Income	31.1%	23.8%	27.6%	18.2%
Disposable Income	24.4%	27.1%	19.2%	17.7%

These figures indicate that the percentage decline in both the personal and disposable income shares of the top 5% was greater in the U. S. than in Britain. The U. S. figures are from Kuznets (p. 36), while the British figures are based on the Inland Revenue classifications of income and family size for 1937–38 and 1948–49. See this writer's "Income Shares of Upper Income Groups in Great Britain and the United States," *AER, 44* (1954).

rectly with increasing and declining prosperity.[7] However, in both
the United States in 1946 and Britain in 1948 government controls
tended to limit factor returns in the form of corporate profits and
rents, and it is primarily the rise of these income components which
often tends to accentuate inequality in prosperous or inflationary
periods. The lessening of factor income inequality in Britain may indicate merely that the government was stricter, or more successful, in
controlling the inflationary rise of these sources of income in comparison with wages and farm incomes.

The decline in income inequality was greatest for personal factor
income, probably as a result of changes in corporate distributions.
Dividend payments in both countries in the postwar years were not
more than double the distributions in 1937–39, but gross undistributed profits increased from £270 million to £1,205 million in
Britain and from $.1 billion to $17.7 billion in the United States. Thus
nonpersonal income, which is distributed more unequally than personal income, was a larger share of private factor income in the postwar years in both countries.

The movement toward equality in disposable incomes was much
greater in Britain both before and after the war. This was due largely
to the comparatively heavier direct taxation of personal incomes in
Britain, direct taxes in that country increasing over the decade from
9% of personal income in 1937 to 15% in 1948–49, and from 3%
in the United States in 1938–39 to 11% in 1946–47.

Line 5 of Table 37 shows that income redistribution was much
greater in Britain both before and after the war, although the relative increase in redistribution in the postwar years was the same for
both countries (i.e. redistribution increased by an amount equal to
2% of total income in both countries). If we compare the net redistribution with the inequality of private factor income, however, it is
obvious that the British redistributive effort was much greater, given
the initial distribution of income. That is to say, Britain went about
one-third of the way toward establishing perfect equality in 1937,
but almost half way in 1948–49, while the United States went only
one-sixth and about one-quarter of the way in the respective prewar
and postwar years.[8] With a more equal distribution of factor income
and a substantially greater redistribution of income, the inequality
of final consumer incomes in Britain was substantially less than that
of the United States, especially in the postwar years.

7. Profits tend to be less stable than other components of income over the trade
cycle, and since such a large share of the income of persons in the highest income
groups arises from profits, these highest incomes tend to fluctuate more than incomes
of other groups.
8. Dividing line 5 by line 3 in Table 37.

Two major conclusions can be drawn from this indication of changing degrees of income inequality. The most apparent one, of course, is that Britain has gone much further in the redistribution of income than has the United States. The other, perhaps equally significant, is the apparent tendency in Britain for the distribution of factor incomes to become considerably less unequal. As will be suggested in the next chapter, this was largely due to the greater relative increase in income than the increase in private capital (i.e. in earned income rather than investment income), 1948–49 income being a little more than double the national income in 1937, while the value of privately held capital increased by not quite 50%.[9] As a result, the proportion of total unearned income (both personal and nonpersonal) to private factor income declined from about 28.1% in 1938 to 26.3% in 1948. Coupled with the relative decline in rent, profits, and interest, the British government since the war has also discouraged the distribution of corporate profits by a differential profits tax. As a combined effect, investment income as a percentage of personal factor income dropped from 24% in 1938 to only 13% in 1948. The accumulation of undistributed profits has been primarily the result of the corporate tax structure. The relative decline of total private investment income (i.e. aggregate rent, interest, and profits) is somewhat difficult to explain, although one suspects that postwar controls and regulations are largely responsible. Corporate gross trading profits increased proportionately more than the national income in the 1938–48 decade, but the jump was not nearly so spectacular as the increase in corporate profits in the United States. Is this, perhaps, an indication of a lessening desire (or ability) to make profits under existing controls and tax regulations? Or an indication of a relatively greater pressure by other productive factors, labor for example, to increase their share of gross corporate revenue? Or an indication of a decline in industrial efficiency? Or perhaps an indication of a greater sense of social responsibility by business leaders? The answer probably requires an extensive analysis of industry which cannot be given here. It is quite possible, however, that what appears to be a rather unusual effect may be natural for Britain but would be foreign for the United States. Looking back over the less prosperous thirties, one suspects that the greater stability of corporate profits in Britain may be merely an institutional characteristic which has been absent in America.[10] While

9. This may be effect as well as cause, for the value of capital assets reflect their capacity to produce future income. The relative decline of total private capital, however, is also the result of a very noticeable decline in the rate of private savings.

10. One element of the apparent stability lies in national accounting techniques. Debenture interest is included as part of corporate trading profits in Britain, while it is excluded in the United States. Net trading profits in the U. S., over and above

British corporate profits since 1938 have not increased nearly so much as have their counterparts in America, on the other hand neither did they sink to such depths in the thirties when the British economy was equally depressed. If British profits are characteristically more sluggish in reacting to general business conditions, relative prosperity (or inflation) may not have the same tendency to increase income inequality that it has had in the United States (at least until 1940).

Figure VII. Distribution of prewar factor and consumer incomes, United States and Great Britain.

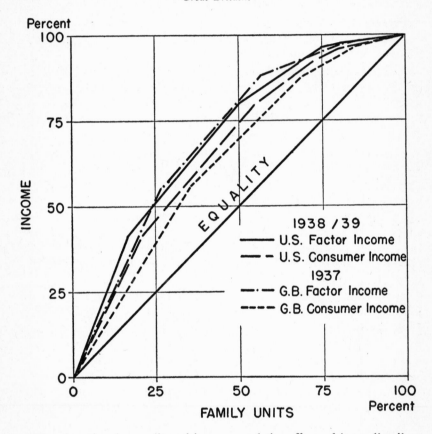

The changing inequality of income and the effect of its redistribution in the two countries can be presented graphically by the use of Lorenz curves. In Figure VII the prewar distribution of private factor

debenture interest obligations, no doubt appear more unstable on the leverage principle, although this does not completely account for the difference between the two countries.

income and consumer income for the United States and Great Britain are shown. As indicated in Table 37 above, prewar inequality of factor income was greatest in Britain, and this is shown in the graph by the slightly larger area between the Lorenz curve and the 45° line of perfect equality. The redistribution of income was comparatively greater in Britain, however, so that consumer income inequality was slightly less in Britain than in the United States.

Figure VIII. Distribution of postwar factor and consumer incomes, United States and Great Britain.

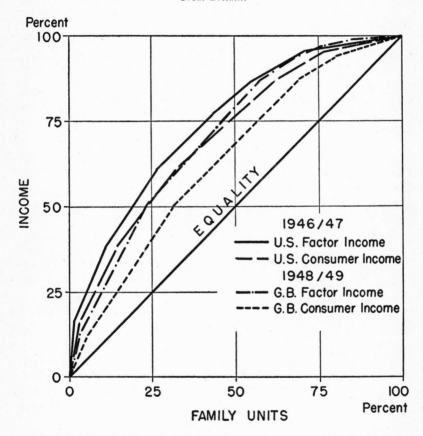

In Figure VIII the postwar situation is shown, and the British distribution of income both before and after redistribution was considerably more equal than the American counterparts.

Before leaving the comparison of the two countries, the other index of inequality used in the last chapter,[11] the percentages of consumer

11. See p. 78.

units and income remaining within the limits of a hypothetical equalitarian range of incomes, might also be applied to the United States. The results are shown in Table 38.

TABLE 38

Percentage of Family Units and Total Income below,
within, and above an Assumed "Ideal"
Range of Incomes

	PERCENTAGE OF UNITS OUTSIDE IDEAL RANGE			PERCENTAGE OF INCOME OUTSIDE IDEAL RANGE		
	BELOW MIN.	WITHIN RANGE	ABOVE MAX.	BELOW MIN.	WITHIN RANGE	ABOVE MAX.
Prewar						
U. S. private income	31 *	67.9	1.1	11 *	73	16
G. B. private income	33 *	65.7	1.3	15 *	64	21
U. S. consumer income	22	77.0	1.0	7	79	14
G. B. consumer income	22	77.2	.8	10	72	18
Postwar						
U. S. private income	37	62.6	.4 *	10	77	13 *
G. B. private income	37	62.1	.9	16	70	14
U. S. consumer income	25	74.7	.3 *	7.0	82.0	11.0 *
G. B. consumer income	12	87.4	.6	5.5	89.1	5.4

* Asterisked figures are subject to a rather wide margin of error, since the process of extrapolation in open-ended income groups is a risky venture, to say the least. These figures, however, should be roughly indicative of percentages above and below the chosen range.

The limits of the hypothetical range of incomes for the United States were roughly $870–8,700 in 1938–39 and $1,950–19,500 in 1946–47. In the prewar year 67.9% of consumer units with 73% of total private factor income were within the range, and after redistribution 77% of consumer units with 79% of the income were within this range. While the percentage of *persons* within the range was slightly greater for the United States than for Britain before the war, the percentage of United States *income* inside this range was considerably greater both before and after redistribution. In the postwar years fewer persons were within this range before redistribution in both countries. The redistribution was proportionately greater in Britain, however, so that Britain had only a little over 10% of her families and consumer incomes outside this range, while the United States still had 25.3% of her consumer units and 17% of her income outside.

Looking more closely at these figures, we find that in Britain there were relatively more persons with a larger percentage of total private income above the upper limits of the assumed range of incomes. At the bottom, however, the British distribution was noticeably more concentrated just below the lower limits of this range. These characteristics were also noticeable on the Lorenz curves above, where the curves representing private factor incomes for the two countries crossed in both years. In terms of the results of efforts to redistribute incomes, this is undoubtedly an important point. In 1948–49, for example, the difference between the total factor income received by persons above the maximum of this range in Britain and the total income these persons would have had if they had only received the maximum was almost four times the amount of income which would have been needed to bring the 37% of families below the minimum up to that lower limit. In the United States in 1946–47, on the other hand, income in excess of the maximum would have been only barely sufficient to raise those on the bottom of the income scale up to the lower limit. In other words, theoretically it would have been a simpler task in Britain than in the United States merely from the point of view of taxing and spending to bring everyone within such a hypothetical range by redistributing income from those above the maximum to those below the minimum. Whereas about the same percentage of family units were within the hypothetical range in the two countries, in Britain there was a slightly smaller excess of income over the maximum, but a substantially smaller deficiency of income below the minimum.[12]

Summary of Income Redistribution in Britain and the United States

The initial distribution of private income in Britain and the United States was of a similar pattern before the war, but in the postwar period there appears to have been a tendency toward greater equality in Britain, while inequality in the United States remained about the same. Both before and after the war the redistribution of income was substantially greater in Britain. Combining a somewhat more

12. This can be represented by a simple formula. If superscript a and b are taken to refer to above and below the hypothetical range, N is the percentage of persons, and Y the percentage of total income, then $\frac{Y^a - 5N^a}{.5N^b - Y^b}$ is the ratio of income in excess of the maximum to the income deficiency below the minimum. Before the war the resulting figures were 9.6 for Britain and 2.3 for the U. S. (e.g. in Britain the excess over the maximum was 9.6 times as great as the deficiency below the minimum; in the U. S. 2.3 times, etc.). In the postwar years these had fallen to 3.8 for Britain and only 1.3 for the U. S. By comparison with the average income in each country, it would appear that the very low incomes were relatively much poorer in the U. S. than in Britain, even before the consideration of income redistribution. (This is not in real terms, only relative to one's compatriots; although, if the lowest incomes are above the level of subsistence, the comparison may appear as important to them as their real living standards.)

equal initial distribution in postwar Britain with a greater redistributive effort, we find that the distribution of final consumer income in postwar Britain was considerably less unequal than in the United States. This is true whether one measures inequality against a yardstick of precise equality or against a hypothetical "ideal" range of income around the average income.

It is unfortunate that the comparison with the United States could not be made for identical years, but it is probable that the findings would have been about the same. In the United States 1946–47 was a fairly typical postwar peacetime year. Demobilization and conversion back to peacetime pursuits was more rapid in America, and between 1946–47 and 1949 there was no substantial change in the patterns of taxing and spending, as there was in Britain. Britain also lagged somewhat behind the United States in beginning large scale rearmaments, so that 1948–49 in Britain is probably a better comparison with 1946–47 in the United States than might at first be concluded. Despite the sharp recession in the United States in 1937–38 the prewar years used for both countries were probably quite typical of the gradual period of recovery.

Having compared the redistribution of income in Britain with the experience of another country in the same period, we have completed the statistical task. In the remaining two chapters of Part I some general conclusions on the means and consequences of the redistribution of incomes will be drawn.

CHAPTER 9

Income, Wealth, and Opportunity

THE MAJOR part of this study has been concerned with measuring the redistribution of income after the fact—that is, given the initial distribution of factor income. In this sense, redistribution is an alteration of what may be felt to be an undesirable original distribution of purchasing power. But does not the existence of programs aimed at redistributing incomes have some effect also on the relative distribution of original incomes in some future period, if not immediately? [1] Pareto suggested at one time that the distribution of original factor income tended to follow a natural law of inequality so that little could be done to alter permanently the pattern of factor income distribution.[2] He did believe that inequality of consumer incomes could be diminished "by periodic redistributions at short intervals," [3] but thought that factor income distribution would be only temporarily disturbed by various programs of taxation. Later economists, however, while agreeing that there may be a tendency toward similarity of income distribution, given similar circumstances and conditions (e.g. laws of inheritance, educational standards, degrees of industrialization, etc.), have held rather that there is no "natural law" concerning the degree of income inequality.[4]

The belief that the conditions which produce a given distribution of income are not immutable, and further, that such conditions are

1. One might also ask whether redistribution does not affect the *level* of income as well as its distribution. As mentioned in the introduction to this study, it has been assumed here that the level of income is unaffected by redistribution, even though this is probably not the case. It is difficult if not impossible, however, to prove that a redistributive program such as that in Britain today tends either to increase or to decrease the real level of income. Granted, it sets up factors working in both directions, but which is the greater, and may it not vary over time? This question cannot be answered positively, although everyone has opinions on it.

2. Vilfredo Pareto, *Cours d'economie politique professé à l'Université de Lausanne* (2 vols., Lausanne, 1896–97), pp. 300–45.

3. P. 360.

4. Cf. Arthur C. Pigou, *Wealth and Welfare* (London, Macmillan, 1912), pp. 71–7, and *The Economics of Welfare* (4th ed. London, Macmillan, 1932), pp. 647–55; Irving Fisher, *Elementary Principles of Economics* (New York, Macmillan, 1911), ch. 25; Hugh Dalton, *Some Aspects of the Inequality of Incomes in Modern Communities* (New York, E. P. Dutton, 1929), Pt. IV.

proper centers of attention in determining public policy, seems apparent in the development of government redistributive programs over the last fifty years in Britain. This view is by no means limited to the Labour Party, but has been shared to a large degree by Liberals and Conservatives alike. There have been two basic methods by which the government has attempted to diminish the inequality of original factor incomes over the past fifty years, aimed at directly reducing excessive inequalities of opportunity and of wealth.

From the long-run point of view, changes in the degree of inequality of opportunity and wealth are probably of more importance than the redistribution of income through taxation at any one moment. The former tend to be permanent and in many cases cumulative, while the latter is but a temporary measure, which must be repeated year after year to most nearly maintain any distribution of consumer income which a community may feel is desirable.

Measures to promote greater fundamental equality in the long run are not nearly so spectacular as current taxation and expenditure programs. Politically there is often a tendency to nearsightedness when it comes to weighing the present against the future, and such measures do not produce immediate results, nor are their effects easily distinguishable or measurable. In contrast with income taxes, which must be reckoned with annually, the income effects of, say, a major change in tax regulations concerning inheritances or a marked improvement in educational services may be hardly discernible for a generation or more. But even though programs aimed at the sources of income inequality are evolutionary in effect, they none the less play important parts in the redistribution of incomes over time. In this chapter, therefore, attention will be focused briefly on some of the measures which may be expected to have a noticeable effect on diminishing the inequality of incomes at the source.

INEQUALITY OF OPPORTUNITY

As long as there is a problem of economizing scarce resources, and as long as men are not held in absolute slavery, differential (i.e. unequal) rewards are necessary incentives to bring about an efficient allocation of manpower. Most Western nations, however, while recognizing the need for income inequality in a free society, have at the same time attempted to mitigate what have been felt to be excessive inequalities of opportunity. There is abundant evidence of a strong movement in this direction in the examples which immediately spring to mind, such as the nineteenth-century political reform movements in Britain and the abolition of slavery in America, the development of publicly supported educational services, the opening of female employment fields and woman suffrage in politics, etc. In Britain since 1908 there has also been the gradual, if somewhat piecemeal, growth of what have come to be called "welfare programs."

The modern program of social welfare services in Britain seems to have begun with the Old Age Pensions Act of 1908.[5] In 1911 both unemployment and health insurance were added, although only about 2¼ million workers were then covered. In the decade following the first World War social security was considerably expanded by the extension of existing programs to cover almost all working people, and by the passage of the Widow's, Orphan's, and Old Age Contributory Pensions Act. From 1925 to the second World War there were no further substantial changes in social security legislation.

Beginning in the 1930's, however, there were increasing demands for more substantial guarantees against unemployment and for the extension of welfare programs to new fields. The 1939–45 war, following as it did on the heels of the depression, acted as a potent catalyst in bringing about a change in public policy, so that when the end of the war appeared in sight, the electorate was as interested in the planning of long-run welfare services as it was in the immediate problems of demobilization and reconstruction.

The basic change in public policy culminating in the 1940's, which Kenneth Galbraith has termed "the most comprehensive, subtle, and worst-described revolution in modern history," [6] is to be found not so much in the specific welfare programs adopted after the war, for these were not particularly revolutionary, nor entirely unprecedented,[7] as in two new concepts of public policy underlying the adoptions of the programs. These concepts were of vast importance and constituted a radical departure from prewar policy.

The first was embodied in the White Paper on postwar employment policy issued by the Coalition government just prior to the invasion of France in 1944.[8] In this policy document it was stated that the government henceforth assumed "as one of their primary

5. The Workmen's Compensation Act of 1897 was perhaps a forerunner, but it merely gave governmental regulation to an industry-administered program.

6. "Europe's Great Last Chance," *Harper's Magazine, 198* (1949), 44.

7. The programs of the Labour government followed precedents set by earlier governments. For example, public aid to those in poverty dated back to the 17th century as a statutory program; nationalization had been resorted to under Conservative and Liberal governments for electricity, transport, port authorities, broadcasting, etc.; compulsory health insurance for the working classes had begun before the first World War; centralized planning had been adopted during both world wars; and aid to persons raising families had been inaugurated in the Finance Act of 1909. Considered individually, the Labour government's accomplishments present nothing extremely novel, although considered en masse, they impress one by the number of changes which came about within such a short period of time.

8. *Employment Policy, Cmd.* 6527 (1944).

aims and responsibilities the maintenance of a high and stable level of employment." This meant that all parties to the coalition agreed that the government should no longer be an interested but relatively inactive spectator in the nation's economy. Rather, the government should direct its policy toward, and if necessary take direct action to ensure, the maintenance of total expenditure consistent with full employment of the nation's working population. For previous centuries the government had taken steps to lessen the hardships of unemployment and poverty, but never before had it accepted the responsibility of guaranteeing to its people that they would not again be subjected to the deprivations of economic depression. It was a guarantee which many persons thought could not be fulfilled, but regardless of future success or failure the British government was apparently committed to the attempt.

The second new concept was evidenced in the thread running through the new and expanded welfare programs, namely the inclusion of *all* persons under the benefit proposals regardless of income or wealth. This is found in the 1942 Beveridge Report,[9] in the 1944 Coalition White Papers on social insurance and health,[10] in the National Insurance, Family Allowances, and National Health Service Acts, as well as in the food subsidy and utility clothing schemes begun during the war. Before the war social insurance and related welfare programs had been almost entirely limited to those employed persons below a moderate level of income. After 1945 there was a departure from the purely redistributive type of program and an introduction of schemes whereby everyone was eligible for benefits regardless of his economic standing in the community. Previously it had been the government's charge to provide for the most needy; now it was evidently the public will (in which all of the major political parties acquiesced) that the community should provide for the minimum needs of all its people in matters of child support and services for the young, health, insurance against unemployment, disablement, and retirement—and to a lesser extent should ensure a supply of adequate but inexpensive food, housing, and clothing.

These "new style" welfare services in Britain probably could not have been adopted at any time in the previous twenty-five years, for the most necessary prerequisite for a successful long-run policy to diminish the inequality of opportunity (and therefore the inequality of future earned incomes) is the abolition of poverty.[11] Until this goal

9. *Social Insurance and Allied Services*, Cmd. 6404 (1942), pp. 53–4.
10. *Government Proposals for Social Insurance Generally and for Family Allowances*, Cmd. 6550 (1944); *Statement of Government Policy Relating to the Establishment of a National Health Service*, Cmd. 6502 (1944).
11. Poverty is defined here as a level of subsistence which is insufficient for the

has been achieved, political and social pressures make it most expedient for any government to concentrate on immediate, although temporary, relief through current taxation and income transfers. A twentieth-century mass democracy cannot safely afford to mortgage present relief for future gains while poverty is still widespread. Thus it would have been difficult for Britain to have concentrated primarily on diminishing long-run inequalities when, as at the turn of the century, about a third of the nation was living in poverty, or when, as in the 1930's, 12%–15% of the working population was unemployed. Postwar Britain is arriving at a phase, however, where there are indications that absolute poverty will be extinguished. At the present moment Britain is beset by problems of international recovery, but assuming that this period of rough water is weathered—and Britain has survived worse troubles—the feat may well be accomplished. Some persons may feel that it is a luxury she can ill afford at this moment, but the fact is that she has very nearly done so.[12]

The successful eradication of poverty is dependent upon three basic things: (1) the maintenance of a general level of productivity such that the average employed worker can purchase the necessities of life with his normal wage income, (2) the maintenance of (relatively) full employment, and (3) at least minimum provision for those who, through one misfortune or another, are unable to provide sufficient income for themselves.

The first of these was fulfilled before the beginning of this century, and the increasing size of the nation's real output over the last fifty years has made it possible for the average employed worker to live substantially above the subsistence line.

The second point—full employment—was achieved in 1940 for the

maintenance of continuing physical efficiency (for a family head and his dependents, if any). This definition is based on that of Seebohm Rowntree, which will be used below. Rowntree also subdivides poverty into primary and secondary, the former meaning that one's income is insufficient to maintain this level, while secondary poverty includes borderline cases where income is just sufficient, but "some portion of it is absorbed by other expenditures, either useful or wasteful." See *Poverty and Progress* (1941), p. 460–1, 101–3). Thus if father imbibed, or mother played the dogs, and the physical efficiency of the family could not be maintained for this reason, such a household would be in secondary poverty. This may be a somewhat unsatisfactory definition as a qualitative absolute, but it is as close as one can come to a working definition. For reference to a critical commentary on this standard, see p. 98 n., below.

12. This is the old argument of whether one should bend his efforts primarily to redistributing the pie, or to baking a larger pie. Within certain ranges, it is not necessarily an either-or choice, but there are some grounds for suspicion that further redistribution might be more harmful than beneficial to the nation's total real output. This is a matter of dialectic, and involves the weighing of social costs against purely economic costs; so there is really no correct answer apart from a value judgment. See also p. 111, below.

first time since the end of the first World War. (Full employment is here defined as less than 5% unemployed.) Americans, judging from their own recent experience, may tend to think that in this century unemployment was a problem/ that existed only between 1930 and 1939; but this is far from the truth in Britain. In the thirty years preceding the 1914 war, unemployment in Britain had averaged slightly less than 5%, but from 1920 to 1939 it averaged 14% of the total work force, and only in one year did it fall below 10% (9.6% in 1927).[13] During the recent war the percentage finally dropped to about .5%, and except for February and March of 1947, when a bitter winter and the coal shortage almost brought production to a halt, unemployment did not rise above 2% in the five years following the war. Thus by 1948–49 Britain had enjoyed almost a decade of full employment, although it was still viewed as a rather novel blessing.

The third prerequisite for the eradication of poverty has been achieved only since the end of the war. By the end of 1948, however, social security and welfare programs were sufficient to provide at least a minimum subsistence for those temporarily unemployed, the injured, the sick, and the elderly. Therefore, assuming no decline in the real level of the national income and no substantial departures from full employment, direst poverty may disappear from the scene in Britain. Certainly hardship exists today, and will continue to exist for many years, but near-starvation-level poverty has been almost completely absent since 1940.

Rowntree's studies for the city of York are an interesting indication of this decline in poverty. In his first study, for 1899, he found that 15½% of the working population of the city of York were living in "primary" (or "abject") poverty, and 33½% in primary and secondary poverty. In 1936 7% were in primary poverty and 31% in primary and secondary poverty, while unemployment was over 40% of the working population in York. By 1950 the percentages had fallen to .4% in primary and only 2.8% in primary and secondary poverty.[14]

As remarkable as the decline in poverty appears from the York study, one would have expected some such movement by merely comparing the level of economic activity in 1936 and 1950. The Rowntree and Lavers study, however, also made an estimate of the number

13. William H. Beveridge, *Full Employment in a Free Society* (1944), pp. 47, 72–3.
14. *Poverty and Progress*, pp. 450–77, and (with G. R. Lavers) *Poverty and the Welfare State* (1951), pp. 30–1. Some question has been raised concerning the strict comparability of the subsistence budgets for 1936 and 1950, and it seems probable that in real terms the latter year's minimum budget may differ by 1%–2% from that in 1936. If this is so, the number of persons in poverty, judged by the earlier year's standard, may have been slightly greater, although the marked improvement in diminishing poverty would still be evident. For a critique of the Rowntree and Lavers study see "Poverty Ten Years after Beveridge," *Planning, 19* (1952), 21–40.

of working class households which would have been in poverty had the scales of welfare benefits remained unchanged since 1936. Their findings have been adapted in Table 39 to show the effect of new programs and rate changes. The indication is that if 1936 welfare programs had existed unchanged in 1950, 4.7% of York's working class households would have been in primary poverty and 22% in primary and secondary poverty. This latter is about ten times the actual percentage estimated for 1950. Given the new welfare programs in existence in 1950, if food subsidies had been discontinued it is estimated that primary and secondary poverty would have increased from the actual 2.8% to 13.7%. On the other hand, if just family allowances were left out of the 1950 calculations, primary and secondary poverty would have increased from 2.8% to 6%. As a last comparison, if unemployment levels in 1950 had been as high as in 1936, primary and secondary poverty would have been increased only to 4.3%. These comparisons indicate that in diminishing the number of families below the poverty line food subsidies were more important than either the level of unemployment or the receipt of family allowances. The effectiveness of the present unemployment compensation program is shown by the estimated small increase in poverty which would have arisen from widespread unemployment in York.

TABLE 39

Poverty in York in 1950, and Estimated Poverty Which Would Have Existed under Reduced Welfare Measures *

	PERCENTAGE IN PRIMARY POVERTY	PERCENTAGE IN PRIMARY AND SECONDARY POVERTY
Actual, 1950	.37%	2.77%
If 1950 welfare measures had been identical to 1936	4.72%	22.18%
If there had been no food subsidies in 1950	2.42%	13.74%
If there had been no family allowances in 1950	.79%	5.97%
If unemployment in 1950 had been at 1936 level	2.38%	4.25%

* Rowntree and Lavers, pp. 40–8.

It has been pointed out that the eradication of poverty is but the first step—albeit a most important one—in attempting to reduce excessive inequalities of opportunity. The succeeding steps might be called environmental, in that they include services primarily directed toward improving the education of the young, the health of the nation's population, and adult training for specialized skills, together with the improvement of the physical environment in the form of housing, public health facilities, and town and country planning. These environmental services have been financed out of general tax revenues, whereas a large share of the social security and welfare programs mentioned above in the discussion of poverty were financed by contributions.[15]

Expenditures on environmental services increased fivefold from 1938 to 1948. Including expenditures on education, scholarships, training allowances, public health, the national health service,[16] and housing, the total expenditure on these services by the central government in 1938 was approximately £103 million, as against £516 million in 1948–49 (or 11.8% of total current expenditures as against 15.4% respectively). Forty per cent of the 1948–49 expenditures were accounted for by the national health service.

The cost of the health program rose to about £400 million by 1950, absorbing about 3½% of the national income. Although it is difficult to judge precisely, this amount was probably about 75% greater than the amount the nation spent on health privately before the new program went into effect. The indirect form of pricing (i.e. through general taxation) removed cost as a prohibitive factor in medical and dental treatment. If there is no great deterioration in the standards of medical services, the national health service may be expected to provide social benefits in the form of preventive medicine which are not necessarily indicated by the public costs of this program. It is still rather early to judge the results of the new service, for it remains beset by the problems which always arise when any article or service in short supply is no longer rationed (in this case, the removal of price rationing), and its supporters and critics have not as yet met on the middle ground of dispassionate appraisal. The new service does, however, provide important benefits for many persons who could not previously afford adequate care, and if successful it should substantially improve the general health environment.[17]

15. Expenditures on social security and welfare programs totaled just over £1,000 million in 1948–49. Of these benefits £390 million were from contributory schemes (under the national insurance acts), £205 million were noncontributory (family allowances, war pensions, and national assistance), and £430 million were in the form of subsidies (milk and welfare foods, general foodstuffs, and clothing).

16. That part of national health service expenditures covered by the contribution of the national insurance fund is excluded from this total.

17. The lower middle income groups may have benefited most from the national health service, for their incomes were too high for them to have come automatically

Central government expenditure on education increased from about £65 million to £170 million over the 1938–48 decade, and centrally financed scholarship allowances increased from £2.2 million to £14.6 million. By 1948–49 over 12,000 university students, including about 15% of all advanced students, were receiving aid direct from governmental sources. The major part of this aid was for students from low and middle income families.

Housing expenditures were four times greater in 1948–49 than in 1938, and the government by mid-1950 had added almost 600,000 new (permanent) houses and flats for rental to low income families. If we include conversions, rebuilt war-damaged buildings, and temporary housing units, about 900,000 government-financed family units of accommodation had been completed since the end of the second World War.[18]

Thus, in the years immediately following the recent war, Britain has turned attention more closely to the long-run problems of inequality of opportunity. Through the combined effect of the war and the relative (domestic) prosperity immediately following it, full employment has been maintained for more than a decade. In conjunction with this, the revised social insurance programs buttressed by noncontributory programs and extensive subsidy schemes have all but completely wiped out dire poverty. Twenty years previously Keynes had written, contemplating the economic possibilities for our grandchildren, "The economic problem, the struggle for subsistence, always has been hitherto the primary, most pressing problem of the human race . . . [but] a point may soon be reached, much sooner perhaps than we are all of us aware of, when these needs are satisfied in the sense that we prefer to devote our further energies to noneconomic purposes." [19] By 1948–49 the first and most important step of abolishing dire poverty had been practically accomplished; only time will tell whether this was a permanent accomplishment and

under the old national health insurance. The old program provided benefits quite similar to the new (free medical attention, choice of participating doctors, free medicines, etc.), and voluntary and charitable medical services were available to low incomes not covered by national health insurance. Some indication of the benefits to middle income families is found in the fact that the greatest deluge of patients in doctors' waiting rooms after the inauguration of the national health service was not in low income districts, but in middle class areas where the doctors' practices had formerly been entirely private. See *Report of the Ministry of Health, 1948–49, Cmd. 7910* (1950), p. 123.

18. Since the central government makes grants-in-aid primarily to local authorities, there is no way of indicating what proportion of these numbers was due directly to central government expenditures. For the housing figures, as of July 31, 1950, see *Housing Summary, Cmd. 8025* (1950).

19. John Maynard Keynes, *Essays in Persuasion* (London, Macmillan, 1931), pp. 365–6.

whether the next eighty years "will lead us out of the tunnel of economic necessity into daylight." [20]

INEQUALITY OF WEALTH

One of the primary causes of extreme inequalities of opportunity and income lies in the distribution of wealth. In 1948–49, for example, 1% of the nation's adult population owned 46% of all private capital and 16% held over 90% of private wealth.[21] Some of the programs discussed above may help to create greater equality in the distribution of earned income, but the inequality in the distribution of wealth still permits a small part of the community to begin the race, in Stephen Potter's words, "one up." There has been only a minute lessening of the degree of inequality in the distribution of wealth over the 1938–48 decade. The figures in Chapter 3 indicated this, but it may be shown more clearly by Lorenz curves. In Figure IX, for example, the area under the 1948–49 curve is only slightly less than for 1936–38. Translated into the type of index used to compare income inequalities in the preceding chapters, in 1936–38 it would have required the redistribution of 76.8% of private capital to have precisely equalized capital holdings among the adult population. In 1948–49 it would have required the redistribution of 75.4% to have accomplished this end. The inequality of wealth was therefore diminished by less than 2% over the period of the decade.

At first thought this may seem a surprisingly small diminution in the degree of inequality of wealth in these days of heavy taxation of income and wealth. There are, however, a number of factors which can account for it. One reason, of course, is that only a relatively small proportion of total private wealth has come under the purview of the Inland Revenue in the last ten years. If the average generation is approximately 32 years, it is probable that in any decade not more than $^{10}/_{32}$ of private capital is transferred because of estate owners' deaths. In addition, since Britain has not had a gift tax, probably between 20% and 50% of all capital has changed hands without becoming liable to death duties.[22] If the higher of these two percentages

20. *Ibid.,* p. 372.

21. See Table 4, p. 33, above. It should be pointed out, however, that the 1% who held 46% of private wealth were scattered among income groups ranging from £750 upward. Similarly, some of the 16% who owned 90% of private wealth had annual incomes as small as £250. By income groups, persons with incomes exceeding £5,000 held only about 23% of private capital, while about 50% of private capital was owned by persons with personal incomes of less than £600. See Table 5, p. 34.

22. Like the U. S. estate tax regulations, death duty is charged on capital transfers made within five years of death, on the basis that such gifts were made in anticipation of death. There is no very accurate way of estimating the extent to which death duties are avoided by gifts *inter vivos,* but judging from the number of advertise-

is more nearly accurate, only about 16% of total private capital was dutiable in the last decade.

A second factor which might help to explain the almost unchanged degree of inequality of wealth is that capital gains have not been subject to tax in Britain. Therefore, even though inheritance taxes

Figure IX. Distribution of private capital, 1936–38 and 1948–49.

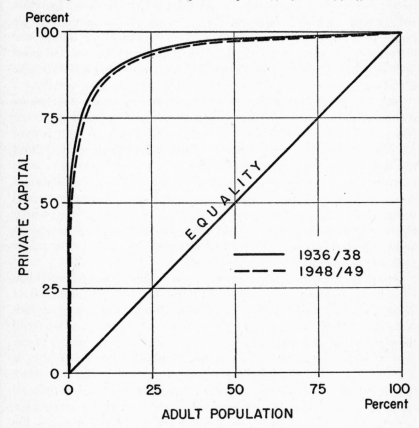

have taken large bites out of medium-large estates, there has been the possibility of considerable appreciation of capital between the time a person inherited an estate and the time of his death. This was more important through the 1940's than it would have been in the 1930's, and there is good reason to believe, as will be pointed out be-

ments in the London *Times'* personal columns reading, "Why Pay Death Duties, see ———— and ————, Tax Consultants," the amount should be considerable. Before the 1939 war, Josiah Wedgewood estimated that about 25% of estates above £50,000 were given away during the estate-owners' lifetimes. See *The Economics of Inheritance* (Penguin ed.), p. 246.

low, that medium-large estates have been more favored in the maintenance of estate values than have small estates.

A third factor is that measuring the degree of inequality is not
necessarily an indication of the relative welfare of any capital-owning
group. From 1938 to 1948 the national income increased 91%, but
the value of private capital increased by only 52%. In terms of
purchasing power, the nation's real income has increased by 5%–
10%, while the real value of the monetary sum represented by
capital holdings has fallen about 12%–20%. In other words, the
importance of wealth has declined in relation to earned incomes,
and the index of wealth inequality indicates only that the loss was
distributed almost proportionately throughout all sizes of estates.

One way of indicating this tendency is to take estates of various
sizes and see what would happen to them over the period of one
generation under present tax regulations. In Table 40 eight estate
sizes have been chosen at random, and the values of these are traced
through a generation. It is assumed that the estate owners are married (no other dependents) and rely solely on investment incomes.
A 4% yield is used to estimate investment income before tax. Consumption is estimated by assuming that large estate owners have been
able to reduce present living standards to one-half of 1938 standards,
and small estate owners to three-quarters, and that these living standards will be maintained for a generation.[23]

Given these assumptions, column 5 of Table 40 estimates the
value of capital after 31 years, but before the estate is submitted to
death duties. In comparison with the original value of any estate, the
reduction in the size of capital holdings due to income taxation and
the rise in cost of living alone is quite evident. The original £1 million estate, for example, after 31 years of dissaving (compounded at
4%) is reduced by £674,000, leaving less than a third of the original
amount to face death duties. Under the assumptions used, no capital
owner in Table 40 could save anything toward meeting death duties.

Column 6 of Table 40 indicates the death duty on each estate, the

23. 1938 living standards refer to the maximum standard which could have been
enjoyed out of income net of unavoidable taxes. In Table 40 a 50% reduction is
assumed for estates of £100,000 or more, a 33.3% reduction for estates of £25,000 and
£50,000, and a 25% reduction for smaller holdings. The smaller reduction for smaller
estates is reasoned to be most likely, since persons with smaller incomes would presumably have fewer superfluous expenditures which they could easily eliminate. Also,
savings out of investment income before the war would probably have been a smaller
proportion of income for the smaller estates, so that the reduction in actual living
standards—as compared to the reduction in the possible *maximum* living standards
used above—would be more nearly equivalent for all estate sizes. In estimating
consumption, the middle-class cost of living index for 1948 is estimated at 200
(1938 = 100). See Seers, p. 21.

TABLE 40

Maintenance of Estate Values over a Generation under Existing Tax Rates

(In Pounds)

SIZE OF ESTATE	INVESTMENT INCOME BEFORE TAX	INVESTMENT INCOME AFTER TAX	ANNUAL CONSUMPTION	ANNUAL NET SAVING	VALUE OF CAPITAL AFTER 31 YEARS	DEATH DUTY	NET VALUE OF CAPITAL AFTER GENERATION	PERCENTAGE CHANGE
	1	2	3	4	5	6	7	8
1,000,000	40,000	4,663	16,968	−11,305	326,222	179,422	146,800	−85.3%
500,000	20,000	4,245	9,893	−5,648	164,379	65,752	98,627	−80.3%
250,000	10,000	3,520	5,806	−2,286	113,754	39,812	73,942	−70.4%
100,000	4,000	2,120	3,364	−1,244	25,858	3,620	22,238	−67.8%
50,000	2,000	1,307	1,830	−523	18,830	1,883	16,947	−66.1%
25,000	1,000	676	960	−284	8,074	323	7,751	−69.0%
10,000	400	342	438	−96	4,279	85	4,194	−58.1%
5,000	200	197	237	−40	2,616	26	2,590	−48.2%

final net estates handed on to the next generation being shown in column 7. It is interesting to note that the reduction in the size of estates over a generation is not much greater proportionately for large estates than for small ones. Under the given assumptions, for example, the £250,000 estate is decreased by 70% and the £25,000 estate by 69%.

The immediate conclusion that might be drawn from Table 40 is that estates of all sizes must be dwindling rapidly, primarily because of dissavings during an estate-owner's lifetime. But while this is a not too unrealistic picture of how tax burdens and the rising cost of living appear to estate owners at any one time, it clearly cannot be valid, if one judges by the estimate of total private capital in Table 55, Chapter 11 below. In that chapter it will be seen that the number of estates of all sizes above £100 increased almost 75% over the last decade and the number of estates greater than £25,000 increased by about 50%.

How can one reconcile these two seemingly divergent conclusions? One possibility, of course, is that estates really are declining rapidly but this trend is not yet apparent in the death duty statistics. For example, taking an extreme case, if all persons inheriting estates since 1945 are adopting a policy of spending their entire inheritances during their lifetimes, this may not become noticeable for a number of years in the statistics of estates falling in. In the meantime, most current estates falling in belonged to persons who inherited them (or possibly amassed them) during the 1920's, and these persons, having been brought up in an era of relative business prosperity and conservative politics, can more reasonably be expected to have followed prudent and conservative policies in handling their estates. In modified form this is undoubtedly a partial explanation of the paradox above.[24]

A second, and undoubtedly more important factor, however, is that in Table 40 it was assumed that the market value of capital assets remained unchanged over the generation. If this assumption is replaced by a more realistic one, the results vary considerably. For example, if alternative assumptions of appreciation in the value of capital assets of 1%, 2%, or 3% annually are postulated, many estates actually increase in size over a generation. In Table 41 the percentage change in the value of any estate over a generation is indicated under assumptions of capital appreciation ranging from zero, as in Table 39,

24. The rate of risk function in estimating private capital should compensate for this, the holdings of young estate owners falling in being subject to a higher multiplier. However, the sex and age distribution of estate owners used in the 1948 capital estimates has been based on prewar experience, since current data were lacking. See p. 145, below.

to 3% annually. Under the assumption of a 1% per year inflation in values, positive savings (out of income and capital appreciation) would be possible for estates of £10,000 and below, although only the £5,000 estate would be larger after death duties than the original value of the estate. Given a 2% inflation, all gross estates (before death duties) would increase by roughly 50%, and those of £50,000 and below would show net increases after death duties. With a 3% inflation the value of all gross estates would approximately double, although death duties would reduce the size of estates of £250,000 and above to less than their original size.

TABLE 41

Percentage Change in the Value of Estates over the Period of a Generation under Different Assumptions of Capital Appreciation

	PERCENTAGE CHANGE IN VALUE UNDER THE GIVEN ASSUMPTIONS			
ORIGINAL ESTATE	0%	1%	2%	3%
1,000,000	−85.3	−67.7	−54.3	−47.0
500,000	−80.3	−58.5	−39.2	−36.6
250,000	−70.4	−47.6	−26.0	−10.4
100,000	−67.8	−39.8	−5.4	+12.8
50,000	−66.1	−24.0	+10.0	+40.6
25,000	−69.0	−19.1	+24.0	+61.1
10,000	−58.1	−9.6	+44.0	+93.6
5,000	−48.2	+8.6	+63.2	+106.8

In the decade from 1938 to 1948 the average annual rate of inflation in the value of capital assets approximated 2.5%. Total private capital increased from £19,000 million to £29,000 million, less than half of this increase arising from additions to private savings. If the estimate of private capital by size distribution in Chapter 3 is indicative of actual postwar holdings, it seems probable that either larger estates have inflated at a faster rate than smaller ones or the wealthier have been more successful in substantially reducing their consumption standards. In either case, inflation of capital assets has played a large part in the maintenance of estate values since 1938. Capital appreciation is, in effect, a form of untaxed income. A person with a £500,000 estate, for example, would receive an investment income of approximately £20,000 per year, netting not more than £4,500 after income and surtax. If his estate appreciated in any one year by 2½%, however, he could realize an additional £12,500, free from tax, while maintaining the total pound value of his estate.

Inflation is sometimes said to be an alternative to taxation in reducing the inequality of wealth. The foregoing has indicated, however, that this has not necessarily been the case in the recent period
with a moderate rate of inflation. But capital appreciation is only a
temporary relief for the wealthy, for the increase in the cost of living
over the decade has been cumulative and it is doubtful if it will
decline as rapidly or as far as it has risen. If a period of stabilized
prices and incomes follows, it is probable that the rate of annual
appreciation of capital will drop nearly to zero again (or possibly below). Thus, the £500,000 estate owner will have to rely solely on his
net income again, or dissave. In the meantime, however, inflation has
considerably retarded the redistribution of wealth which was foreseen
as a result of postwar tax policy. Many persons have been able to
keep up their living standards and pass their estates on intact (in
money terms), providing they invested in inflatable assets and avoided
estate duty on at least part of their holdings by giving some capital
away before death.[25]

Owners of large estates gain more than proportionately in the
early years of an inflationary period, but lose progressively after their
initial period of well being. The reverse, of course, is true during a de-
flationary period, capital depreciation at first being more rapid than
decreases in the general price level.

One thing does seem relatively certain concerning holders of
large estates in Britain: they are becoming a much more static and
exclusive group, primarily as a result of government tax policy. High
inheritance taxes coupled with only moderately progressive taxes on
income would tend to make the wealthy a considerably more fluid
group, rather like Schumpeter's analogy of the capitalist "hotel,"
always full, but the occupants always changing. But the extremely
high taxes on income today, plus moderately high inheritance taxes,
make it virtually impossible for newcomers to join the ranks of the
exalted. If a capital gains tax should be enacted, large estates would
decline more rapidly, but about the only remaining possibility of
accumulating wealth would be shut off. With current tax regulations
it will probably be many generations before this class will lose its
prominence. Under such circumstances it is perhaps fortunate that
the wealthy classes in England traditionally have had a strong
sense of social responsibility.

The Labour Party in its period in office leavened its attack on in-

25. The temporary nature of this situation arises because a constant rate of inflation
in consumer prices would necessitate an ever increasing rate of inflation in the value
of capital if one were just to keep pace. Even if the inflation of consumer prices
should cease now, capital appreciation would have to continue at its present rate if
estate owners were not to be worse off than they currently are. Capital appreciation,
however, is largely dependent on inflation in the prices of consumer goods.

equality of wealth with Fabian faith in gradualness and evolution. But a somewhat less moderate element in the party has called repeatedly for a capital levy as an economic measure to meet the heavy expenses of rearmament (and/or debt retirement). In periods of full employment, however, such a levy is of very dubious economic value, since the receipts come almost entirely out of savings and release no resources for the real economic problem of producing more consumption and investment goods. A capital levy would become economic only when it became desirable to shift the burden of taxation to savings rather than consumption. It may also be argued that even at such times the psychological effect on incentives might more than offset any advantages to be gained. Thus it would seem that the argument over the use of a capital levy must rest primarily on the question of the social desirability of diminishing the inequality of wealth.

The special contribution in 1948 was a sort of capital levy—that is, it was aimed at taxing capital even though it was technically a tax on investment income. The maximum rate on capital was about 2%,[26] and it is unlikely that it accomplished anything more than nullifying part of the inflation in the value of capital assets in that one year. If we compare the yield of this levy with private capital held by persons with incomes above £2,000, it did not reduce total holdings by much more than 1%. By nature such a levy can be used only as an infrequent weapon,[27] and only then as a surprise (or retroactive). At the rates charged, the special contribution had only negligible effect in reducing inequality, and probably close-to-zero effect in aiding the solution of Britain's postwar inflationary problem.

One last possibility in the reduction of inequality of wealth should be mentioned, if only because it concerns a principle on which schemes for the reform of inheritance taxes are sometimes based. This is the possibility that if the accumulation of capital in large holdings was halted, the normal division of estates among beneficiaries would automatically tend to break up these holdings. An interesting sample of estates was made in 1944–45 in an effort to discover the exact importance of splitting estates among beneficiaries.[28] It was found that for estates larger than £400,000, 59% of the average net estate was left to a single beneficiary. For estates between £100,000 and £400,000 this percentage was 61%, and 64% for those below £100,000. It may be misleading, however, to conclude that the splitting of estates

26. The maximum rate on investment income was 50%, and assuming a 4% return on capital, 2% of capital was its maximum rate.

27. If it had been a recurring tax, it would have raised the sum of all direct taxes on income to 147.5%.

28. G. Z. Fijalkowski-Bereday, "The Equalizing Effects of the Death Duties," *OxEP*, n.s., *2* (1950), 176–96.

necessarily makes for the diminution of large holdings. If all the beneficiaries of estates of, say, £400,000 and above are in roughly the same social and economic classes, it is equally possible that inheritances may be consolidated again.[29] One possibility, although rather unromantic for this day and age, is that marriage may bring together two people who have each inherited, say, 50% of their fathers' estates. Another is that X's son may receive only 60% of his parents' estate, the rest going to assorted cousins, etc., but X's son may in turn get small bequests from the estates of his various uncles and aunts so that his total inheritance about equals his father's total net estate. Although not enough is known about estate splitting to justify a conclusive answer, in the absence of taxing inheritances instead of the gross estates of the deceased, it seems likely that the effect on the inequality in the distribution of wealth is not very substantial.

Summary

Apart from the taxing of current incomes to provide temporary benefits, the government has also attempted to mitigate excessive inequalities of opportunity, which in turn help to determine the distribution of future income. The first necessary step has almost been accomplished, the eradication of dire poverty. In addition, the expansion of environmental services and the heavier taxation of wealth since 1945 can be expected to have some effect on diminishing the inequality of both earned and investment incomes in future years. In 1948–49 about 15% of current expenditures were devoted to environmental services (i.e. health, housing, education), as compared to less than 12% in 1937. The relative importance of wealth has been declining over the decade, and 88% of personal income in 1948 was earned, as compared to 80% in 1937. The inequality of capital holdings has diminished only slightly in the last 10 years, but as the rate of inflation of capital values declines, a much more rapid decline in the number and value of large capital holdings can be expected, given the present tax rates on income and capital.

It would be incorrect to imply that these two types of programs were designed only to reduce the inequality of future incomes, for they have immediate as well as long-run effects. However, the expansion of environmental services and the gradual decline in large inheritances, if these are permanent features, will undoubtedly have a tendency to diminish extreme inequalities of opportunity for future generations.

29. Especially since the reproduction rate of high income families is less than 1. See *Report of the Royal Commission on Population, Cmd.* 7695 (1949), pars. 64–71.

CHAPTER 10

Conclusion

THE CONCLUDING pages of this last chapter of Part I are intended as a summing up—rather than a passing of judgment—on the program of income redistribution in postwar Britain. The material which has been presented, and which is outlined in more detail in Part II, may perhaps be useful in forming personal judgments, but it is felt that such an evaluation is outside the scope of this study and cannot be purely economic. Indeed, the decisions to redistribute incomes and the myriad consequences of such decisions are not themselves necessarily, or even primarily, economic.[1] In these circumstances a statistical study can be no more than a partial guide.

Before summarizing, however, two factors are necessary to give perspective to the statistical conclusions which have not been adequately discussed in the preceding chapters. One is the question of how the redistribution of income affected families of various sizes, and the other concerns the effect of the wartime experience on postwar developments in public finance. To handle either of these subjects adequately would probably require another book, but it is necessary to discuss them briefly here because of their importance in making judgments concerning the redistributive program.

INCOME REDISTRIBUTION AND THE FAMILY[2]

In the allocation of taxes and benefits all family units have been treated alike. That is to say, although the estimates of total taxes paid

1. Even to the extent that consequences may be more purely economic, it remains true that a monetary calculus of redistributive gains and losses is not an adequate indicator of changes in real welfare, for welfare is not adequately measured by a price system. This is especially true when considering communal action, for the activities of government tend to be concentrated in those areas where the welfare of private persons is interdependent. Also, as has been emphasized in earlier chapters, benefits have been valued rather arbitrarily (i.e. at factor cost), and the very statistical measure of tax burdens and benefits is subject to considerable difficulties which make precision impossible, even given the theoretical assumptions concerning incidence.

2. The material in this section is based on the author's "Income Tax Allowances and the Family in Great Britain," *Population Studies, 6* (1953), 218–32, and *Memorandum on British Income Tax Allowances and Family Allowances,* Royal Commission on Taxation, Document No. 63 (1951).

and benefits received by any income group reflected the average size of the tax family in that group, no distinction was made between the redistributive gains or losses incurred by size of family. It should be obvious, however, that the average single income recipient with an income of, say, £500 pays more in direct taxes and receives fewer direct benefits than does the average man supporting a wife and children on the same income. Less income tax is paid by the family supporter because of the deduction of personal allowances for dependents in calculating taxable income. In addition, the spending pattern of the family supporter differs considerably from that of the single man, and this would be reflected in the payment of indirect taxes on goods purchased. On the expenditure side, government subsidies on food and clothing would probably be an appreciably larger benefit to the family man; the father of children would benefit more directly from expenditures on education and health; family allowance payments would be received for each child below the school-leaving age (after the first); and transfer incomes received under the national insurance programs (or the equivalent noncontributory welfare programs) would be greater for a person with dependents than for the single man. This does not exhaust the list of differences, but these are the major ways in which the state attempts at least partially to alleviate the relatively less fortunate economic position of the family supporter.

It would be a difficult task to calculate the redistributive gain or loss for each size family within any income group. One recent study has attempted this for five family sizes for 1937–38 and 1941–42,[3] but no comparable work has been done for the postwar period. With one exception, therefore, it will be suggested here merely that there are differential gains or losses by size of family within any income group and that these may be fairly substantial amounts. Because the exception—income tax allowances—is often overlooked, and because these allowances are probably the most important single item mentioned above, costing the government approximately £360 million in 1948–49, they will be discussed in more detail.

Income tax allowances for dependents result in savings in income tax liability, and these savings in turn result in higher posttax incomes for taxpayers with dependents than those without. There is perhaps little difference in the distinction between the aid received by family-supporting taxpayers under the tax allowances program and under the family allowances scheme. In the latter case the government takes money from persons in the form of taxes and gives it back to some in the form of allowances for second and succeeding

3. Shirras and Rostas.

children. This transaction is therefore observed as a flow of funds through the government account. In the case of tax savings, however, partly for administrative reasons and partly because of political accident, the government informs the taxpayer that he may deduct a certain sum directly from his tax and merely pay the balance. In this situation there is no observable flow of funds through the government account, although the government is just as certainly giving financial aid in support of a taxpayer's family as it would if it were actually paying out cash benefits. In effect the government was saying to a taxpayer in 1948–49 who had, to use an example, £1,000 earned income, "If you are a single man you must pay to the government £265 10s., leaving you £734 10s. for yourself; but if you are a married man with three children you need a larger net income than the single man, so you will have to pay only £153, leaving you £847." The tax saving made by the family supporter, £112 10s. in this case, was granted because it was felt that his need was greater than that of the taxpayer with no dependents.

It might be argued, of course, that the single man actually pays a penalty for *not* having a family, rather than the difference being a reward for *having* a family.[4] In the development of income tax regulations, however, this has not been the case. Until the Finance Act of 1909 all taxpayers were assessed similarly, regardless of family size. That act first introduced tax relief for dependent children, and the Finance Act of 1918 included allowances for wives and adult dependents. Over the last generation both the size of the allowances

4. A colleague has raised the argument that once you start viewing differences in tax applications in this manner, it can be carried to absurd ends. For example, by this reasoning he feels that since the state places heavy customs and excise duties on, say, alcoholic beverages and tobacco, one could argue therefore that in effect the government is really subsidizing all other commodities not so taxed. This, however, is not an identical case. Wherever the state sets up a general tax rate pertaining to a particular class of persons (e.g. those above the exemption limit) or class of goods, and then makes specific exemptions or reduction in rates for a segment of that class, one can reasonably say that the government is discriminating in favor of that segment. If the government announced that henceforth the manufacturers of Austin motor cars or Craven A cigarettes would no longer be liable to profits tax, a very good case could be made that these manufacturers were in fact being subsidized by the government. However, in the case of income tax allowances for dependents, one does not have to accept the argument that tax savings are really a form of subsidy, for the important point is that the government, whether subsidizing or penalizing, is taxing in such a way that the single man and the family man with the same initial income have different net incomes after tax. If these tax savings are viewed as a subsidy, however, this program may appear quite unusual, for it is unlikely that the government would ever adopt a welfare program of paying cash benefits to high income families to the complete exclusion of families raising about 50% of the nation's children. For a further discussion of possible anomalies in tax relief programs, see the author's article in *Population Studies* referred to above, n. 2.

and the tax rates have increased, so that tax savings were possible in 1948–49 amounting to £31 10s. for a wife, £27 for a child, and £22 10s. for an adult dependent.

The amount of tax saving and its effect on disposable income can best be seen by the illustration in Table 42 using four random incomes and different family circumstances. Unlike national assistance, which is determined largely by need, or family allowances, which are a fixed sum regardless of income, the amount of tax saving varies directly with the taxpayers' marginal rate of income tax. The taxpayer whose income is already so low that he is exempt from tax

TABLE 42

Tax Savings for Persons of Selected Incomes under
Various Family Circumstances, 1948–49

TAXABLE INCOME BEFORE DEDUCTION OF DEPENDENT'S ALLOWANCES (IN POUNDS)	TAX SAVINGS FOR A FAMILY CONSISTING OF TAXPAYER, PLUS:			
	WIFE	WIFE AND 1 CHILD	WIFE AND 3 CHILDREN	WIFE AND 5 CHILDREN
	£ s d	£ s d	£ s d	£ s d
150	1 10 0	1 10 0	1 10 0	1 10 0
300	21 0 0	31 10 0	31 10 0	31 10 0
600	31 10 0	57 0 0	93 0 0	121 10 0
1,000	31 10 0	58 10 0	112 10 0	166 10 0

does not benefit from these allowances, and his disposable income is the same as that of the single person who has the same original income. But the taxpayer with five children and income so high that his marginal rate of tax is the standard rate may find his disposable income as much as 23% greater than the disposable income of the single taxpayer with the same original income.

The total cost to the government of dependents' allowances (in the form of lost tax revenues) in 1948–49 was about £360 million (approximately £450 million in 1952). This is more than the total benefits paid out under the national insurance programs in 1948–49, or the Exchequer cost of the national health service, housing, the BBC, and educational scholarships combined. The estimated distribution of these tax savings is indicated in Table 43.

The program of income tax allowances is, in a sense, redistributive in either (or both) of two directions. It may be considered redistributive horizontally in that in any one income group single taxpayers and those with families of less than average size pay more income tax than do taxpayers with larger than average families. It may be redistributive vertically in that the tax savings of family supporters in any income group are not necessarily made up for by the remaining taxpayers in that same group. Whether the redistribution is primarily from the rich to the poor (or vice versa), or from single to family-supporting taxpayers cannot be determined without making some assumption as to what the alternative program might be. Although there are an unlimited number of alternatives to the existing tax regulations, it may be interesting to examine three rather obvious ones which would leave the balance of the government account unchanged.

TABLE 43

Estimated Tax Savings on Dependent's Allowances, 1948–49

INCOME RANGE (IN POUNDS)	TOTAL TAX SAVING (IN MILLION POUNDS)	AVERAGE TAX SAVING PER FAMILY HEAD * (IN POUNDS)
Under 135	0	0
135–250	30.0	7.1
250–500	209.6	35.5
500–750	60.6	44.2
750–1,000	23.7	48.4
1,000–2,000	26.4	61.1
2,000 and above	10.1	56.7
	360.4	(23.4)

* The number of family heads has been estimated by subtracting the number of single, dependent-free taxpayers from the total number of taxpayers in each income group. See *Cmd.* 8052, table 87, for the classification of incomes by family circumstances, 1948–49.

First, if the existing tax allowances were abolished and every taxpayer calculated his tax as the single taxpayer now does (i.e. on his actual income, minus only the single person's allowance) and then reduced his tax payment by 24%, the same total income tax revenue would be raised. Comparing the existing program with this alternative, one would conclude that the current redistribution was chiefly horizontal, from single to family-supporting taxpayers.

A second alternative, instead of making a flat percentage reduction in tax liability, would be the raising of the present exemption limit from £135 to about £400. (In 1948 £400 was about the same level of real income that the exemption limit was before the first World War, when dependents' allowances were first introduced.) Compared with this alternative, the 1948 tax allowances program could be said to have redistributed £360 million from low income taxpayers to middle and high income families.

A third alternative might be to have everyone pay taxes at the single man's rates and then for the government to pay out the additional £360 million revenue in cash payments to all persons with dependents. If the payment were a flat rate per dependent, this would have meant about £14 each in 1948–49. Compared with this third alternative, the existing program redistributed income both vertically from low to high incomes and horizontally from single to family-supporting taxpayers.

However one looks at it, income tax allowances are both expensive and redistributive, but since one cannot be certain in what direction income is really redistributed, these tax savings cannot be added to, or subtracted from, the estimate of aggregate redistribution arrived at in Chapter 6. It can certainly be concluded, however, that there is present in Britain an additional force not included in the previous estimates, redistributing incomes *to* persons with large families.

WARTIME AND POSTWAR FINANCE

In a previous chapter the redistribution of income in 1948–49 was compared with that of a prewar year, and it was estimated that the aggregate net redistribution had increased from about 8.8% of the national income to roughly 13.1%. It might be misleading, however, to draw conclusions from this fact without any reference to the events which occurred between these years. To carry the war through to a successful conclusion without an uncontrolled inflation, the government resorted to high taxation, price and wage controls, rationing of consumer goods, and various other controls and regulations. The standard rate of income tax was raised from 5s. (25%) in 1938 to 10s. (50%) in 1941, where it remained for the duration of the war. Surtax rates increased correspondingly, so that whereas the marginal rate of income and surtax combined had reached 50% at £8,000 in 1937, it reached 50% at only £165 of taxable income in 1941, and rose to 85% at £8,000. The first profits tax since the end of the 1914 war was enacted in 1937, and by 1940 profits above a standard rate were being taxed at 100%. Death duties rapidly increased, customs and excise duties rose, and a purchase tax was imposed in 1940. As mentioned in the introductory chapter, the existing tax structure was greatly extended, and from past experience it could have been predicted that postwar tax revenues would not return to their original position in either form or amount.

At the same time that revenues were expanding, government expenditures also soared to new levels, so that about half of the nation's real output was being consumed by the government in 1941. The figures in Table 44 give some indication of the rapid rise of taxes and expenditures in relation to private income subject to tax.

In 1946 income taxes were reduced slightly, while surtax rates were increased, the effect being a reduction in the yield from taxes on income both absolutely and as a percentage of income. With some duty increases and an increased volume of trade, however, receipts from customs and excise duties continued to increase after the war. Current expenditures began to taper off in 1945 but remained at least three times as great as prewar expenditures. Beginning in the latter half of 1948–49 expenditures began to rise again in absolute terms, partially as the result of expanded welfare services (e.g. food subsidies, the national health service, etc.) and increasingly because of pressures for rearmament arising from the international situation.

TABLE 44

Change in Tax Yields and Current Expenditures since 1938,
in Pounds and as Percentages of Gross Income *

Year	INCOME AND SURTAX (In Million Pounds)	(Percentage)	CUSTOMS AND EXCISE (In Million Pounds)	(Percentage)	CURRENT EXPENDITURES (In Million Pounds)	(Percentage)
1938	336	8.8	340	8.8	944	22.7
1940	524	10.7	532	10.7	3,884	79.3
1942	1,007	15.1	887	13.3	5,637	86.1
1944	1,317	18.0	1,075	14.7	6,063	83.0
1946	1,156	14.0	1,183	14.3	4,058	49.2
1948	1,368	13.3	1,555	15.1	3,153	30.6
1950	1,553	13.4	1,520	13.1	3,455	29.8

* Since there are no adequate figures for the national income during the war years, gross income as reported by the Inland Revenue has been used in estimating the percentages. Gross income is similar to private income as defined in Ch. 1, except that tax-exempt income is not included.

Not shown in Table 44 is the proportion of expenditures devoted to normal peacetime services. If expenditures were further broken down it would be seen that those not related directly to the war steadily increased up through 1948–49, remaining relatively constant from 1949 to the present (1952) at a level equal to about 27%–28% of the national income (24% of gross income).

The effect of the war on the enlargement of peacetime government budgets cannot be overestimated, for without the war it is very doubtful if government services would have expanded as rapidly as they have done. To establish the new postwar welfare programs it was not necessary to raise taxes—actually many taxes were reduced. In this sense it was a much simpler task to expand peacetime expenditures immediately after 1945 than it would have been in 1938.

The war made larger peacetime tax revenues more acceptable in two

ways. First, although there was little change in the income tax structure between, say, 1940–41 and 1948–49, because of the inflation of
the national income in money terms many persons who had paid no
income tax before the war now found their incomes taxed, even
though their real income remained unchanged. This is clearly indicated by the Inland Revenue figures showing the number of persons
who were actually chargeable with tax; although the exemption
limit was £15 higher in 1948–49 than in 1940–41, the number of
persons chargeable with tax increased from 5,900,000 in 1940–41 to
14,495,000 in 1948–49. In other words, the increase in money incomes brought an additional 8½ million persons within the taxable
income range who had not previously been liable to income tax. In
terms of real income the exemption limit was in effect lowered slightly
each year after 1938, dropping from £125 in 1938 to only £70 (in
1938 pounds) in 1948. Even though tax rates were slightly higher
for all incomes in 1941–42 than in 1948–49 the Exchequer receipt of
income taxes in the earlier year was only 56% as great as in 1948–49.
Because of this increase in incomes the government could, after the
war, reduce income tax rates slightly and still have a greater absolute
revenue than during the peak war years.

The second way in which the war made larger peacetime tax revenues more acceptable concerns incentives and the relationship of
any given tax structure to its immediate predecessor. If the London
Times, one day in 1937, had announced to its morning readers that
the government had decided the night before to raise taxes and expenditures tremendously (i.e. instituted tax rates and expenditure
programs comparable to those of 1948–49), it is quite possible that
everyone from captain of industry to bus driver would have joined in
a general strike against the government. Persons with incomes over
£10,000 would have found their incomes net of taxes cut to about a
fifth of accustomed amounts, the average worker would have found
his marginal tax rate almost doubled, companies which had not had
profits taxed for almost 20 years would have received bills from the
government for 25% of their undistributed profits, the prices of goods
in the shops would have jumped alarmingly—many items doubling in
cost—and dying would have suddenly become so expensive that one
would have hoped to live forever or die retroactively.

What actually happened when the budget for 1948 was introduced?
Some cheered, many grumbled, the House of Commons gave a substantial majority to the government, and life seemingly went on without more than a slight ripple of disturbance.

This only serves, perhaps more dramatically than necessary, to
emphasize that given tax rates do not have a fixed effect upon one's

incentive to earn, to invest, or to save, and that people become at least partially accustomed to losing a share of their income in the form of taxes. Without the intervening war years it is most unlikely that taxes could have been raised as rapidly, or to the same heights, as they were without more disastrous effects upon the economy.

A century earlier McCulloch had written of taxation in his day, "the severity of its pressure in England is but too apparent. . . . the evil is one of a very marked character; and . . . till it be materially mitigated, it will furnish matter for perennial agitation and discontent, and be a formidable obstacle to our progress." [5] In 1948, when the national income was roughly fifteen times larger, total tax revenues were about 130 times greater. McCulloch's strictures might bear repeating today.

But even if higher tax rates have been accepted in the postwar years with relative equanimity, this does not necessarily mean that these higher rates are not more damaging to desirable incentives. Britain's total real output has been climbing since the end of the war, despite some dire predictions to the contrary; on the other hand, despite many optimistic predictions her real output has not increased as rapidly as that of some other western nations. Unfortunately, it is impossible to draw a direct relationship between the effect of tax rates on incentives and actual production, since one cannot isolate the causes of changes in productivity. The English businessman says publicly that all incentive has disappeared and the executive no longer cares about efficient performance, while the Labourite says publicly that workers now have a stake in the economy, and because of less insecurity, more medical care, inexpensive food and clothing, etc. working efficiency will increase. There is probably a good deal of truth in both views, although each side perhaps overstates its own case. If Britain continues on the road she has followed in the first seven years since the end of the war in Europe, her economic future may largely depend on the balance of these two forces. High taxes are obviously damaging to incentives; will the benefits of a welfare state be sufficient to counterbalance this? Roy Harrod, a supporter of the Conservative Party in recent elections, has expressed the hope that

these social benefits will be ultimately remunerative, that better health, education and security will eventually give rise to increased output per man, which will, so to speak, in the long run cover the cost of the services for the nation as a whole. The redistribution has taken place and is being borne without great complaint; it is independent of the shortages and austerities

5. John R. McCulloch, *A Treatise on the Principles and Practical Influence of Taxation and the Funding System* (London, Longman, Brown, Green, and Longmans, 1845), pp. 389–91.

with which we are now threatened and which prevent the consumer satisfying his needs with the income that remains to him after all these charges have been met.[6]

Summary of Conclusions

In gathering up the threads of the analysis of Part I, one who is familiar with postwar Britain does not find the major conclusion surprising. The redistribution of income has been substantial, and many people have gained while a somewhat smaller number have lost. The total amount redistributed has been estimated, at the outside limits, as between approximately £640 million and £1,680 million, with £1,260 million chosen on the basis of the median assumption concerning the allocation of indivisible benefits.[7] The latter figure was about 13.1% of the national income in 1948–49, and it seems probable that this is the high-water mark of redistribution in modern industrial Britain.

The dividing line between redistributive gains and losses has been estimated to be near the middle of the £500–750 range, so that one can fairly safely conclude that about 80% of the population was on the gaining end, and at least 10% was on the losing end. This would seem to imply that if voters acted with pecuniary rationality an overwhelming majority would have favored the redistributive program. But for a number of reasons this can by no means be a proper conclusion. Quite obviously, elections are not determined entirely on a utilitarian or precise pecuniary calculus. Similarly, many persons lost against their will, but many also gained against their will. More important, however, is the definition of gains and losses. What people felt they lost was probably greater than the amounts estimated here, and what others have been estimated to have gained is undoubtedly far greater than most gainers felt they had received. This results largely from the allocation of what has been called indivisible benefits, benefits arising from general governmental expenditures, national defense, etc. If these amounts are excluded, as they were in the discussion in the first half of Chapter 6, the gainers appear to be persons in the two lowest income groups (i.e. below about £225). They were the only ones who received more in the way of tangible benefits than they paid in taxes. If political elections depended solely upon the weighing of these tangible benefits, it could equally well be concluded that 75% of the people would have favored much less redistribution.

Practically, political elections are not held on a single issue, nor

6. *Are These Hardships Necessary?* (1947), pp. 16–7.
7. See p. 59, above.

has the voter in Britain been given a clear choice in postwar elections between more or less redistribution. Each of the three major parties has supported substantially all of the welfare programs adopted since the war, although each has recommended its own individual modifications. Each party has recognized the need for continued high taxation in the effort to control inflation, although each has suggested particular adjustments in the interests of equity and incentives. Except for the issue of nationalization, there has been no clear-cut difference of opinion on domestic economic matters. Even if there had been no other important issues at stake, the voters in 1950 and 1951 could have done no more than express an opinion in favor of a little bit more or a little bit less redistribution, or for a change or continuance of administrators.

The difference between redistributive gains as estimated here and the consciously realized gains of the low income groups helps to illustrate the dangers inherent in attempting to make welfare judgments from such a statistical analysis. It should be emphasized again that if one is interested in looking at Britain as an example of a "welfare state" (with all the good or bad connotations that phrase may engender), the redistribution of income does not tell the whole story. One important reason, as pointed out in the first part of this chapter, is that the redistribution of income is not solely between persons of differing income levels. Income is equally shifted from the employed to the unemployed, from the healthy to the sick, from the working-age population to the young and the old, from the able to the disabled, etc. In many cases benefits depended not upon income but on particular circumstances. Thus the redistribution of incomes from high to low income groups was due partly to the fact that a larger proportion of the elderly, the unemployed, the larger families, the disabled, etc. happened to be in the lower income groups.

A second and related reason why the figures do not tell the whole story is that many welfare programs were contributory insurance schemes. Rates were not progressive, so that the average contributor was paying for most of the benefits he would some day receive when he was disabled, unemployed, or retired. The social insurance program appeared mildly redistributive in 1948–49 chiefly because when a contributor finally drew benefits he had usually stopped working temporarily or permanently and therefore naturally fell to a lower income group than that in which he made his contributions. Also, as pointed out previously, after July, 1948, all persons had to contribute to the national insurance program even though the new high income group contributors were not yet eligible for full benefits.

A third reason why the redistribution of income is not a perfect guide to the results of the expanded welfare programs is that many of these new programs have been literally equalitarian in their benefit provisions. They have not been designed to redress inequality, but have been planned for equal participation in benefits regardless of income. The redistribution of income could have been greater if all persons in the upper income groups had been omitted from the benefits of family allowances, the national health service, education, etc., but it appears to have been felt that equal participation (or equal right to participate) in benefits was a more desirable and workable goal.

One final and rather obvious reason why the amount of income redistributed cannot be used as a guide to achievement is that the amount which could conceivably be redistributed from high to low incomes is limited by the degree of inequality of original factor incomes. It goes without saying that in a perfectly equalitarian community there would be no scope for income redistribution (except in the creation of inequality).

It also bears repeating that the expansion of redistributive programs immediately after the end of the war should not be attributed entirely to the Labour Party. The Conservatives would be the last ones to admit that the Labourites had brought about any reforms (other than the nationalization of too many industries too quickly). They have stated quite frankly that "this new conception [of the social services] was developed [by] the Coalition Government with its majority of Conservative Ministers and the full approval of the Conservative majority in the House of Commons. . . . [We] set out the principles for the schemes of pensions, sickness and unemployment benefit, industrial injuries benefit and a national health scheme." [8] On the other hand, even if the Labour Party had never won a majority in the House of Commons, one would still have to conclude that they were partly responsible for the increased emphasis upon the redistribution of income. A strong opposition party usually has the effect of modifying its opponent's policies, and the Liberal and Labour opposition in the interwar years helped to modify the Conservative platform, just as the Conservative and Liberal opposition had a similar effect upon the Labour program from 1945 to 1951. The relative strength of the Conservative and Labour Parties, almost exactly balanced in the last few years, was probably the principal reason why, in the 1950 and 1951 elections, there was so little difference between the parties in their proposed domestic programs. Public opinion has been almost evenly divided, and the strong

8. *The Right Road for Britain,* the Conservative Party's statement of policy for the 1950 election, pp. 41–2.

competition for votes has brought the major parties closer together than they were before the war.

A review of the 1950 and 1951 election platforms of the three major political parties indicates that except for the nationalization of private industries each party has accepted with only minor qualification the expanded role of the government in the maintenance of national welfare. They differ on the administration of some of the newer programs and on which groups within the population should be given additional relief from taxation or additional benefits. They substantially agree, however, on the principle of income redistribution, and each party has made major contributions toward this end in its periods in office in this century. The Liberals, before the first World War, introduced progressive taxation of income and estates, old age pensions, and health and unemployment insurance. The Conservatives between the wars made the direct tax system quite steeply progressive, inaugurated a peacetime profits tax, introduced the first national scheme of contributory pensions, and when they were the majority party in the wartime coalition, began family allowances and drafted the proposals for extended social security and a national health program. The Labourites, since 1945, put into operation the expanded national insurance and national health service, expanded food subsidies, and continued the steeply progressive wartime tax structure.

Certainly the experience of income redistribution in Britain since 1945 seems to have a mixed heritage. It has resulted from a curious combination of liberal reform, socialist zeal, and conservative social responsibility, plus the historical tragedy of depression and war, flavored with a pinch of disillusion and a liberal sprinkling of faith. Perhaps all shades of political sentiment could trace their heritage back to that Briton who was so deeply concerned with the welfare of his nation—Adam Smith. His words could well have been those of a twentieth-century Beveridge, Churchill, or Atlee, when he said:

What can be added to the happiness of the man who is in health, who is out of debt, and has a clear conscience? . . . Notwithstanding the present misery and depravity of the world, so justly lamented, this really is the state of the greater part of men. . . . But though little can be added to this state, much may be taken from it. Though between this condition and the highest pitch of human prosperity, the interval is but a trifle; between it and the lowest depth of misery the distance is immense and prodigious.[9]

9. *Theory of Moral Sentiments,* Section III, Chapter 1.

PART TWO

CHAPTER 11

The Construction of Income and Wealth Estimates, and a Breakdown of the Government Account

In Chapter 3 the distribution of income and wealth by income groups was summarized, and a general classification of the government account was given. In this chapter the manner in which these estimates have been constructed will be explained in more detail.

Family Classification of the "under £135" Income Group

Table 1 indicated the constitution of each income group by family circumstance. For persons with incomes above the tax-exemption limit, the data were merely a summary of information published in the 1948–49 Inland Revenue report.[1] The Inland Revenue figures account for about 92% of the population in 1948–49, leaving roughly 3.8 million persons below the tax-exemption limit. It would be incorrect, however, to assume that the division of persons by family classification in this income group was the same as for higher income groups. The Inland Revenue figures indicate that there was a major difference in the constitution of the average tax family between the £135–250 and the £250–500 groups, and it is to be expected that the average size of tax family in the under £135 group was considerably smaller than either of these.

It is impossible to make a precise classification of families in the lowest income group, but there is considerable data which can be used in an attempt to fill out the picture for this group. In the following pages such an attempt is made, and the classification is summarized in Table 45 below.

In the report of the National Assistance Board [2] the number of persons receiving relief, and therefore presumably having incomes of less than £135, is given. Based on a sample inquiry made in November, 1948, the Board estimated that of the 1,464,880 persons re-

---

1. *Cmd.* 8052 (1950), p. 87, table 86. A slight adjustment has been made in number of persons in the groups between £250 and £1,000. See p. 138, below.
2. *Report of the National Assistant Board, 1948–49, Cmd.* 7767 (1949), pp. 41–7.

ceiving relief directly, or dependent upon relief applicants, 963,460 were family heads, supporting 213,960 wives, 272,320 children, and 15,140 adult dependents.

Similarly, unemployment statistics can be used to add another piece to the puzzle. Using information from the report of the Ministry of National Insurance for 1948–49 [3] and assuming that women unemployed in excess of ten weeks and men in excess of 20 weeks had incomes of less than £135, a total of 33,335 wage earners would fall into the under £135 group (allowance being made so as not to double count those unemployed already on the rolls of the National Assistance Board). Assuming these wage earners had dependents in the same proportion as all unemployed persons, 4,860 wives, 6,410 children, and 2,265 adult dependents may be added.

War pension data is to be found in the annual report of the Ministry of Pensions for 1948–49.[4] 26,850 pensioners may be added if we assume the following had incomes not exceeding £135 : all persons 70% (plus) disabled, 10% of all other partial disablements, one-half of those receiving lowered standard allowances, all persons receiving constant attendance allowances, and all receiving unemployability allowances. If all pensioners had dependents in the same proportion regardless of income, these would have supported 18,526 wives, 16,378 children, and 5,095 adult dependents.

If we compare the 1948–49 defense estimates with the services pay code, it appears that slightly over half a million men in the forces had incomes of less than £135. These were largely young men doing their compulsory training and therefore could be expected to have had fewer dependents than the average member of the forces. Members of the forces in this income group have been estimated at 534,400, and their dependents as 38,500 wives, 20,000 children, and 15,500 adult dependents.

Another large group with small income would be those who had just left school and were beginning work. For want of a better estimate, it has been assumed that all persons under the age of 18 leaving school had incomes in their first year at work below £135.[5] These

3. *Report of the Ministry of National Insurance, 1944–49, Cmd.* 7955 (1950), pp. 34–7, 92–6.

4. *Report of the Ministry of Pensions, 1948–49,* H.C. 260 (1949), appendices 3–10, pp. 38–43.

5. Or, alternatively, that ⅓ of those between the age of leaving school and 18 had incomes below £135. This is not an unlikely assumption, for many children of this age do not work full time from the moment of leaving school. It should be remembered, however, that a sizable proportion of this group have excellent (family) means of support and are not, from a welfare standpoint, members of the lowest income group.

would number 582,000. Only a small proportion of this number would be married; so dependents have been estimated at 6,000 wives, 10,-000 adult dependents, and no children.

Adding up these five categories of persons, we have totals of 2,140,045 independent adults over 16, 281,846 wives, 315,108 children, and 48,000 adult dependents, or 2,785,000 total. This leaves the difference between this sum and 3,795,000 (1,010,000) unaccounted for. From population statistics it is known that there were in 1948 11,245,000 children under 16 in Great Britain. In addition, approximately 169,000 children aged 16 and 17 remained in secondary schools, 106,000 were in "further education," and 17,000 were in other full-time training without pay (or pay of less than £60 annually).[6] Thus, 11,537,000 were eligible to be claimed as child dependents by parents for income tax purposes. This would mean that after subtracting the number of children known to be in the other income groups there should be roughly 370,000 children in families in the lowest income group. Therefore another 55,000 children must be included in this residue of persons unaccounted for in the lowest income group. The proportion of wives and adult dependents to family heads in the £135–250 income group has been used to estimate the division of adults in this unaccounted-for group. The division of the 1,010,000 remaining persons with incomes below £135 has therefore been assumed as 653,000 family heads, 180,000 wives 55,000 children, and 125,000 adult dependents. Three types of persons would commonly fall into this low—but nonrelief—income group. A large portion would be retired persons living on tax-free annuities or on capital, over and above investment incomes of less than £135. Or, if they had incomes of between £120 and £135 and were living with relatives, they could not be claimed as adult dependents and would fall into this category of independent adults. Another portion would include workers with low incomes who for one reason or another did not qualify (or did not wish to qualify) for relief. Among others, a large share of agricultural laborers would fall into this class, as would most of Britain's gypsy population. The remaining persons might be those who temporarily were living on past savings.[7] If one were living on a capital sum of even £4,000, all of which was invested in assets whose yield was less than 3½%, one's investment income would probably be less than £135.

6. See *Annual Abstract of Statistics, No. 86, 1938–48,* Central Statistical Office (1949) pp. 78–88, 92–3.

7. In Britain casual receipts of capital, such as cash receipts from football pools, competitions, and sweepstakes, are not classified as income and therefore are not subject to income tax.

Table 45 summarizes the foregoing paragraphs, giving the estimate of persons in the lowest income group by family classification.

TABLE 45

Estimate of the Population in the "under £135" Income Group, by Family Classification Great Britain, 1948–49

DESCRIPTION	TAX-FAMILY HEADS 1	WIVES 2	CHILDREN 3	ADULT DEPENDENTS 4	TOTAL 5
1. Recipients of national assistance	963,460	213,960	272,320	15,140	1,464,880
2. Recipients of unemployment benefits	33,335	4,860	6,410	2,265	46,870
3. Recipients of war pensions	26,850	18,526	16,379	5,095	66,850
4. Members of armed forces	534,400	38,500	20,000	15,500	608,400
5. Persons under 18	582,000	6,000	—	10,000	598,000
6. Others	653,000	180,000	55,000	125,000	1,013,000
Totals	2,790,045	461,846	370,109	173,000	3,798,000

It is difficult to label the first column adequately, for all are not literally "income recipients" or taxpayers or family heads or independent adults. "Tax-family heads" has been adopted as the most descriptive term, for every person in column 1 would be liable to tax under his own name if his income were slightly higher. (The income of wives, children, and adult dependents would presumably be added to the family income, reported singly.)

The average size of the tax family in the lowest income group, based on this estimate, is 1.36, as compared to 2.22 for all other income groups as reported by the Inland Revenue.

The totals shown at the bottom of Table 45 are the same as those in parentheses on line 1 of Table 1, above, p. 27.

NATIONAL INCOME IN 1948–49

The national income of the United Kingdom by distributive shares, as given by the White Papers, is indicated in Table 46 for 1938, 1948, and 1949.[8] The 1948–49 fiscal year, on which the present study has been based, covers the last three quarters of 1948 and the first quarter of 1949; so column 2 of Table 46 most nearly approximates the income of the 1948–49 fiscal year. To indicate the relative

8. *Cmd.* 8203, p. 17.

increase in the various income components, column 4 divides the 1948 figures by those for 1938 showing the ratio of increase. The entire national income increased 2.1 times, the largest advances having been made by farm incomes and corporate profits. The smallest increases were for rent and profits of unincorporated businesses, while wages, salaries, and professional earnings all increased by about the same proportion as did total income.

TABLE 46

National Income by Distributive Shares

ITEM	1938 1	1948 2	1949 3	1948÷1938 4
Wages	1,735	4,025	4,230	2.3
Salaries	1,110	2,200	2,350	2.0
Pay and allowances of the armed forces	78	246	246	3.2
Employers' national insurance contributions	54	157	195	3.0
Professional earnings	84	161	172	2.0
Income from farming	64	261	304	4.1
Profits of sole traders and partnerships	440	810	815	1.8
Trading profits of companies	536	1,580	1,488	3.0
Trading profits of public enterprises	29	79	72	2.7
Rent of land and buildings	416	470	483	1.1
Income arising in U. K.	4,553	10,058	10,439	2.3
Net income from abroad	164	−1	27	.2
National income	4,716	10,057	10,466	2.1

The White Paper estimates are very useful, but they do not provide the exact data which is required here. This is true for a number of reasons: (1) The White Paper estimates are for calendar years, while the budget data used in analyzing taxes and expenditures refer to fiscal years (April 6 to April 5); (2) the White Paper estimates are for the United Kingdom, whereas only Great Britain is being treated here; and (3) social accounting methods are used to measure the flow of actual income and expenditure within a given period, while this investigation is concerned with incomes liable to tax under the current year's finance act (even if they should be incomes earned in previous years) and expenditures arising from grants made in the current year (even though part of these funds may be spent in a succeeding year).[9]

9. See p. 5, above.

The first two difficulties are not serious, and adjustments have been made in the estimates below. The national income has been estimated for the fiscal year—i.e. from the second quarter of 1948 to the end of the first quarter of 1949—by comparing the White Paper estimates with quarterly estimates made by the Oxford Institute of Statistics.[10] For a part of the national income, this has been checked against income as reflected in monthly tax receipts under the pay-as-you-earn program. The adjustment for Northern Ireland has been made on the basis of Northern Ireland income reported to the Inland Revenue in 1948–49.

The third difficulty calls for more complicated adjustments. Many taxes imposed by the Finance Act of 1948 for the fiscal year 1948–49 actually were charged on incomes earned in a previous year. For example, the profits tax for 1948–49 was charged on corporate income earned in the accounting year which ended between April 5, 1947, and April 6, 1948; the surtax was charged on the income of fiscal year 1947–48. The income tax varied according to the different schedules, income liable under schedules A, B, C, and E being current income and that under schedule D the same as under the profits tax.[11]

Any measure of the national income, therefore, which would represent income subject to tax in the 1948–49 fiscal year must be a composite one. In the estimate below, from the usual national income figures all profits and professional earnings have been removed and those for previous periods substituted. Professional earnings for 1947–48 have been used, as have profits of the calendar year of 1947. The surtax presents the only theoretical problem. It is a tax on upper incomes used to extend the progressiveness of the income tax, but it is not deducted under the pay-as-you-earn scheme and is charged on income of a different year from the income tax. Since both income tax and surtax are on personal incomes, however, it is impossible to have any one figure of personal income in the composite national income which will be correct for both taxes. This problem is insoluble, and one must choose either one year's income or the other if an estimate of national income applicable to 1948–49 tax legisla-

10. Dudley Seers and others, "Quarterly Estimates of the National Income," *BOxIS, 11* (1949), 293–306, 373–81.

11. The Inland Revenue report agrees that "Ideally the statistics should relate to the assessments for a particular year irrespective of the date when the assessment is made. As, however, an assessment may be made at any time within six years of the end of the year of assessment, this would mean that no final figure could be presented except after a long period of time. It has, therefore, always been the practice to relate the statistics to assessments made in a particular year." (*Cmd.* 8052, p. 41) Statistics relating to special trade groups based on assessments for a particular year have been made for prewar years, but it is unfortunate that the Inland Revenue does not attempt this for all taxes once in every, say, ten years.

tion is to be made. Actually such a precise income estimate is not crucial to the estimate of income redistribution, but it would be useful to have one. Since the income tax is the more important revenue-raising tax, current income will be used in the estimate below for all types of personal income except profits and professional earnings. From a practical viewpoint there is no real problem for 1948–49, for incomes currently assessed for surtax (but earned in 1947–48) differed by less than one-tenth of one per cent from actual 1948–49 incomes assessed to surtax in the succeeding year.[12]

Table 47 shows the composite national income for Great Britain, indicating incomes actually liable to tax in the 1948–49 fiscal year.

TABLE 47

Composite National Income, Fiscal Year 1948–49

ITEM	(MILLION POUNDS)
Wages	3,996
Salaries	2,177
Pay and allowances of the armed forces	244
Employers' national insurance contribution	171
Professional earnings	159
Income from farming	274
Profits of sole traders and partnerships	782
Trading profits of Companies and public enterprises	1,512
Other public income	78
Rent of land and buildings	462
National income	9,855

Having estimated the composite national income, we can rearrange it to show personal, nonpersonal and public incomes to better advantage. This is done in Table 48 below, items 1 through 5 showing the income totals as defined in Chapter 3. The resulting national income is item 8.

Turning to the Inland Revenue reports, one finds no exactly comparable estimates of income. The Inland Revenue defines five types of income totals which are used in their tax summaries.[13] These are: (1) *gross income,* the aggregate income brought under review, not including some incomes under the exemption limit; (2) *gross true income,* being gross income less reductions for overcharges, reliefs for loss, and certain interest deductions; (3) *net true income,* being gross true income less allowances for repairs and depreciation; (4) *actual income,* being net true income liable to tax (excluding incomes under exemption limit and charities); and (5) *taxable in-*

12. See p. 158.
13. See *Cmd.* 8103, p. 33.

come, being actual income less personal reliefs and allowances. For 1948–49 these totals for Great Britain were:

(MILLION POUNDS)

Gross income	10,170.7
Gross true income	9,261.9
Net true income	8,743.3
Actual income	8,627.7
Taxable income	4,789.5

None of these has an exact counterpart in social accounting, since they are defined for legal purposes.

TABLE 48

Personal, Private, and Public Income, 1948–49
(In Million Pounds)

ITEM	PERSONAL INCOME	NON-PERSONAL INCOME	PRIVATE INCOME (1 + 2)	PUBLIC INCOME	TOTAL INCOME (3 + 4)
	1	2	3	4	5
Wages	3,996		3,996		3,996
Salaries	2,177		2,177		2,177
Pay of allowances of armed forces	244		244		244
Employer's National Insurance contribution		171	171		171
Professional earnings	159		159		159
Traders' profits	776		776	7 *	783
Income from farming	274		274		274
Dividends and interest	819	193 †	1,012	18 *	1,030
Other public income				78 ‡	78
Rent	446		446	19 *	465
Companies and public enterprises:					
Provision for tax		636	636		636
Addition to reserves		443	443		443
1. Personal factor income	8,891				
2. Transfers	716		716	12 ‖	728
3. Total personal income	9,607 §				
4. Nonpersonal income		1,443			
5. Total private income			11,050		
6. Public income				134	
7. Total income					11,184
Less:					
Interest on national debt					−601
Transfers					−728
8. National income					9,855

* Income of charities not listed in the Registrar's Field.

† Includes £73.5 million income of life assurance funds and £119.3 million income of nonprofit societies and bodies listed in the Registrar's Field.

‡ Trading profits of governmental boards and authorities.

§ Includes £308 million personal factor income-in-kind, and £61 million transfer income-in-kind. See p. 141.

‖ Government grants to universities.

Some income—e.g. much of the income of persons below the exemption limit, income-in-kind, income of tax exempt government agencies, income illegally evading tax—is excluded from all these totals, so that we would expect the Inland Revenue figures to be below any similar social accounting aggregates. Except for these omissions, gross income is similar to private income as defined in Chapter 3. Gross true income has no counterpart in social accounting, but net true income, if one could correct for omissions and subtract transfer incomes subject to tax, would approximate national income. Taxable income is purely a legal fiction. Actual income is the most important aggregate for the purpose at hand, since it is from this figure that the only available data on the distribution of incomes by income range is obtained. It is therefore useful to attempt to reconcile this aggregate with the composite national income estimate. This is done in Table 49 below, using a procedure similar to Bowley's comparison of his estimates with White Paper figures for a prewar year.[14]

In looking at the deductions made from national income in Table 49 to arrive at Inland Revenue "actual income," we see that actual income is that part of the national income liable to tax, plus taxable transfer incomes.[15]

TABLE 49

Reconciliation of Composite National Income with Inland Revenue Assessments

INCOME TAX SCHEDULE	COMPONENTS OF NATIONAL INCOME	DE- DUCTIONS	INLAND REVENUE "ACTUAL INCOME"
A Rent	466.6		
Less: Adjustments		—38.5	
Underassessments		—31.0	
Income of charities		—19.0	
Incomes under exemption limit		—19.8	358.1
B Farmers' Profits (Under £100)	86.3		
Less: Adjustments		—9.0	
Value of produce consumed		—30.0	
Underassessments		—8.3	
Incomes under exemption limit		—13.0	26.0

14. Arthur L. Bowley, ed., *Studies in the National Income* (1942), pp. 83–4. See also Barna, p. 241.

15. The White Papers on national income use a similar aggregate in showing the distribution of income before tax, for example in *Cmd.* 8203, p. 22, table 12. No information is given, however, on the way in which this figure is estimated. The White Paper merely states that "in addition to the income shown in the table there are amounts accruing to persons that cannot be allocated to particular ranges of income. These are estimated to have been . . . £1,460 mn. in 1949."

TABLE 49 *(continued)*

*Reconciliation of Composite National Income with
Inland Revenue Assessments*

INCOME TAX SCHEDULE	COMPONENTS OF NATIONAL INCOME	DE-DUCTIONS	INLAND REVENUE "ACTUAL INCOME"
C Interest on government securities	235.6		
Less: Adjustments		—24.5	
Income of charities		—3.3	
Incomes under exemption limit		—10.0	200.8
D Farmers' profits	197.4		
Professional earnings	161.2		
Traders' profits	787.4		
Trading profits of companies	1,512.7		
Other company income (excluding £80.2 million in C)	329.7		
Other public income	78.0		
Less: Adjustments		—172.3	
Value of farm produce consumed		—74.0	
Investment income of nonprofit bodies		—142.6	
Profits tax liability		—274.4	
Interest accrued on national savings certificates		—36.7	
Earnings on own account		—30.0	
Income of charities		—22.0	
Incomes under exemption limit		—10.3	
Plus: Net income due to residents abroad		+2.0	2,302.1
E Wages	3,996.1		
Salaries	2,178.6		
Pay and allowances of armed forces	246.0		
Transfer incomes	728.0		
Less: Adjustments		—303.3	
Armed forces income-in-kind		—39.0	
Armed forces incomes under exemption limit		—101.0	
Other income-in-kind and untaxed allowances		—273.0	
Other income under exemption limit		—371.4	
Transfer incomes exempt from tax		—320.4	5,740.7
Totals	11,013.4	—2,385.7	8,627.7
Plus: Employers' national insurance contribution		+171.0	
Less: Interest on the debt		—601.0	
Transfer payments		—728.0	
National income		9,855.4	

This table will be useful in constructing a complete distribution of
the national income, for the deductions column gives an idea of
items and amounts which must be added to the published distribu-

tion of actual income. Ideally, beginning with a complete distribution of actual income and then working backward and allocating all items in the deductions column which are applicable to private persons, one could arrive at a distribution of private income. Unfortunately the process is not quite so simple, but the technique followed in the succeeding section is the same.

DISTRIBUTION OF PERSONAL INCOME

The 92nd report of the Inland Revenue classified income by ranges of income before tax for 1948–49.[16] Twelve ranges of income were used, and the total income allocated was £7,800 million. This table was based partly on actual tax returns and partly on the distributional pattern established in the income census of 1937–38.[17]

The 1949 and 1950 White Papers on national income also give distributions of income in six income classifications for both 1948 and 1949. These estimates, while quite similar to the Inland Revenue's for incomes above £1,000, differ substantially below that level in both the number and amount of incomes in each income group. The difference between the sets of figures is much greater than can reasonably be accounted for by the fact that one is for the calendar, and the other for the fiscal, year. Since some choice between them had to be made, the White Paper figures have been assumed to be more nearly accurate in relation to the number and amount of incomes in each income group. The only basis for this choice was that the White Papers use common social accounting techniques, and it is simpler to work from fairly well defined income aggregates than from Inland Revenue figures the constitution of which remains something of a mystery.

Personal income in the White Papers is given as £8,541 million for 1948 and £9,048 million for 1949.[18] Adjusting these to fit the fiscal year, and excluding Northern Ireland, personal income under the White Paper's definition would be approximately £8,465 million for the 1948–49 fiscal year. It is felt that this figure is more nearly correct than that given by the Inland Revenue, and the Inland Revenue

16. *Cmd.* 8052, p. 83.

17. The report states: "Unfortunately current information is not available in . . . accessible form, except for the small number of people in the Sur-tax sphere. . . . This is because Income Tax assessments are not made on an individual's total income but on each source of income separately" (p. 82). Where there is more than one source of income an income recipient is reported more than once in the assessments; hence it is necessary to rely on the prewar income census. A new census has been taken for incomes in 1949–50, but it has not yet been published. For a description of the original census see 83d report, *RCIR, 1940, Cmd.* 6769 (1946), pp. 28–39.

18. *National Income and Expenditure of the United Kingdom, 1946 to 1949, Cmd.* 7933 (1950), p. 16; *Cmd.* 8203, p. 22.

data on family classifications has been slightly adjusted to fit the White Paper distribution.[19]

The White Paper estimates of personal income include tax-exempt transfer incomes but exclude about £1,140 million of income which are "amounts accruing to persons that cannot be allocated to particular ranges of income," [20] so that the figure of £8,465 million personal income mentioned above is not equivalent to either "actual income" as the Inland Revenue defines it, nor personal income as defined here in Chapter 3. The distribution of the latter can be estimated, however, by working backward and forward from the White Paper figures.

In Table 50, column 1, is given a distribution based on the White Paper personal income data adjusted for the fiscal year and to exclude Northern Ireland.[21] Untaxed transfer incomes in 1948–49 amounted to £320.4 million, consisting of the following:

	(MILLION POUNDS)
Old age tobacco coupons	8.8
Sickness and maternity benefits	57.0
Industrial injuries benefits	5.6
Unemployment compensation	23.5
Outdoor relief	2.1
School milk and meals	59.0
War pensions	86.6
Training allowances	9.0
Scholarships	24.0
National assistance	44.8
	320.4

19. The major difference between the two is that the White Paper distribution shows fewer persons in the £250–500 group, and more in the £500–1,000 range, than the Inland Revenue. The average income in each of these groups is identical for the two sets of data, the total income of all groups therefore being greater for the White Paper estimate. Using the White Paper figures will not distort the relative weight of taxes for each income group, for direct taxes on income are estimated in Ch. 12 in terms of the effective rate of tax on each group given by the Inland Revenue. The total income tax revenue will be slightly greater than shown in the Inland Revenue reports, since the effective rate is higher in the £500–1,000 group than in the £250–500 group, but the difference is not more than £30 million (2% of total income tax revenues).

20. *Cmd.* 7933, p. 16, n.

21. Northern Ireland's "actual income," as a percentage of total "actual income," was 1.4% in 1948–49. This proportion has been deducted from each income group to give the distribution for Great Britain. It is likely that there are more low incomes and fewer high incomes in Northern Ireland than in the United Kingdom as a whole, but the error in making a standard deduction for all income groups should be slight. See *Cmd.* 8052, p. 44, for Inland Revenue estimates of "actual income" for Northern Ireland and the U.K.

In column 2 of Table 50 the distribution of these untaxed transfer incomes is shown.[22] Subtracting these amounts from column 1 results in an estimated distribution of personal "actual income" shown in column 3. The total, £8,145, differs from total "actual income" in Table 49 above, by undistributed corporate profits net of profits tax liability.

TABLE 50

Estimated Distribution of Personal "Actual Income"
(In Million Pounds)

INCOME RANGE (IN POUNDS)	PERSONAL INCOME (BASED ON WHITE PAPERS) 1	TAX-EXEMPT TRANSFER INCOME 2	PERSONAL "ACTUAL INCOME" (1 MINUS 2) 3
Under 135	400	79.7	320.3
135–250	1,894	96.9	1,797.1
250–500	3,008	116.1	2,891.9
500–750	1,007	18.4	988.6
750–1,000	516	5.9	510.1
1,000–2,000	722	2.1	719.9
2,000–3,000	275	.7	274.3
3,000–5,000	247	.4	246.6
5,000–10,000	201	.2	200.8
10,000–20,000	113	—	113.0
20,000 and above	82	—	82.0
	8,465	320.4	8,144.6

Starting now with personal "actual income," we can attempt to build back up to total personal income, including all those portions of income which were untaxed. The difference between personal "actual income" in Table 50 and total personal income as given in Table 3 of Chapter 3 is £1,471 million. Of this amount about 60% can be identified, and it is worth the effort of trying to estimate the distribution of those items which can be identified. The distribution of £320 million of the difference between "actual income" and total personal income has already been indicated in Table 50, i.e. tax-exempt transfer incomes. In addition, there were employees' national insurance contributions of £207 million, cooperative dividends of £37 million, interest on national savings certificates of £66 million, income-in-kind of approximately £39 million to members of the armed forces,

22. See pp. 206–19 for an estimate of the distribution of transfer incomes by specific programs.

income-in-kind of farmers of an estimated £104 million, and approximately £165 million other income received in noncash forms.

In Table 51 these items are allocated to income groups. Considerable guesswork is necessary in the attempt to allocate these amounts to specific groups, but it seems more desirable to make a rough approximation than merely to allocate the remaining £1,150 million in proportion to all other income.

In Table 51 national insurance contributions have been allocated in relation to the number of income earners in each income group.[23] Cooperative dividends have been spread over the five lowest income groups on the assumption that these groups respectively (from the lowest) spent 15%, 12%, 8%, 3%, and 1% of their total incomes in cooperative stores and received dividends in proportions to these expenditures. Interest on national savings certificates has been divided among income groups up to the £5,000 level in proportion to their initial income before tax. There was a greater incentive for persons in the higher income groups to invest in these certificates, since they were tax free, but their small denomination (10s. units) and the limit on holdings (roughly £1,700 in 1948–49) were deterrents. For persons with incomes above £5,000 it was assumed that the full £1,700 was held, since distribution strictly in proportion to initial income would have resulted in holdings far above the legal limit.

The cost of issue of food and clothing to members of the armed services has been allocated roughly in proportion to estimated armed forces incomes. A little over a third of total farm income has been assumed to be produce consumed, and this has been allocated primarily to the three lowest income groups. Other unreported income-in-kind of domestics, agricultural laborers, miners, presents from employers, professional services provided on own account, etc. have been estimated at roughly 2% of total income and have been allocated in inverse proportion to the total income of each group, ranging from 5% for the lowest income group down to .5% for the £2,000–3,000 group.

23. The new national insurance act, making insurance compulsory for all employed, self-employed, and unoccupied persons (with the exception of full-time housewives) went into effect on July 5, 1948. Therefore, contributions for ¾ of the fiscal year were allocated in proportion to the number of income earners in each income group. Although contributions were slightly higher for self-employed and unoccupied persons (who are chiefly in the higher income groups), more wives of persons in the lower income brackets were working. Thus the average contribution per tax family should have been about equal in all ranges. For the first quarter of the fiscal year, under the old unemployment, national health, and contributory pension schemes, insurance was only compulsory for persons with incomes not exceeding £420. (The number of voluntary contributors was small, not exceeding 25,000 in the contributory pensions scheme.) The £30 million contributions between April 6 and July 5, 1948, have been distributed in proportion to the number of income earners in each of the three lowest income groups.

TABLE 51

Allocation of Untaxed Portions of Personal Income
(In Million Pounds)

Income Range	Transfer Incomes	National Insurance Contribution	Cooperative Dividends	National Savings	Income-in-Kind of:			Total
					Farmers	Armed Forces	Other	
Under 135	79.7	20.0	3.4	2.2	22.0	11.0	15.7	154.0
135–250	96.9	80.0	15.1	13.3	50.0	17.0	55.8	328.1
250–500	116.1	78.0	16.2	24.5	18.0	5.0	53.7	311.5
500–750	18.4	16.0	2.1	8.4	9.0	3.0	25.5	82.4
750–1,000	5.9	6.0	.2	4.5	3.0	2.0	7.5	29.1
1,000–2,000	2.1	5.0	—	6.4	2.0	1.0	5.2	21.7
2,000–3,000	.7	1.1	—	2.5	—	—	1.6	5.9
3,000–5,000	.4	.5	—	2.3	—	—	—	3.2
5,000–10,000	.2	.3	—	1.6	—	—	—	2.1
10,000–20,000	—	.1	—	.5	—	—	—	.6
20,000 and above	—	—	—	.1	—	—	—	.1
Totals	320.4	207.0	37.0	66.3	104.0	39.0	165.0	938.7

After estimating the allocation of identifiable tax-exempt incomes, £523.9 million still remains unaccounted for. This amount probably consisted of certain allowances for losses and overcharges recognized by the Inland Revenue, some miscellaneous expenses which were deductible for tax purposes, earnings "on own account" not reported, tax evasions, etc. There is no adequate basis, however, on which to allocate this income, so that it will be assumed that this income was distributed among persons in proportion to their income reported to tax. This is a rather unsatisfactory arrangement, but it is necessary in order to obtain a distribution of all personal income.

TABLE 52

Distribution of Personal Incomes
(In Million Pounds)

INCOME RANGE (IN POUNDS)	PERSONAL "ACTUAL INCOME" 1	TAX-EXEMPT INCOME 2	UNIDEN-TIFIABLE INCOME 3	TOTAL PERSONAL INCOME 4
Under 135	320.3	154.0	19.4	493.7
135–250	1797.1	328.1	114.4	2,239.6
250–500	2891.9	311.5	187.2	3,390.6
500–750	988.6	82.4	63.3	1,134.3
750–1,000	510.1	29.1	32.6	571.8
1,000–2,000	719.9	21.7	45.4	787.0
2,000–3,000	274.3	5.9	17.0	297.2
3,000–5,000	246.6	13.2	16.5	266.3
5,000–10,000	200.8	2.1	13.9	216.8
10,000–20,000	113.0	.6	8.2	121.8
20,000 and above	82.0	.1	6.0	88.1
Totals	8,144.6	938.7	523.9	9,607.2

In Table 52 the estimated distribution of personal income is shown, column 1 indicating personal "actual income," column 2 the identifiable tax-exempt incomes allocated above, and column 3 the unidentifiable income. The distribution of total personal income shown in column 4 is the same as that given in Table 3 of Chapter 3.

DISTRIBUTION OF NONPERSONAL INCOME AND PRIVATE INCOME

In addition to personal income there was £1,433.3 million nonpersonal income in 1948–49 which can be imputed to individuals by income groups. This amount included:

(MILLION POUNDS)

Gross undistributed corporate profits	1,079.6
Income of life assurance companies	73.5
Income of societies	119.3
Employers' national insurance contributions	171.0
	1,443.4

Undistributed profits can be allocated to income groups on the basis of shareholdings. In the latter part of this chapter, following the discussion of the distribution of wealth, an index is developed relating the holding of shares to persons by income range. Column 1 of Table 53 shows the estimated distribution of undistributed profits.

TABLE 53

Distribution of Nonpersonal Income
(In Million Pounds)

INCOME RANGE (IN POUNDS)	UNDIS-TRIBUTED PROFITS	INSUR-ANCE INCOME	SOCIETY INCOME	EMPLOYERS' NATIONAL INSURANCE CONTRI-BUTIONS	TOTAL NON-PERSONAL INCOME
	1	2	3	4	5
Under 135	4.28	2.4	13.3	9.0	28.9
135–250	16.7	13.7	59.8	71.0	161.2
250–500	114.0	20.5	46.4	70.0	250.9
500–750	102.5	8.6	13.3	13.0	137.4
750–1,000	60.7	8.9	—	4.4	74.0
1,000–2,000	151.6	13.0	—	3.0	167.6
2,000–3,000	107.7	6.1	—	.5	114.3
3,000–5,000	124.5	7.9	—	.1	132.5
5,000–10,000	140.1	5.7	—	—	145.8
10,000–20,000	98.3	3.7	—	—	102.0
20,000 and above	125.5	3.3	—	—	128.8
Totals	1,045.8	93.8	132.8	171.0	1,443.4
Insurance income *	20.3				
Society income *	13.5				
	1,079.6				

* These amounts are included in columns 2 and 3.

The income of life assurance companies is distributed among income groups in column 2 of Table 53. The total of insurance income in this table is £20.3 million greater than listed above, since this is the share of undistributed corporate profits which must be imputed to

the holdings of insurance companies. An insurance index similar to
the share index is given at the end of this chapter, and the £93.8 million insurance income has been allocated to income grades on this
basis.

Income of societies [24] was an estimated £119.3 million in 1948–49,
to which must be added their imputed share of undistributed corporate profits of £13.5 million. In allocating society income in column
3 of Table 53 it has been assumed that 10% of society benefits went
to the lowest income group, and 45%, 35%, and 10% to the three
next highest groups respectively.

Employers' national insurance contributions have been allocated
similarly to employees' contributions, as explained in the preceding
section.[25]

The distribution of total private income can now be estimated by
adding personal incomes from Table 52 and nonpersonal incomes
from Table 53. This distribution is shown in Table 54, the figures
in column 3 being the same as those in Table 3 of Chapter 3.

The distributions of personal factor and private factor incomes
given in Chapter 3 were found by deducting transfer incomes, which
are allocated in detail in Chapter 16 below.

TABLE 54

Distribution of Private Income
(In Million Pounds)

INCOME RANGE (IN POUNDS)	PERSONAL INCOME 1	NONPERSONAL INCOME 2	PRIVATE INCOME (1 + 2) 3
Under 135	493.7	28.9	522.6
135–250	2,239.6	161.2	2,400.8
250–500	3,390.6	250.9	3,641.5
500–750	1,134.3	137.4	1,271.7
750–1,000	571.8	74.0	645.8
1,000–2,000	787.0	167.6	954.6
2,000–3,000	297.2	114.3	411.5
3,000–5,000	266.3	132.5	398.8
5,000–10,000	216.8	145.8	362.6
10,000–20,000	121.8	102.0	223.8
20,000 and above	88.1	128.8	216.9
Totals	9,607.2	1,443.4	11,050.6

24. Most of these societies were savings and insurance institutions, e.g. friendly
societies, trade union benefit funds, thrift clubs, etc.
25. See p. 140.

DISTRIBUTION OF PRIVATE CAPITAL

In Table 4 of Chapter 3 a distribution of private capital by size of holding, based on the 1946–50 period, was given which was estimated by the estate method. This method is based on data of the age and sex grouping of persons leaving estates of particular sizes in any year or period of years. Taking the death duty data as a sample of living estate owners, for each estate size one can then determine the average probability of death within one year of the average person holding any particular size estate by reference to mortality tables. For example, the probability of death in one year for the average male, aged 50, in England is approximately .011, i.e. 1.1% of males aged 50 can be expected to die within an average year. Therefore, for each male aged 50 who did die in 1948–49 there can be assumed to be 91 others of similar circumstances still living. The reciprocal of the probability of death in one year (in this case, 91) can be used as a multiplier to estimate the number of living persons of the same age, and similarly to estimate the amount of capital possessed by living estate owners of that age.[26]

For 1946–50 the average estate multiplier was 33.74, and the total value of private capital was £29,907 million.[27] This estimate includes the market value of all privately held realty, securities, and personal property, and exceeds the value of physical assets by the inclusion of government securities and the total value of insurance policies (not amounts paid up). It is also greater than the value of income-producing assets, in that idle cash, unused land, household possessions, etc. are similarly included. Unearned incomes (e.g. rent, dividends, and interest) in 1948–49 totaled approximately £1,100 million; so in terms of the Griffen (income) method of estimating private capital, current capital values represented an average 26 years' purchase of income.

In Table 55 the distribution of capital by size of holding for the 1946–50 period is compared with Barna's prewar estimate and Langley's prewar and postwar estimates. The difference between the two postwar estimates is more apparent than real, Langley's 1946–47 estimate having been based on a year when an unusually small number of estates came under the Inland Revenue's purview.

26. For a more detailed description of this method, see H. Campion, *Public and Private Property in Great Britain* (1939), pp. 1–24. For other illustrations of its use with English data, see Bernard Mallet, "A Method of Estimating Capital Wealth from Estate Duty Statistics," *JRSS, 71* (1908), 65–84; H. Campion and G. W. Daniels, *The Distribution of the National Capital* (1936); Barna, pp. 259–71; Kathleen Langley, "The Distribution of Capital in Private Hands in 1936–38 and 1946–47," *BOxIS, 12* (1950), 339–59, and *13* (1951), 33–54; and Cartter, *Eca, 20,* 247–58.

27. See Table 4, p. 33, above. For the appropriate multipliers for different sizes of estates, see table 1 of Cartter, n. 26 above.

In the past it has been difficult to relate capital holdings to income groups, but recently the Inland Revenue reports have provided some useful information which can be adapted for this purpose. The 1948–49 and 1949–50 reports included tables indicating the receipt of investment incomes by size to gross incomes by size.[28] For example, by looking at these tables it can be found that for investment incomes ranging between £12,000 and £15,000, 8.8% was received by persons whose gross incomes were greater than £20,000, and 91.2% was received by persons whose incomes fell in the £10,000–20,000 range. Therefore, if we knew approximately what size capital holdings were represented by investment incomes of £12,000–15,000, the amount of capital in the equivalent range could be allotted to income groups in these proportions.

TABLE 55

Estimates of Private Capital by Size of Holding *

	LANGLEY 1936–38		BARNA 1937–38	
SIZE OF HOLDING (IN POUNDS)	NUMBER (IN THOUSANDS)	VALUE (IN MILLION POUNDS)	NUMBER (IN THOUSANDS)	VALUE (IN MILLION POUNDS)
Under 100	19,190	1,015	—	—
100–1,000	4,548	2,208	5,625	2,360
1,000–5,000	1,294	3,348	1,480	3,580
5,000–10,000	231	1,931	293	2,190
10,000–25,000	156	2,813	195	3,110
25,000–100,000	70	3,694	90	4,090
100,000 and above	13.1	4,304	14.7	3,610
Totals	25,502	19,313	7,700	18,940

	LANGLEY 1946–47		1946–50 ESTIMATE	
SIZE OF HOLDING (IN POUNDS)	NUMBER (IN THOUSANDS)	VALUE (IN MILLION POUNDS)	NUMBER (IN THOUSANDS)	VALUE (IN MILLION POUNDS)
Under 100	18,892	1,233	19,633	883
100–1,000	8,441	2,958	8,448	3,479
1,000–5,000	2,706	5,832	2,389	5,607
5,000–10,000	420	3,070	510	3,854
10,000–25,000	279	4,436	338	5,453
25,000–100,000	117	5,223	137	6,229
100,000 and above	16.8	4,501	18.8	4,402
Totals	30,872	27,152	31,474	29,907

* See Barna, p. 260; Langley, *12,* 351–4; *13,* 403. Langley's maximum and minimum estimates for each range have been averaged.

28. *Cmd.* 8052, table 102; and *Cmd.* 8103, table 45.

To match investment incomes to capital holding, a yield estimate must be introduced. The Inland Revenue data of estates falling in gives the property breakdown by estate sizes, so that an estimate of the yield of different types of capital can be converted into an average rate of yield by size of estate. The average yields of different kinds of capital are estimated for 1948–49 to have been approximately as follows: British government securites 2.9%;[29] other government securities 3.2%; shares 4.3%; cash 1%; mortgages 5%; land 4.6%; house property 6%; ground rents 4.5%; other realty 5%; and other personalty 3%. When these are weighted by the relative holdings in each estate range, the resulting yield estimates are approximately 2.9% for estates of less than £10,000, 3.5% for estates of £10,000–15,000, 3.6% for £15,000–100,000, and 3.65% for estates above £100,000. The investment income ranges given by the Inland Revenue can now be translated into equivalent capital ranges, as shown in the left-hand columns of Table 56 below.

The equivalent capital range for the £12,000–15,000 investment income range used in the example above can now be estimated as £330,000–410,000. Therefore, 8.8% of the capital falling within this range can be assumed to have belonged to persons with incomes exceeding £20,000, and 91.2% to persons with incomes between £10,000 and £20,000. This process can be followed for all incomes of more than £2,000. The percentages shown in Table 56 (above and to the left of the dotted lines) have been adapted directly from the Inland Revenue tables already referred to.

Below the investment and gross income level of £2,000 the task of relating income and capital is more difficult. The total amounts of investment incomes of less than £2,000 received by persons with gross incomes exceeding £2,000 is known from surtax returns, and the yield estimates indicate approximately the total investment income from any particular capital range. In this way percentages of capital in small holdings possessed by persons with gross incomes exceeding £2,000 can be worked out.[30] These are shown in Table 56 (below and to the left of the dotted lines).

29. The average 1948 yield of national savings certificates, consols, 3½% war loans, and 3% savings bonds, weighted by the relative amounts in private hands.

30. This is easier to explain by reference to Table 56. In the gross income column headed £3,000–5,000 (for example), is the figure 12% for capital holdings of £27,500–55,000. This percentage was estimated in the following manner: investment incomes ranging between £1,000–2,000 (equivalent to the £27,500–55,000 capital range) for persons in the £3,000–5,000 gross income range totaled approximately £15.5 million. The total amount of capital in the £27,500–55,000 capital range was roughly £3,590 million. (by extrapolation of Table 4, p. 33, above). Applying the yield estimate outlined above (3.6% in this case), we estimate total investment income from this capital range at £129 million. The £15.5 million is 12% of £129 million. All figures below and to the left of the dotted lines in Tables 56 and 57 have been estimated in this manner.

For gross incomes below £2,000 there is no available information on investment incomes, so that one can only follow the pattern established for incomes above that level. The percentages in Table 56 to the right of the vertical line, therefore, must be accepted with a considerable degree of caution. For the purpose of later chapters, however, the probable errors in determining the relative holdings of capital for incomes below £2,000 is not very important, for over 90% of all capital taxes in 1948–49 were paid by persons in income groups above £2,000. It should be recognized, nevertheless, that the error in relative amounts of capital held by these lower income groups may be substantial.[31]

Converting the percentages in Table 56 into actual amounts of capital, we may formulate Table 57, which gives the estimated distribution of capital among income groups. The figures along the bottom of this table are the same as those given in Table 5 of Chapter 3.

INSURANCE POLICY AND CORPORATE SHARE HOLDINGS BY INCOME GROUP

In order to allocate some portions of income and taxes to income groups, it is necessary to know something about the relative holdings of insurance policies and corporate shares. The method used in estimating the ownership of capital by income group above can be adapted for this purpose.

The Inland Revenue annually publishes a breakdown of types of property in estates falling in. From the 1948–49 table[32] the percentage of insurance and share values can be determined by estate range. Then using Table 56 above, indices by estate range can be

31. A partial cross-check has been made on the capital estimates, the results of which are about what one would have anticipated. After capital holdings have been estimated (in Table 57), the yield estimates can be applied to determine the approximate investment incomes of each income group. If these investment incomes are then calculated as percentages of total income, the percentages should vary directly with the level of income if the distribution of capital by income group is anywhere near correct. Investment income as a percentage of total income, followed this procedure, worked out as follows:

Gross Income Range	Percentage of Investment Income
£1,000–2,000	16.7%
500–1,000	15.7%
250–500	10.4%
Less than 250	5.8%

This pattern is almost identical with that found in the last published Inland Revenue figures on investment incomes, for 1938 (*Cmd. 6769*).

32. *Cmd.* 8052, table 112.

TABLE 56

*Percentage Distribution of Investment Incomes and Capital
Holdings, by Size Distribution, among Gross
Income Groups*

Investment Income Range (In Thousand Pounds)	Equivalent Capital Range (In Thousand Pounds)	Gross Income Groups											Total
		Above 20,000	10,000–20,000	5,000–10,000	3,000–5,000	2,000–3,000	1,000–2,000	750–1,000	500–750	250–500	135–250	Under 135	
Above 20	Above 550	100.0											100.0
15–20	410–550	29.0	71.0										100.0
12–15	330–410	8.8	91.2										100.0
10–12	275–330	5.1	94.9										100.0
8–10	220–275	3.7	37.6	58.7									100.0
6–8	165–220	1.6	18.6	79.8									100.0
5–6	135–165	1.2	9.8	89.0									100.0
4–5	110–135	.8	5.5	35.6	58.1								100.0
3–4	82–110	.5	3.7	25.4	70.4								100.0
2–3	55–82	.3	2.0	11.1	25.2	61.4							100.0
1–2	27.5–55	.2	.9	4.8	12.0	13.1	69.0*						100.0
.5–1	14.3–27.5	.1	.3	1.7	4.4	5.6	8.2	29.0	50.7				100.0
.25–.5	7.8–14.3	—	.1	.7	2.2	3.2	5.7	8.9	16.0	63.2			100.0
Under .25	Under 7.8	—	—	.4	.4	.8	3.9	7.3	15.2	48.0	20.0	4.3	100.0

* This percentage can be included in the relatively certain area, since it is a residuum.

TABLE 57

Distribution of Capital, by Income Groups
(In Million Pounds)

CAPITAL RANGE (IN THOUSAND POUNDS)	GROSS INCOME GROUPS											TOTAL BY CAPITAL GROUPS
	Above 20,000	10,000–20,000	5,000–10,000	3,000–5,000	2,000–3,000	1,000–2,000	750–1,000	500–750	250–500	135–250	Under 135	
Above 550	1,120											1,120
410–550	101	244										345
330–410	26	269										295
275–330	14	261										275
220–275	15	150	235									400
165–220	8	95	407									510
135–165	6	51	468									525
110–135	5	40	254	416								715
82–110	4	31	211	584								830
55–82	4	28	158	358	872							1,420
27.5–55	7	32	173	431	470	2,477*						3,590
14.3–27.5	4	12	68	176	222	328	1,155	2,020				3,985
7.8–14.3	—	4	26	82	119	213	332	597	2,357			3,730
Under 7.8	—	—	12	49	97	475	890	1,861	5,840	2,420	523	12,167
Total by Income groups	1,314	1,217	2,012	2,096	1,780	3,493	2,377	4,478	8,197	2,420	523	29,907

* See note to Table 56.

translated into indices by income range. In Table 58 these resulting indices by income range are given.

TABLE 58

Percentage Distribution of Insurance Policy and Corporate Share Holdings, by Income Group

INCOME RANGE (IN POUNDS)	INSURANCE POLICIES (PERCENTAGE)	CORPORATE SHARES (PERCENTAGE)
Under 135	2.6	.4
135–250	14.6	1.6
250–500	21.8	10.9
500–750	10.2	9.8
750–1,000	8.5	5.8
1,000–2,000	13.8	14.5
2,000–3,000	6.5	10.3
3,000–5,000	8.5	11.9
5,000–10,000	6.1	13.4
10,000–20,000	3.9	9.4
20,000 and above	3.5	12.0
	100.0	100.0

CLASSIFICATION OF GOVERNMENT EXPENDITURES

The sources of government tax revenue are not difficult to classify, but the expenditure programs are many and varied. To allocate specific expenditures to income groups requires a rather minute breakdown, and as explained in Chapter 3 it will simplify allocation to divide expenditures into those representing transfers, other divisible expenditures, and indivisible expenditures.

The expenditures side of the budget in Britain is divided into civil votes and service votes, the latter being almost entirely military and the former having to do with all the government civil services. There were ten classes of civil votes in 1948–49. In the listing which follows, under each of the ten headings expenditures are broken down by the administering agency and by type of expenditure where necessary.

Wherever an attempt in succeeding chapters has been made to allocate specific amounts, these items are shown in greater detail. The national insurance expenditures are included at the end of the listing, and Exchequer grants to the extrabudgetary funds are shown in the civil votes in parentheses, not added into the totals until actually disbursed by the national insurance funds.

The following is the combined expenditure account of the central government and the national insurance funds, representing expenditures authorized during the 1948–49 fiscal year.[33]

CLASSIFICATION OF EXPENDITURES	INDIVISIBLE EXPENDITURES	TRANS- FERS	DIVISIBLE EXPENDITURES
	(IN THOUSAND POUNDS)		
CIVIL VOTES			
Class I—central government and finance	£11,835		
Class II—foreign and imperial	70,341		
Class III—home, law, justice	41,791		
Class IV—education and broadcasting			
General	12,260		
University grants	12,503		
BBC overseas services	4,500		
Scholarships		£14,563	
Education			£171,570
Class V—health, housing, town and country planning, labour, and national insurance			
Ministry of Health			
General	9,487		
Hospitals			7,615
Housing			69,599
National health service			
Exchequer contribution *			226,838 *
National insurance fund contribution			27,000
Ministry of Labour			
General	721		
Administration	7,315		2,000
Training allowances		10,301	
Employment and transference			6,205
National insurance			
National insurance fund		(93,185)	
Industrial injuries fund		(4,071)	
Health and unemployment funds		(11,930)	
Contributory pensions fund		(31,151)	
Family allowance payments		59,494	
Family allowance administration			1,235
National assistance			
Benefits		64,005	
Administration			4,485
Miscellaneous	6,994		

* The Exchequer grant for the cost of the national health service is given here as £18.5 million more than in the civil estimates. This sum represents the transfer of superannuation funds from local sources to the national health service, and it has been considered here merely as a capital transfer, rather than income to the national health service.

33. This listing is based primarily on the 1948–49 and 1949–50 *Civil Estimates, H. C.* 68, 1–10 (1948) and *H. C.* 77, 1–10 (1949), the former showing the budgeted amounts for 1948–49, and the latter actual amounts spent during the fiscal year. The total amounts under each civil vote equal grants issued during the fiscal year, less the net surplus balance from prior years (i.e. surplus balances not written off during the year), plus unspent balances at the end of the year. The balance of unissued grants at the end of 1948–49 was less than 1% of all grants in 1948–49, so that this adjustment was relatively unimportant quantitatively. See *H. C.* 189. Detailed breakdowns of expenditures by agency are based on the annual reports of the various ministries.

CLASSIFICATION OF EXPENDITURES	INDIVISIBLE EXPENDITURES	TRANS-FERS	DIVISIBLE EXPENDITURES
	(IN THOUSAND POUNDS)		
Class VI—trade, industry and transport			
Board of Trade			
General	£18,048		
Utility cloth rebates			£1,760
Assistance to cotton manufacturers			200
Assistance to furniture industry			25
Ministry of Agriculture			
General	10,332		
Agricultural machinery services (England and Wales)	1,263		1,262
Agricultural machinery services (Scotland)	409		409
Marginal farming (Scotland)			300
Lime fertilizers			5,000
General assistance, development, and improvement services			3,450
County executive			9,122
Hill and Grassland (England and Wales)			4,458
Hill and Grassland (Scotland)			2,000
Calf rearing (England and Wales)			2,500
Calf rearing (Scotland)			1,750
Roads	19,864		6,955
Miscellaneous	70,608		
Class VII—common services	89,793		
Class VIII—pensions			
War pensions		£81,675	
Medical benefits		4,502	
Administration			3,819
General	6,602		
Class IX—contributions to local authorities	56,717		
Class X—supply, food, and miscellaneous services			
Fuel operations			2,875
Ministry of Supply			
General	108,948		
Net trading losses			11,991
Agency factory losses			876
Ministry of Food			
General	19,975		
Milk and welfare foods		35,452	
Sugar, deficiency payment			3,441
Net trading expenditure			387,852
Miscellaneous	39,760		
Total, civil votes	£620,075	£269,992	£1,007,003
SERVICE VOTES			
Army	349,000	11,000	
Navy	163,500	5,000	
Air	184,400	5,000	
Ministry of Defense	632		
Total service votes	£697,532	£21,000	
Net revenue Departments	29,707		
Total current expenditures	£1,347,314	£290,992	£1,007,003

CLASSIFICATION OF EXPENDITURES	INDIVISIBLE EXPENDITURES	TRANS- FERS	DIVISIBLE EXPENDITURES
	(IN THOUSAND POUNDS)		
National Insurance Fund Expenditures			
Contributory pensions and allowances		£243,818	
Health benefits		60,625	
Industrial injuries benefits		5,675	
Widows and guardians benefits		16,150	
Unemployment benefits		20,180	
Contribution to national health service			(£27,000)
Administrative less other income			2,846
Adjustments			
Negative revenues			
Old age tobacco duty relief		8,750	
Postwar income tax credits		18,800	
Less: government income from property	£—24,000		
Combined expenditures on transfers, goods, and services	£1,323,314	£664,990	£1,009,849
Debt Charges †	500,000		
National insurance fund surplus ‡	144,043		
Surplus on current account	430,934		
Total expenditures and surpluses	£2,398,291	£664,990	£1,009,849
Combined total		£4,073,130	

† Total debt charges were £519,933,081, but the balance over £500 million was met from receipts under various acts, e.g. Local Authority Loan Act of 1945, Housing Act of 1944, and Coal Industry Nationalization Act of 1946. See *H.C.* 189, pp. 30–1.

‡ The surplus of the national insurance fund was a surplus by accounting technique only. If there had been no exchequer grants in 1948–49 the fund would have had a deficit of £31 million. In the two following years the fund had a surplus in its own right, since new contributors were not eligible for full benefits until they had made a certain number of payments under the new program.

CHAPTER 12

The Allocation of Direct Taxes
on Personal Incomes

THE ESTIMATED distribution of direct taxes on personal incomes was given in Table 7 of Chapter 4; in this chapter the method by which this estimate was determined is explained in more detail. The income tax, surtax, and employees' national insurance contribution are discussed separately.

INCOME TAX AND SURTAX RATES, 1948–49

The income tax is an annual measure, created in the finance act of each year. It consists of a standard rate of tax which is made progressive in the lower income brackets through the operation of reliefs, allowances, and two special ranges of reduced rates. In the upper income groups, i.e. above £2,000, the tax structure is made progressive by the operation of the surtax. In Table 59 the income tax rates and reliefs and surtax rates are shown for typical prewar and wartime years, as well as 1948–49.

The reduced rates on taxable incomes of less than £250 make the marginal rate of income tax for 1948–49 increase in three steps, 15% to 30% to 45%. Once a taxable income of £250 has been reached, the marginal rate of income tax is constant at 9s. (45%). From £2,000 onward the surtax raises the effective marginal rate in 11 steps, the surtax reaching 10s. 6d. (52½%) at £20,000. The effective average rate of tax, i.e. the average rate of income and surtax combined, is progressive through all ranges approaching a maximum of 9s. income tax, plus 10s. 6d. surtax, or 19s. 6d. (97.5%). This was shown diagrammatically in Figure III (p. 38).

The British income tax is charged on five different schedules, each corresponding to a particular type or types of income.

Schedule A is for "Income from the Ownership of Lands, Houses, etc.," chargeable on the net annual value of the property.[1] Any rents received in excess of tax valuations are assessed under Schedule D.

---

1. *Cmd.* 8103, pp. 38–44. The gross annual value is determined every five years in reference to the previous five years' rent. Actually there has been no re-evaluation under Schedule A since 1936, so that a large portion of rent is assessed under Schedule D.

Schedule B pertains to "Profits from the Occupation of Lands, etc." (mainly farmers' profits), with tax chargeable on the annual

TABLE 59

Income Tax Rates and Allowances

	1937–38	1944–45	1948–49
Standard rate	5s.	10s.	9s.
Allowances and reliefs			
Exemption limit	£125	£110	£135
Earned income allowance	1/5	1/10	1/5
(Maximum)	£300	£150	£400
Age allowance	1/5	1/10	1/5
Single allowance	£100	£80	£110
Married allowance	£180	£140	£180
Wife's earned income allowance,			
Maximum	£45	£80	£110
Child allowance	£60	£50	£60
Housekeeper allowance	£50	£50	£50
Dependent relative allowance	£25	£50	£50
Reduced rates	1s. 8d. on first £135	6s. 6d. on first £165	3s. on first £50 6s. on next £200

Minor reliefs:
Allowances for life insurance premiums at defined rates. Dominion income tax relief, according to statutory provisions. In effect, allowance for national insurance contributions.

SLICE OF INCOME (IN POUNDS)	SURTAX RATES		
	1937–38	1944–45	1948–49
	(IN SHILLINGS AND PENCE)		
2,000–2,500	1/0	2/0	2/0
2,500–3,000	1/4.5	2/3	2/6
3,000–4,000	2/2.4	3/3	3/6
4,000–5,000	3/3.6	4/3	4/6
5,000–6,000	3/10.2	5/0	5/6
6,000–8,000	4/4.8	5/9	6/6
8,000–10,000	5/6	7/0	7/6
10,000–12,000	6/0.6	8/3	8/6
12,000–15,000	6/0.6	8/3	9/6
15,000–20,000	6/7.2	9/0	10/0
20,000–30,000	7/1.8	9/6	10/6
30,000–50,000	7/8.4	9/6	10/6
Above 50,000	8/3	9/6	10/6

value (determined similarly to Schedule A). Where the annual value is in excess of £100, all income is assessed under Schedule D.

Schedule C is for "Income from British, Dominion, and Foreign Government Securities, where tax is deducted at the source." Included are most payments of government interest to persons. Excluded are some interest payments under £5 annually, interest on national saving certificates (which are tax free) and on a few special securities such as the 3½% war loan.

Schedule D is a catch-all, including "Business Profits, Professional Earnings, Certain Interests, Income from Abroad, and various miscellaneous sources of Income."

Schedule E, including the largest share of income assessed to tax, is for "Income from Offices, Employments, or Pensions." More than 98% of Schedule E income is withheld under the pay-as-you-earn scheme, adopted in the last year of the war.

As was mentioned in Chapter 3, the finance act of any one year does not apply to incomes wholly earned within that year. The Finance Act of 1948 covers the fiscal period April 6, 1948, to April 5, 1949, but incomes charged under Schedule D were those for the previous year (and in some cases, incomes almost two years previous). Thus, in estimating the distribution of pretax and posttax incomes for 1948–49, professional earnings, excess farmers' profits, and traders' profits for the fiscal year 1947–48 have been used. Since corporations are allowed to use a fiscal year of their choice, corporate income is likely to be charged about 16 months (on the average) after earnings, and 1947 calendar year profits are used in the estimate of private income.[2]

DISTRIBUTION OF PERSONAL INCOME TAXES

The Inland Revenue estimated the ultimate yield of income taxes charged under the Finance Act of 1948 at £1,317.1 million for Great Britain.[3] Part of this yield, however, consisted of income taxes on nonpersonal incomes. This latter amount was approximately £385 million in 1948–49,[4] leaving £932 million to be allocated to personal incomes.

The 1949 Inland Revenue report estimated the distribution of income tax and surtax combined for 1948–49.[5] The distribution of surtaxes was also given separately, so that the amount of income tax on each income group can be estimated by subtracting surtaxes from to-

2. See Ch. 11, p. 132, above.
3. *Cmd.* 8103, p. 35.
4. See Ch. 13, p. 160.
5. *Cmd.* 8052, table 85.

tal taxes on income. The allocation of personal income taxes given in Table 7 of Chapter 4 was based on this Inland Revenue estimate, an adjustment having been made for Northern Ireland and for the slight difference in the number and amount of incomes in groups below £1,000, discussed in the previous chapter.[6]

DISTRIBUTION OF SURTAXES

Incomes liable to surtax in 1948–49 were incomes earned in the previous fiscal year. This creates a slight difficulty, for the distribution of incomes above £2,000 given in Chapter 11 is based primarily on incomes earned in the 1948–49 fiscal year. The difference in the total number and amount of incomes liable to surtax earned in 1947–48 (taxed in 1948–49) and 1948–49 (taxed in 1949–50) is slight, as can be illustrated by the Inland Revenue summaries in the year of assessment.

SURTAX RETURNS	INCOMES EARNED IN:	
	1947–48	1948–49
Number of incomes	166,942	168,718
Amount of income	£762.4 million	£761.9 million
Tax assessed	£109.9 million	£108.9 million

There was, however, a slightly greater difference in the number and amount of incomes in particular income ranges above £2,000. For example, in 1948–49 there were fewer persons in the £2,000–3,000 and £10,000–20,000 ranges and more in the other ranges than in 1947–48. In allocating surtaxes, therefore, the relative distribution of this tax among 1947–48 income ranges has been used. An adjustment has then been made to relate these amounts to the 1948–49 distribution of income. In effect, it has been assumed that about 4% of incomes in the £2,000–3,000 range in 1947–48 moved up to the next income grade in 1948–49 and that about 1½% of incomes in the £10,000–20,000 group also moved up to the next bracket. The approximately 2,000 new persons in 1948–49 subject to surtax have been assumed to be newcomers whose incomes rose to just slightly over £2,000. This tax adjustment is slight but is an attempt to keep within the original plan of using taxes originating under the 1948 finance act.

6. See p. 138. The average income tax rate on each income group indicated in the Inland Revenue table has been applied to the estimated distribution of "actual income" shown in Table 52 of Ch. 11, above p. 142. The total yield of personal income taxes determined in this manner is £932.6 million, as compared with the Inland Revenue's £947 million. The difference is the approximate amount of tax arising from Northern Ireland incomes.

The estimated final yield of the surtax in 1948–49 is £126.9 million, and it is assumed that the published returns in the 1949 Inland Revenue report were 84% complete for each income range.[7] The allocation of surtaxes is shown in Table 7 of Chapter 4.

DISTRIBUTION OF NATIONAL INSURANCE CONTRIBUTIONS

In one sense national insurance contributions are not really a tax, but a form of compulsory insurance contribution, since the resulting revenues are devoted to a specific purpose and are handled by an extrabudgetary fund. Since the pension, health, and unemployment insurance programs are not organized on a strict insurance principle, however, these contributions have been considered here as a direct tax on personal incomes. Contributions by both employees and employers have been included in the distributions of personal and non-personal incomes in Chapter 3.

The allocation of these contributions to income groups has been determined on two separate bases, since the insurance programs changed in July, 1948. Insurance was compulsory only for persons with incomes below £420, before that month; so for the first quarter of the fiscal year contributions have been allocated in proportion to the number of incomes in the three lowest income groups. For the remaining three quarters they have been allocated in proportion to the number of incomes in all income ranges.[8] Contribution rates were slightly higher for self-employed and nonemployed persons (other than housewives) who were presumably grouped chiefly in the upper income groups, but a larger percentage of wives in the lower income groups were working, so that contributions have been assumed roughly proportional to the number of income recipients.[9] The estimated distribution of these contributions is given in Table 7 of Chapter 4.

7. See *Cmd.* 8052, table 98.
8. See pp. 206 ff. for a discussion of the old and new national insurance programs.
9. Incomes of working wives are usually combined with husbands' incomes and reported singly.

CHAPTER 13

The Allocation of Direct Taxes on
Nonpersonal Income and Wealth

In ADDITION to the direct taxes discussed in the preceding chapter there were direct taxes on nonpersonal income in 1948 amounting to £952 million. These consisted of income and profits taxes on corporate profits, and direct taxes on capital in the form of death duties and the 1948 special contribution. The allocation of each of these taxes is dependent upon the ownership of capital. In Chapter 11 the ownership of capital by income groups was estimated, and this information will be used to allocate the taxes in this chapter. Each of the four taxes mentioned above will be discussed separately.

INCOME TAXES ON NONPERSONAL INCOME

Income tax in Britain is deducted from corporate earnings at the source at the standard rate of tax (9s. in 1948–49, or 45%). That portion of income taxes which fell on distributed earnings has already been included in the allocation of personal taxes in Chapter 12. Gross undistributed profits of companies liable to income tax in 1948–49 was £1,070 million, from which the profits tax of £274.4 million must be deducted to find taxable income.[1] Net taxable undistributed profits were therefore £805.2 million, the gross income tax £362.3 million, and the net tax allowing for double taxation relief approximately £332.4 million. Two per cent of this amount is estimated to have fallen on insurance companies for their share in the ownership of undistributed profit, and 1½% on societies, leaving £321 million corporate income tax to be imputed directly to shareholders. This amount has been allocated on the basis of the index of shareholdings developed in Chapter 11[2] and is shown in column 1 of Table 60 below.

Income tax on life insurance income of £73.5 million was approximately £29.4 million, to which must be added their share of income tax on undistributed corporate profits of £6.8 million. Income tax on societies is estimated at £22.7 million on income of £90.7 million, plus

1. See p. 163.
2. See p. 151.

the £4.6 million share of income tax on undistributed corporate profits.[3] These amounts are allocated to income groups in columns 2 and 3 of Table 60 on the basis of indices developed in Chapter 11.[4]

TABLE 60

Distribution of Income Tax on Nonpersonal Incomes
(In Million Pounds)

INCOME RANGE (IN POUNDS)	INCOME TAX ON:			
	UNDISTRIBUTED PROFITS	INSURANCE COMPANIES	SOCIETIES	TOTAL
	1	2	3	4
Under 135	1.28	.99	2.23	4.50
135–250	5.14	5.37	9.54	20.05
250–500	34.90	8.03	12.76	55.69
500–750	31.47	4.27	2.72	38.46
750–1,000	18.62	2.39	—	21.01
1,000–2,000	46.56	5.06	—	51.62
2,000–3,000	33.07	2.42	—	35.49
3,000–5,000	38.21	2.71	—	40.92
5,000–10,000	43.03	2.26	—	45.29
10,000–20,000	30.19	1.46	—	31.65
20,000 and above	38.53	1.29	—	39.82
Totals	321.0	36.25	27.25	384.50

The amounts shown in column 4 of Table 60 are the same as those given in Table 9 of Chapter 4.

PROFITS TAX

The profits tax rates from January, 1947, to October, 1949, were 25% on all distributed profits and 10% on undistributed profits. The tax applied only to companies, societies, and other bodies not subject to surtax.[5] Certain types of undertakings were completely exempt, e.g. certain non-nationalized public utilities, industrial undertakings in developmental areas, the BBC, etc. Other groups, including nationalized enterprises, cooperatives, and businesses carried on by

3. Societies listed in the Registrar's Field are either exempt from tax completely, e.g. friendly societies, trade unions, and industrial and provident societies (cooperatives), or pay at a rate somewhat less than the standard rate. Reduced rates are permitted by the government on the assumption that members of these societies are in low income groups where they would normally be paying tax at less than the standard rate. A total of £90.7 million income of building societies, collecting societies, industrial assurance, and miscellaneous clubs and groups has been charged here at an average rate of 25%.

4. See pp. 149–51.

5. Private unincorporated firms had been subject to the national defense contribution and the wartime excess-profits tax until January, 1947.

companies not resident in the United Kingdom, were charged at the flat rate of 10% regardless of distributions. Building societies paid at a further reduced rate, not exceeding 6%.

Companies with incomes below £12,000 received an abatement amounting to one-fifth the amount by which profits fell short of £12,000, those below £2,000 being completely exempt from tax. To avoid the double taxation of profits, no tax was charged on "franked investment income." Such franked income is that which is received in the form of dividends from other companies also liable to profits tax.

The receipt of profits taxes by the Inland Revenue lags considerably behind assessment, and assessments are often a number of years behind the period in which income has actually been earned. Thus, in 1948–49 one-third of the profits taxes received were from excess profits assessments, even though the excess profits tax had expired two years previous.[6] Assessments in 1948–49 (excluding excess profits assessments) amounted to £255 million on £1,955.9 million profits.

Company profits in Great Britain liable to tax in 1948–49 were approximately £1,923 million.[7] Of this amount £163.6 million was not liable to tax. This exempt amount included £69.1 million income of nonprofit-making bodies,[8] £73.5 million franked investment income of life assurance companies, and £21.0 million miscellaneous income of statutory undertakings, royalties, etc. Of the remaining £1,759 million, £256.5 million belonged to companies with incomes below £12,000. According to Schedule D income tax data on the distribution in ranges of profit for companies, 89.9% of all companies with an aggregate income amounting to 11.6% of all company income were in income categories below £12,000.[9] Another 66.9% with 3.2% of the aggregate income were completely exempt from tax, having incomes of less than £2,000.

The tax on companies between £2,000 and £12,000 has been estimated by assuming 60% distributions and working out the average tax for each group within this range. The total tax on companies with incomes of less than £12,000 is estimated £24.4 million. Building societies, paying tax at a maximum of 6% were liable for profits

6. For a decade, up to 1938, the Inland Revenue was receiving on the average a million pounds a year for excess profits tax from the first World War.

7. *Cmd.* 8203, table 34. This is the figure for the calendar year 1947, less an adjustment for Northern Ireland. See also p. 136, above.

8. All income of non-profit societies has been estimated at £109.3 million. From this, however, £30.6 million income of building societies and £9.6 million income of industrial and provident societies, taxed at special rates, have been deducted.

9. *Cmd.* 8103, p. 43, tables 27, 28.

tax of £3.0 million and industrial and provident societies at 10%, £.9 million.

After subtracting the income of companies and societies fully or partially exempt (or paying at special rates), £1,462.5 million remained to be charged at the full rates. Of this, £669.3 million was distributed to persons and therefore liable to tax at 25%, and £793.2 million was retained and liable to tax at 10%. The yield of the tax at the full rates was £167.5 million on distributions and £79.3 million on undistributed profits. The profits tax for 1948–49 thus amounted to £274.4 million, arising as follows:

Profits tax on building societies	£1.8 million
" " " industrial and provident societies	1.0
" " " companies with incomes below £12,000	24.8
" " " companies with incomes above £12,000	246.8
	£274.4 million

In imputing the profits tax to shareholders, 2% has been allocated to persons in relation to the insurance index in Chapter 11, 1½% by the society index, and the remaining 96½% on the basis of the share index.[10] The first two items make due allowance for the holdings of corporate shares by insurance companies and societies. The final estimated distribution of the profits tax by income groups is given in Table 9 of Chapter 4.

DEATH DUTIES

Ideally, all death duties should be able to be expressed as rates on the value of estates. Actually, however, minor duties were levied on estates *net of estate duty* and depended upon the size of bequest, so that they had no necessary relationship to the size of estate falling in. In earlier investigations into the burden of death duties, it has often been assumed that minor duties were proportional to estate duties.[11] As estate duties have increased, however, this has tended to give an increasingly distorted picture. Take the example of an estate left as a legacy to a charity, liable to 10% legacy duty. At the end of the 1914–18 war, an estate of £100,000 net of estate duty would have amounted to £90,000, so the 10% legacy duty expressed as a rate *on the initial value* of the estate would have been 9%. In 1948–49 the net estate would have been £65,000, and legacy duty £6,500 or only 6½% of the initial estate. This would also be true for estates of different

10. See p. 151.
11. The report of the Colwyn Committee (*Cmd.* 2800) followed such a method, as have most of the other estimates up to the recent war.

size in the same year, the rate of minor duties expressed as a percentage of the initial estate tending to vary inversely with the size of estate. Recognizing this, the 1942 study by Shirras and Rostas estimated minor duties as more realistic rates on the initial value of estates, based on information in the 81st report of the Inland Revenue (1937–38).[12] In calculating the burden of minor duties two rates were applied to estates *net* of estate duties, 1.9% on estates between £1,000 and £15,000, and 2.5% on estates greater than £15,000. Legacy and succession duty rates, however, have doubled in some categories since before the war. For 1948–49, therefore, the two rates on net estates of the same two classes have been estimated at 2.8% and 3.6% respectively. After the actual amount of minor duties has been estimated in this manner, they have been translated back into rates on initial estates. In Table 61 the rates of minor duties on initial estates are shown, along with estate duty rates and the effective rate of all death duties.[13] When applied to the value of estates falling in during 1948–49, a total of £180.9 million is estimated as the death duty liability incurred during the fiscal year. The average rates were 19.4% for estate duty and 2.9% for minor duties on estates greater than £2,000. Minor duties, while proportional over wide ranges to the amounts received by beneficiaries,

TABLE 61

Death Duties, by Size of Estate Falling In

ESTATE RANGE (IN THOUSAND POUNDS)	AMOUNT FALLING IN (IN MILLION POUNDS)	ESTATE DUTY RATE (PERCENTAGE)	MINOR DUTY RATE (PERCENTAGE)	EFFECTIVE RATE (PERCENTAGE)	DEATH DUTIES (IN MILLION POUNDS)
1–2	(32.0) *	0	2.8	2.8	.90
2–5	104.6	1.2	2.8	4.0	4.17
5–10	117.9	3.1	2.7	5.8	6.84
10–15	75.6	6.4	2.6	9.0	6.80
15–20	54.9	9.8	3.6	13.4	7.25
20–25	39.7	11.8	3.5	15.3	6.06
25–50	124.0	16.7	3.3	20.0	24.80
50–100	104.0	25.1	3.0	28.1	29.21
100–200	68.4	35.5	2.6	38.1	26.03
200–300	32.3	45.1	2.2	47.3	15.26
300–500	28.9	53.9	1.9	55.8	16.10
>500	57.7	63.8	1.2	65.0	37.48
Totals	808.0	(19.4)	(2.9)	(22.3)	180.90

* Estimated.

12. *Burden of British Taxation*, pp. 95–6.
13. The rates of estate duty shown in Table 61 are average rates, weighted by the amount of capital falling in in each duty range. The average rates have been reduced 2% to allow for deductions. The estimated total yield of estate duties based on the rates shown in Table 61 is £156.7 million, whereas actual Inland Revenue receipts in 1948–49 totaled £155.2 million.

become mildly regressive when translated into rates on initial estates, but the effective rate of all death duties is progressive through all ranges.

Table 61 estimates death duties by size of estate; these amounts now need to be related to income groups. In Chapter 11 a method of relating capital holdings to income groups was developed, and the percentage distribution of capital by size of holding among income groups, illustrated in Table 56 of that chapter, can be used here in allocating death duties. In Table 62 this is shown, the bottom line indicating the estimated amount of death duty for each income group. These amounts are the same as those given in Table 10 of Chapter 4.

SPECIAL CONTRIBUTION

The Finance Act of 1948 included Britain's first experiment with a capital levy, the special contribution. According to that act, it was to be a levy on individuals whose total incomes in the previous fiscal year were greater than £2,000, and whose investment income exceeded £250. Payments were to be made on or before January 1, 1949, by which time about three-quarters of the Inland Revenue estimate of the total yield had been received.

The rates of special contribution were as follows:

Slice of Investment Income * (In Pounds)	Rates per Pound (In Shillings)
250–500	2
500–1,000	4
1,000–2,000	6
2,000–5,000	8
5,000 and above	10

* For incomes only slightly in excess of £2,000 the amount of contribution was not to exceed the excess of income over £2,000.

In the language of the Finance Act of 1948 the special contribution was based on income, but it can be considered a capital tax. In the case of death duties all types of capital are subject to valuation for tax purposes, but this is not a simple method of taxing capital at intervals during one's lifetime for both personal and administrative reasons. The only alternative to taxing capital values is to tax income arising from the ownership of capital, even though it may be a less equitable alternative in many instances.[14] Taxes on income obviously

14. Most of the inequities arise in cases where persons have extremely specialized capital holdings, the tax year not being one of normal returns. The choice of a particular year for assessment is of less importance in terms of treating all capital owners equally if holdings are widely diversified.

TABLE 62

Distribution of Death Duties, by Income Range and Capital Range

(In Million Pounds)

CAPITAL RANGE (IN THOUSAND POUNDS)	20,000 AND ABOVE	10,000–20,000	5,000–10,000	3,000–5,000	2,000–3,000	1,000–2,000	750–1,000	500–750	250–500	135–250	UNDER 135	TOTAL DEATH DUTIES BY CAPITAL RANGE
	GROSS INCOME GROUPS											
Above 550	34.38											34.38
410–550	2.62	6.41										9.03
330–410	.61	6.35										6.96
275–330	.30	5.67										5.97
220–275	.29	2.98	4.65									7.92
165–220	.14	1.63	6.98									8.75
135–165	.10	.78	7.10									7.98
110–135	.09	.60	3.87	6.31								10.87
82–110	.05	.39	2.69	7.41								10.54
55–82	.05	.32	1.76	3.99	9.71							15.83
27.5–55	.05	.23	1.29	3.20	3.49	18.39						26.65
14.3–27.5	.02	.06	.32	.84	1.04	1.53	5.38	9.42				18.61
7.8–14.3	—	.01	.06	.19	.28	.49	.77	1.37	5.40			8.57
Under 7.8	—	—	.01	.04	.07	.34	.64	1.35	4.24	1.78	.37	8.84
Total death duties by income group	38.70	25.43	28.73	21.98	14.59	20.75	6.79	12.14	9.64	1.78	.37	180.90

cannot exceed 100%, and the effect of the special contribution, if considered as a tax on income, would have been to raise the maximum marginal rate of tax to 147.5%. The tax, in fact, must in almost every case have been paid out of capital. Considered as a capital tax, the maximum effective rate was roughly 2%, i.e. one-half the rate of return on capital.

TABLE 63

Estimated Final Yield of Special Contribution

	No. of Persons (In Thousands)	Gross Income (In Million Pounds)	Invest. Income (In Million Pounds)	Total Tax (In Million Pounds)
Returns as of 6/4/49	113.8	581.7	330.7	103.2
Less Northern Ireland	−1.5	−6.8	−3.8	−1.0
	112.3	574.9	327.2	102.2
Incomes to be assessed	+10.1	+50.3	+26.2	+10.1
Estimated total	122.4	625.2	353.4	112.2

The Inland Revenue estimated the ultimate yield of the special contribution at £105 million in its 1949 report.[15] Receipts ran considerably ahead of estimates in the year of assessment, and after comparing surtax returns it appears that the final yield will be about 8% greater than originally estimated. In Table 63 an estimate is made of expected total receipts, based on surtax data and on special contribution returns up to mid 1949.[16]

In Table 64 the slices of investment incomes taxed at the various rates, and the resulting amounts of tax, are estimated.

Now that the amounts of special contribution for each investment income range have been estimated, the index of capital ownership by income group in Chapter 11 can be used to allocate these amounts to income groups.[17] Table 65 indicates the resulting distribution of the special contribution by gross income groups. The totals along the bottom of this table are the same as those given in Table 10 of Chapter 4.

15. *Cmd.* 8052, p. 102.
16. *Cmd.* 8103, table 47.
17. The investment income ranges shown in Table 65 are broader than those shown in Table 56, p. 149; so the percentage distribution had to be estimated from Table 57, p. 150, showing actual amounts of capital.

TABLE 64

Incomes Taxed, and Tax Yield of Special Contribution, by Investment Income Ranges
(In Million Pounds)

Investment Income Range (In Pounds)	No. of Persons (In Thousands)	Total Investment Income	Total Tax	Slices of Investment Income Taxed at:					
				0%	10%	20%	30%	40%	50%
250–500	18.3	**7.8** *		**4.6**	**3.2**				
			.32	—	*.32*				
500–1,000	24.9	**19.7**		**6.2**	**6.2**	**7.3**			
			2.08	—	*.62*	*1.46*			
1,000–2,000	25.8	**39.8**		**6.5**	**6.5**	**13.0**	**13.8**		
			7.39	—	*.65*	*2.60*	*4.14*		
2,000–5,000	37.3	**128.1**		**9.3**	**9.3**	**18.6**	**37.2**	**53.7**	
			37.29	—	*.93*	*3.72*	*11.16*	*21.48*	
5,000 and above	16.1	**158.7**		**4.1**	**4.1**	**8.1**	**16.2**	**48.4**	**78.8**
			65.15	—	*.41*	*1.62*	*4.86*	*19.36*	*38.90*
	122.4	354.1		30.7	29.3	47.0	67.2	102.1	78.8
Totals			*112.23*	—	*2.93*	*9.40*	*20.16*	*40.84*	*38.90*

* Investment income in bold face; liability in italics.

TABLE 65

Estimated Distribution of the Special Contribution by Investment Income and Gross Income Ranges
(In Million Pounds)

Investment Income Range (In Pounds)	Gross Income Groups					Total Tax by Investment Income Range
	20,000 and Above	10,000–20,000	5,000–10,000	3,000–5,000	2,000–3,000	
5,000 and above	22.79	22.16	20.20	—	—	65.15
2,000–5,000	.15	1.43	7.44	17.16	11.11	37.29
1,000–2,000	.05	.21	1.15	2.40	3.58	7.39
500–1,000	.02	.05	.30	.63	1.08	2.08
250–500	—	—	.03	.11	.18	.32
Total tax by gross income group	23.01	23.85	29.12	20.30	15.95	112.23

CHAPTER 14

The Allocation of Customs and Excise Duties

INDIRECT taxes in 1948–49 provided £1,684 million in revenue to the government. Ninety per cent of this amount was raised in customs and excise duties. These duties will be allocated in this chapter, and other indirect and miscellaneous taxes will be treated in the succeeding chapter. After customs and excise duties have been classified, personal expenditures by income classification will be analyzed to determine an index on which basis these taxes on consumption may be distributed. Then each major classification of duty will be briefly discussed and its allocation explained. The distribution of these duties is presented in Table 70 at the end of the chapter.

CLASSIFICATION OF CUSTOMS AND EXCISE DUTIES

In 1948–49 44% of all central government revenue arose from customs and excise duties, equal in amount only to revenues arising from all direct taxes on personal income. This was almost five times the amount collected in the last year before the war and almost 50% greater than customs and excise revenues in the first postwar year. The amounts collected in each of these years from customs and excise duties and their combined percentage of all government revenue is shown below.

	1938–39	1945–46	1948–49
	(IN MILLION POUNDS)		
Customs duties	226	570	822
Excise duties	114	541	732
Total customs and excise	340	1,111	1,554
Percentage of all government revenue	39%	35%	44%

The particular taxes and amounts collected in 1948–49 are shown in Table 66. The three most important sources of revenue were tobacco duties, duties on alcoholic drinks, and purchase taxes on luxury goods respectively, these three accounting for roughly 85% of all customs and excise duties.

In distributing customs and excise duties it has been assumed that consumption taxes raise the price of taxed articles by the exact amount of the tax.[1] This method has also been used by the previous studies in income redistribution in Britain.[2] It is impossible to define the margin of error, but insofar as these taxes are distributed accurately in relation to consumption it is felt that this margin is negligible for the middle income groups and not more than about 10% for the highest and lowest groups. Whatever error there may be with the highest and lowest ranges, the tax on the latter will tend to be overstated in most instances.

TABLE 66

Classification of Customs and Excise Duty Receipts, 1948–49 *
(In Million Pounds)

Spirits	90.8
Beer	307.3
Wines and table waters	19.6
Tobacco	610.1
Tea	10.5
Cocoa and coffee	1.5
Sugar and preserved fruit	37.9
Matches and mechanical lighters	7.5
Hydrocarbon oils	14.4
Entertainments	47.2
Silk and artificial silk	3.1
Import Duties Act (1932)	41.7
Ottawa duties (1932)	5.1
Beef and veal duties	2.1
Liquor and club licenses	5.0
Other licenses	.1
Betting duties	23.4
Purchase tax	291.1
Total	1,513.3

* £50 million is excluded. See below, p. 171.

The classification of customs and excise duties in Table 66 above follows that used by the customs and excise commissioners in their annual reports.[3] In addition, these duties might be classified as taxes directly on consumption or business in general and as protective or revenue-raising (and/or consumption-restricting) duties.

About 3.2% of all customs and excise receipts were not directly al-

1. See Ch. 2, pp. 19–20.
2. E.g. Barna, 141–3; Shirras and Rostas, pp. 103–5.
3. E.g. *Report of the Commissions of Customs and Excise, 1949*, Cmd. 7834 (1949), pp. 7–18.

locable to personal consumption, but fell on business in general. These can be enumerated as follows:

	(IN THOUSAND POUNDS)
Key industries duty	881
Import act duties (part)	5,217
Excise licenses (part)	320
Monopoly value duty	810
Power alcohol duty	2
Oils (part)	42,839
	50,070

Thus, the burden on personal consumption is estimated at only £1,513 million in 1948–49. Only this latter amount will be distributed in this chapter, taxes falling on business in general being dealt with elsewhere.[4]

It is difficult to make an exact classification of customs duties as "protective" or "revenue-raising." The problem is made even more complex in postwar Britain by the presence of other limitations on trade. In an open exchange economy the distinction is much simpler, the general rule being to classify all customs duties on articles which are also produced at home as "protective" duties, and duty on all imported articles not domestically produced as "revenue-raising" duties. While the same distinction may be made for 1948–49, import and foreign exchange controls were probably more important than customs duties in restricting foreign trade. The primary concern of Britain was not so much to protect certain home industries as to prevent what the government felt was relatively wasteful use of limited foreign exchange. Thus, many home industries were protected not by tariffs but by import limitations. A further complication lies in the fact that Commonwealth preference on almost all items makes almost every import duty a protective one in a very limited sense. The purely protective duties were duties under the Key Industries, Ottawa, and Import Duty Acts, plus those duties on silk and artificial silk, and beef and veal. In 1948–49 these amounted to £52.8 million, or 6.4% of all customs duties and 3.4% of all combined customs and excise duty receipts. Partially protected articles were those where there was also an excise duty, but the excise duty was considerably less than the customs duty on imported goods. Included in this list, with the percentage differential between the full customs duty and excise duty, were lighters (40%), sugar (25%), playing cards (25%), matches (14%), spirits (1.2%), and beer (.8%). The major "revenue-producing" duties were tea, cocoa, coffee, entertainment, betting,

4. See Ch. 15, below.

licenses, tobacco, and oils. In many of these there was a large element of intended restriction of consumption (or more politely, conservation of resources), e.g. tobacco, alcoholic beverages, oils, and all items subject to purchase tax.

Each of the major classifications of articles subject to customs and excise duties will be treated separately below and allocated to income ranges on the basis of personal consumption expenditures.

DISTRIBUTION OF PERSONAL EXPENDITURE

Before the recent war a number of family budget studies were conducted by governmental and private groups, but since the war little of a comparative nature has been undertaken.[5] Some estimate of the distribution of personal expenditure by income group is necessary, however, to allocate taxes on consumption. Consumption taxes could be allocated to income groups in proportion to disposable incomes, as estimated in Chapter 12. Aggregate personal savings were not more than about 3% of disposable income in 1948–49; so the fact that disposable incomes do not represent actual amounts expended would not be a very great source of error. However, since consumption taxes did not fall more or less uniformly on all classifications of personal expenditure, it would appear desirable to attempt some estimate of the relative expenditure of each income group on various kinds of goods.

There is some information available which can be used in making such an estimate of the distribution of personal spending. The White Papers give a breakdown of consumer expenditure by sixteen expenditure classifications for each postwar year.[6] Thus the total amounts spent on food, clothing, rent, etc. are known. As mentioned above, disposable income for each income group is also known. The relative distribution of expenditures by income group for prewar years is quite well documented, and there is some scanty information on working class household expenditures in the postwar years. If we combine these data, and add a modicum of "enlightened guesswork," it should be possible to arrive at a roughly accurate distribution.

The estimated distribution of consumer expenditures by income range is shown in Table 67. Total expenditure by income range is based on disposable income after an allowance for personal savings.[7]

5. The most complete of the prewar surveys was that conducted by the Ministry of Labour for working-class households; see the *Ministry of Labour Gazette,* Dec., 1940. Also William S. Crawford and H. Broadley, *The People's Food* (1938) ; J. B. Orr, *Food, Health, and Income* (1936) ; Rowntree; and Shirras and Rostas.

6. See *Cmd.* 7933, table 22, for 1948.

7. It has been assumed that savings in the two lowest income groups were zero, and approximately 2½%, 4%, 4%, and 2½% of disposable incomes, respectively, for the next highest groups. It seems most probable that there was considerable dissaving in the highest income groups among persons whose disposable incomes sharply declined in the 1938–48 decade, thus the assumption of a declining rate of savings for

To estimate the expenditures on particular types of commodities by income groups, two methods have been used, based on the pre-war distribution.[8] First, it was assumed that per capita consumption of different types of goods and services in real terms was the same for each income group in 1948–49 as in 1937. For example, prewar food expenditures per capita for each income group were first determined. Then these amounts were multiplied by the 1948 price index as given by the White Papers [9] to translate them into current prices. Finally, these amounts in 1948 prices were multiplied by the number of persons in each income range in 1948–49. The total food consumption for 1948–49 estimated in this manner turned out to be about 20% greater than actual amounts spent on food, so that expenditures for each income group were reduced by 20%, the same relative distribution among groups being retained. This method, when used for all types of expenditures, takes into account relative changes in consumption and prices.

The second method, used in conjunction with the above, required the assumption that approximately the same percentage of disposable income of each income group was spent on any particular class of commodities in the prewar and postwar years. In this case the amounts spent on any particular class of commodities by each income group were multiplied by the percentage change in disposable incomes for each group. The resulting amounts were then inflated by the 1948 price index. If the total amount spent on any class of commodities was then greater or smaller than the actual amount spent in 1948–49, the expenditures for each income group have been increased or decreased proportionately. This method takes into account the relative changes in prices and in disposable incomes (after direct taxes on income and transfer receipts) for each group.

Estimates of the distribution of personal expenditures based on these two methods have been worked out and then averaged. A few further adjustments have been made for goods where the pattern of expenditure has quite obviously changed markedly since the prewar years. Because of food rationing and price controls, for example, it seemed unlikely that the highest income groups spent as large amounts per capita, or even as large a percentage of their disposable income, on food in 1948–49 as in 1937. Here, therefore, the resulting esti-

persons with incomes above £1,000. This was also the finding of one postwar survey of savings by income groups. See H. F. Lydall, "A Pilot Survey of Incomes and Savings," *BOxIS 13* (1951), 257–91.

8. For an estimate of the distribution of personal expenditures by income group for 1937, see Barna, p. 153. Barna's estimate was based primarily on Crawford and Broadley, the *Ministry of Labour Gazette,* Shirras and Rostas, and a number of other smaller surveys for particular income levels.

9. *Cmd.* 7933, table 23.

mates have been adjusted, and estimated expenditures on food in the two highest income groups have been reduced about 20% and food expenditures of the two lowest income groups increased proportionately. Similarly, in the case of expenditures on private motoring, the initial price of automobiles was so high in 1948–49 that most low income families were priced out of the market by the cost of purchasing a car as well as the cost of running it. Expenditures on private motoring have therefore been shifted up almost entirely to income groups above £500. A small amount of clothing expenditure has also been shifted from low to high income groups, since the differential pricing of clothing under the utility programs probably meant proportionately greater expenditures by the high income groups than before the war.

TABLE 67

Estimated Distribution of Personal Spending
(In Million Pounds)

EXPENDITURE CLASSIFICATION	UNDER 135	135– 250	250– 500	500– 1,000	1,000– 3,000	ABOVE 3,000	FOREIGN VISITORS	TOTAL
1. Food	146	700	918	298	110	26	5	2,203
Rationed *	(62)	(277)	(346)	(98)	(29)	(5)	—	(817)
Unrationed *	(84)	(423)	(572)	(200)	(81)	(21)	(5)	(1,386)
2. Drink	58	228	291	114	52	20	3	766
3. Tobacco	54	252	313	106	42	7	—	774
4. Rent, rates, water	31	125	225	119	67	33	—	600
5. Fuel and light	23	82	131	59	29	10	—	334
6. Durable household goods	13	73	141	86	80	38	—	431
7. Other household goods	2	14	22	19	16	9	—	.82
8. Clothing	39	184	319	161	111	44	5	863
9. Printed matter	5	23	37	27	23	8	—	123
10. Private motoring	1	5	14	40	32	12	—	104
11. Travel	14	76	124	68	39	16	4	341
12. Communication	2	10	18	12	10	4	—	56
13. Entertainment	15	47	66	28	16	6	3	181
14. Domestic service	—	2	17	33	27	15	—	94
15. Other services	42	160	255	132	72	34	—	695
16. Other goods	20	78	120	77	38	26	16	375
Total expenditure	465	2,059	3,011	1,379	764	308	36	8,022

* Estimated expenditures on rationed foods have been determined by the total cost of all food items which could have been purchased on a single ration book, multiplied by the number of persons in each income group. Comparing the aggregate entitled ration of many food items with actual amounts consumed in 1948, however, indicates that not all rations were actually purchased. To allow for this, it has been assumed that only 65% of entitled rations were purchased by persons in the lowest income range, 85% in the £135–250 range, 95% in the £250–500 range, and 100% above £500. Total consumption of rationed foods is estimated, therefore, at approximately 93% of entitled rations. This accords with the wartime experience of low income budgets. Cf. Charles Madge, *War-time Pattern of Spending and Saving* (1943), pp. 70–4, and Shirras and Rostas, p. 109.

The estimates in Table 67 are not entirely satisfactory, but they should be a fairly close approximation to the actual distribution of expenditures in 1948–49. Wherever possible, they have been checked against the few limited studies of family spending which have been made since the war.[10] The chances of accuracy are also much greater when attempting to make an estimate of *total* spending rather than merely estimating expenditures by income groups on specific commodities. In Barna's words, "If the distribution of taxes takes the whole distribution of expenditure into consideration . . . the margin of error in the estimates is necessarily reduced because available income for each class and national expenditure on each commodity or service have been independently estimated."[11] Since the totals by income group and by expenditure classification in Table 67 were given to start with, inaccuracies in the distributions should be comparatively minor.

In the following pages, particular customs and excise duties will be allocated to income groups on the basis of the distribution of consumer expenditures estimated in Table 67.

ALLOCATION OF SPECIFIC CUSTOMS AND EXCISE DUTIES

Tobacco Duty

The customs duty on tobacco in 1948–49 was 600% higher than it was in 1938–39, representing, in 1948–49, two-thirds of the price of an average packet of cigarettes. Consumption over the decade has also increased by 20 million pounds (in weight) annually, although in 1948–49 it was about 21% lower than the peak consumption year of 1946–47. A comparison of the basic duty per pound, annual consumption, and net tax receipts is given here for three selected years over the last decade.

	1938–39	1945–46	1948–49
Basic duty per lb.	9s.6d.	35s.6d.	58s.2d.
Consumption (million lbs.)	192	239	212.3
Tax receipts (million pounds)	85	416	610.1

The preferential rate for Empire tobacco was 1s.6½d. below the full rate and 30.1% of all tobacco entered under preferential rates. Rates on imported manufactured tobacco were considerably higher, so that 99.8% of tobacco imports entered in unmanufactured form. The

10. E.g., T. Schulz's surveys, "Working Class Household Expenditure in 1948," *BOxIS, 12* (1950), 81–97; "Family Expenditures in 1949," *BOxIS, 13* (1951), 128–40. Also, Rowntree and Lavers; and M. Abrams, *British Standards of Living,* Bureau of Current Affairs, No. 63 (London, Sept. 18, 1948).

11. Barna, *Redistribution,* p. 149.

breakdown of duty receipts and quantities consumed in 1948–49 was as follows:

		DUTY RECEIPTS	LB. CONSUMPTION
Excise			
Domestic tobacco		294	104
Customs			
Manufactured:	Empire ⎱ Other ⎰	1,333,540	184,719 242,780
Unmanufactured:	Empire ⎱ Other ⎰	608,744,294	63,683,451 148,222,889
Total		£610,078,128	212,333,839 lbs.

The average consumption per adult (16 and over) was 5.6 lbs., or approximately 500 cigarettes annually. The average duty per adult was £16 1s. 3d.

Tobacco duty has been distributed among income groups in proportion to the total expenditure on tobacco, as shown in column 2 of Table 70 below. The duty is such a large part of the final price of tobacco products that there was only about a 5d. variation between the cheap and expensive brands of cigarettes (i.e. 3s. 3d. to 3s. 8d.). The tobacco duty is a flat rate per pound, not an ad valorem duty, and the duty has been assumed to be a roughly constant percentage of the retail price for consumers in each income range.[12]

Alcoholic Beverages

Alcoholic drinks are divided into three major duty classes: spirits, beers, and wines. The duty on the latter two has increased by roughly 600% since 1938, while that on the former is not quite 300% higher. Rates, net receipts, and amounts consumed are shown below for various years in the last decade.

	1938–39	1945–46	1948–49
Spirits			
Basic duty per gallon (£.s.d.)	3/12/6	7/17/6	10/10/10
Customs receipts (million pounds)	4.7	16.9	44.1
Excise receipts (million pounds)	30.9	51.2	46.7
Consumption (million gallons)			
Imported	9.0	6.8	4.8
Domestic	1.2	1.9	3.9

12. The price difference between cheap and expensive cigarettes was due as much to differences in amount of tobacco in each packet as to differences in quality; hence, this assumption should be relatively accurate.

	1938–39	1945–46	1948–49
Beer			
Basic duty (bulk barrels) (*£.s.d.*)	1/4/0	7/0/7½	8/18/10½
Customs receipts (million pounds)	3.2	10.8	12.6
Excise receipts (million pounds)	62.4	295.3	294.7
Consumption (million bulk barrels)			
Imported	.7	.7	.7
Domestic	24.7	32.6	27.0
Wine (imported)			
Basic duty per gallon			
Light (*s.d.*)	4/0	17/0	1/5/0
Heavy (*s.d.*)	8/0	34/0	2/10/0
Customs receipts (million pounds)	4.8	5.0	15.7
Consumption (million gallons)	15.2	3.3	7.5
Wine (domestic)			
Basic duty per gallon (*s.d.*)	3/6	14/6	22/6–30/6
Excise receipts (million pounds)	.5	2.2	3.8
Consumption (million gallons)	6.4	2.9	3.0

Preference was given to Empire spirits amounting to 2s. 6d.; the beer duty for non-Empire beer was £1 per bulk barrel higher than the basic duty; the preferential rate on wines was 2s. lower on light wines, and 10s. on heavy wines. The average consumption per adult in 1948–49 was .23 gallons of spirits, .29 gallons of wine, and .78 gallons of beer. In addition to the above, there was almost £21,000 collected on table waters, bringing the total customs and excise duties on beverages to £417.7 million for 1948–49.

Because of the different composition of expenditures on beverages by different income groups, the allocation of these duties is difficult. Allotting the duty in direct proportion to total expenditure on drink by the different income groups would be unsatisfactory, overstating the burden appreciably on the upper income groups. This fact, the reverse of what one might at first expect, would be caused by two things: first, the duties are not ad valorem and therefore often represent a smaller part of the retail price as the price increases, and second, the duty on beer represents on the average 57% of the retail price, while on wines the duty may be no more than 15% or 20%.[13] With higher income groups one would expect to find beer a smaller part of expenditure on drink, and wines and spirits a much larger share. To account for this, expenditure on drink has been allocated to income groups on two bases. The duty on beer has been assumed to be equal per male adult in each income group. Since the exact num-

13. The duty on beer may vary upward depending on the degree of gravity. The standard barrel is 36 gallons at 1027°, but there was an additional 6s 7½d. tax for each degree above that amount. Spirit duty is similarly based on the proof gallon.

ber of males in each income group is not known, the number of income recipients (family heads) has been used, the two lowest groups being reduced by 50% and 10% to account for the large proportion of single women and young persons under twenty in these groups. The expenditure on spirits and wines has been assumed to be a direct function of disposable income. The combined duties for each income group are shown in column 1 of Table 70 below. Duty on alcoholic drink, as a percentage of total expenditure on drink for all income groups, declines from 53% for the lowest income group (whose consumption is mostly in the form of beer) to 34% for the highest income group (who spend more on wines and spirits than on beer).

Tea

There has been little change in the tea duty since before the war and correspondingly little variation in net customs receipts. The full duty for non-Empire tea has been 2*d.* higher in each of these years, but non-Empire tea has been only about 1% of total imports. In 1948–49 73% of all tea import came from India and Pakistan and 23% from Ceylon.

	1938–39	1945–46	1948–49
Duty per lb. (preferential)	4*d.*	6*d.*	6*d.*
(Apr. '38)	6*d.*		
Net customs receipts (million pounds)	10.8	9.6	10.5
Consumption (million lbs.)	447.4	399.5	426.9

From 1940 to 1952 tea was rationed, the size of the ration during 1948–49 being 2 ounces per week for persons over 5, plus a 4-ounce bonus at Christmas. On this basis, approximately 303 million pounds was purchased on ration, the remaining 117 million pounds being consumed outside the home, e.g. in restaurants. The duty on rationed tea has been allocated on a per capita basis, and tea consumed outside the home is assumed to vary in proportion to unrationed food expenditures. This distribution is shown in column 3 of Table 70.

Cocoa, Coffee, and Chicory

The duties on cocoa and coffee remained unchanged during the last decade, the rates per hundredweight being 14*s.* full and 11*s.* 8*d.* preferential on cocoa, and 14*s.* full and 4*s.* 8*d.* preferential on coffee. Quantities consumed and customs receipts for selected years varied roughly in inverse proportion to tea imports.

	1938–39	1945–46	1948–49
Cocoa			
Net customs receipts (million pounds)	1.1	1.0	1.1
Consumption (million lbs.)	150	163	166
Coffee			
Net customs receipts (million pounds)	.14	.53	.40
Consumption (million lbs.)	31	92	89

The duty on raw chicory was 13s. 3d. per hundredweight, but receipts over the decade were negligible. Neither cocoa nor coffee were rationed in 1948–49, so that duty receipts have been distributed to income ranges in proportion to their total expenditure on unrationed foods. This is shown in column 4 of Table 70.

Sugar

Sugar and similar products produced £37½ million in revenue in 1948–49. Quantities consumed (in equivalent of refined sugar), full and preferential rates, and duty receipts, are given below.

	1938–39	1945–46	1948–49
Quantities consumed			
(thousands of hundredweights)	36,444	20,611	26,070
Rates: Full	11s. 8d.	23s. 4d.	23s. 4d.
Preferential	5s. 10d.	17s. 6d.	17s. 6d.
Duty receipts (million pounds)	13.0	30.0	37.6

Receipts include amounts arising from sugar, molasses, glucose, saccharin, and sweetened imported articles. The total duty has been allocated in relation to expenditures on rationed foods, and is given in column 5 of Table 70.

Matches and Mechanical Lighters

The duty on matches and lighters has remained the same since the outbreak of the war, while consumption of both increased after the end of hostilities. Before the war domestic and foreign manufacturers shared the market almost equally, but in recent years about 75% of all matches and practically all lighters have been domestically produced. There is no preferential rate for Empire products.

In allocating this duty, one-half of the duty on matches and all that on lighters has been distributed in proportion to expenditure on tobacco and the remaining half on matches in proportion to all food expenditures. This distribution is shown in column 6 of Table 70.

	1938–39	1945–46	1948–49
Matches			
Basic customs duty (gross)	4s. 9d.	9s.	9s.
" excise " (")	4s. 2d.	8s. 4d.	8s. 4d.
Net customs receipts (million pounds)	2.1	.4	1.9
Net excise receipts (million pounds)	2.1	4.6	5.2
Consumption (million gross boxes)	16.6	10.1	14.9
Mechanical Lighters			
Basic customs duty	1s. 6d.	3s. 6d.	3s. 6d.
Basic excise duty	1s.	2s. 6d.	2s. 6d.
Net customs receipts (thousand pounds)	65.7	10.8	1.2
Net excise receipts (thousand pounds)	117.6	622.3	394.9
Consumption (millions)	1.9	5.0	3.2

Oils

The customs duty on all hydrocarbon oils used as fuel by road vehicles remained at 9d. per gallon from 1938 to 1949. Until 1947 lubricating oils were subject to a 1d. per gallon duty (with the exception of oils for certain limited purposes), but in 1947 this tax was eliminated by increasing the heavy oil rebate. Other lesser duties were also removed in 1947, so that in 1948–49 only light and heavy oils used as motor vehicle fuel were taxed. The quantities consumed and net customs receipts are shown below.

	1938–39	1945–46	1948–49
Consumption (thousand million gallons)	2.15	2.44	1.65
Net customs receipts (million pounds)	57.9	65.4	57.3

In 1948 there were 3¾ million mechanically propelled vehicles licensed, of which 1.9 million were passenger cars.[14] Of the remaining number, goods vans accounted for just over 20% of the total, hackneys for 4%, and agricultural engines and tractors for 6%. These latter groups can be assumed to be much heavier consumers, per license, of petrol and lubricating oils than private motor cars. Accordingly, one-fourth of the duty on light oils and one-eighth of the duty on heavy oils has been allocated to income groups in proportion to their expenditure on private motoring. Also, one-twentieth of both light and heavy oils has been distributed in proportion to expenditure on

14. *Mechanically Propelled Road Vehicles, Great Britain,* Ministry of Transport, Return, No. 144 (1948), 4.

travel, this representing the fuel consumption of busses and hackneys. The combined distribution of the duty on oils among private persons is shown in column 7 of Table 70. The remaining duty, £42.8 million, is assumed to fall on business in general and will be dealt with in Chapter 15. The amount allocated in Table 70 includes £12.0 million on private motoring and £2.4 million on travel.

Entertainment

Entertainment duty was charged on two scales, depending upon the type of entertainment. Roughly classified, all live performances (except racing events) were charged on a reduced scale, cinemas and racing being charged under the full scale. The former rate in 1948–49 was about 15½%, the latter 25%. Tax receipts by type of entertainment in 1948–49 were as follows:

Entertainments duty	(IN THOUSAND POUNDS)	
Full rate		
Cinemas	38,380	
Horse racing	1,800	
Dog racing	1,590	
Other racing	520	
Miscellaneous	200	42,390
Reduced rates		
Theatres and music halls	2,900	
Football	720	
Cricket	70	
Other sports	250	
Miscellaneous	490	4,430
Unclassified		335
Total Entertainment duty		47,155
Playing card duty		62
Total duty		47,217

Total receipts for entertainments duty increased rapidly to 1946–47, declining slightly after that year.

	1938–39	1945–46	1948–49
Entertainments duty (million pounds)	8.15	51.53	47.15
Playing card duty (million pounds)	.07	.03	.06

The total of these two duties, £47,217,000, has been allocated to income ranges in proportion to expenditure on entertainments as shown in column 8 of Table 70.

Silk and Artificial Silk

The duty on silk varied according to the type of item, i.e. cocoons, raw silk, yarn, finished articles, etc. and the weight or value of the silk. Empire articles were given one-sixth preference in most cases. Customs receipts were £4 million before the war and climbed back from almost zero in the early years of the war to £3¼ million in 1948–49. Excise duties on artificial silks domestically produced averaged about £1 million annually until 1947, after which time drawbacks exceeded duty payments. The duty on silk products has been allotted in relation to the expenditure on clothing by income group, and is shown in column 9 of Table 70.

Import Act Duties

The Import Duties Act of 1932 imposed an ad valorem tax of 10% generally on all goods not subject to other customs duties or specifically entered on the free lists. Empire products, except for a few items such as motor cars, watches, etc. were exempt. By general classification, the net duty paid for various years was:

CLASSIFICATION	1938–39	1945–46	1948–49
I. Food and drink	6.44	5.92	15.72
II. Raw materials	3.57	2.03	5.26
III. Manufactured articles	17.25	7.63	20.71
IV. Animals (nonfood)	.01	—	.01
Total receipts	27.24	15.56	41.65

Class I receipts have been distributed according to expenditures on unrationed food in column 10 of Table 70. Class III and IV receipts have been allocated in proportion to the sum of expenditures under items 6, 7, and 16, in Table 67 above, as shown in column 11 of Table 70. Class II receipts have been assumed to fall on business in general, and will be allocated in Chapter 15.

Ottawa Duties

Under the Ottawa Agreements Act of 1932 duties were imposed on numerous non-Empire products which are also produced within the Empire. Rates varied for different articles, but the average rate was about 10% to 15% of the value of the products in 1948–49. All items included under the list were agricultural products, chiefly food articles (e.g. fresh fruit and dairy products), vegetable oils, and leathers. Net receipts have been published only for 1938–39, 1947–48, and 1948–49, the three totals being £8.1 million, £8.0 million, and £5.1 million respectively. The latter amount has been distributed among income ranges in relation to expenditures on all food items, since almost half of the duty receipts arose from butter, eggs, and cheeses. This is shown in column 12 of Table 70.

Beef and Veal Duty

Duties on imported beef and veal are partially ad valorem and partially specific. The ad valorem duties since 1936 (with the exception of the last six months of 1939) have amounted to 20% on tinned boneless beef and veal and 10% on other tinned beef and veal articles and extracts. Specific duties were 3/4d. on chilled fresh meat and 2/3d. on other kinds. Net receipts for 1938–39 were £3.4 million, £5.3 million for 1947–48, and £2.1 million for 1948–49. This latter amount has been allotted in proportion to expenditures on rationed foods, shown in column 13 of Table 70.

Liquor and Club Licenses

Receipts from licenses on brewers and dealers in wines, spirits, and beer remained fairly constant during the decade, while club duty increased fourfold. The number of licenses and clubs and the net receipts from both types of excise duty are shown here.

	1938–39	1945–46	1948–49
Liquor licenses			
Number (thousands)	193	167	200
Net receipts (million pounds)	4.3	4.1	4.2
Club duty			
Number (thousands)	18	17	20
Net receipt (million pounds)	.2	.6	.8

The total duty from these two sources, £5,029,000, has been allocated in proportion to expenditure on alcoholic drink. This is shown in column 15 of Table 70.

Other licenses amounting to £320,000 in 1948–49 were levied on various manufacturers and traders. This amount will be allocated in Chapter 15. Gun, game, and dog licenses in 1948–49 totaled £1,276,100, but only £97,000 was a central government excise receipt. The remaining amount was collected by the Post Office for the county borough councils. The total of £97,000 has been divided between income groups on the basis of their aggregate disposable income, included with liquor and club licenses in column 14 of Table 70.

Betting Duty

Betting duties were first imposed in 1948 and included a pool betting duty and a bookmaker's license duty. The former applies to all organized pools and to totalizators on dog tracks. The rates were originally 10% of total stakes, but in April of 1948 the rate on pools was raised to 20%. Receipts totaled £21.7 million in 1948–49, 41% arising from dog totalizator betting and 59% from football and other pools.

The bookmaker's license duty came into operation in August of 1948, the duty ranging from £6 to £48 per meeting of 8 races depending upon the enclosure in which a bookie operated and the number of enclosures on a track. Altogether, 138,097 licenses were issued, net receipts for the fiscal year being £1.7 million.

Little is known about the relationship between income and gambling expenditures. The recent royal commission investigating betting, lotteries, and gaming estimated that the cost of gambling in 1948 was £67.5 million, and £70.2 million in 1949.[15] This amount represented net expenditure, i.e. stakes less annual winnings. Total stakes were estimated to have been in the neighborhood of £500 million to £750 million. Of the two types of duty above, the pool betting duty is directly dependent upon the volume of stakes. Stakes for football pools in 1948–49 are estimated to have been £61.5 million, and stakes on dog totalizators £93.6 million.[16]

TABLE 68

Estimate of Stakes in Football Pools, by Income Range

INCOME RANGE (IN POUNDS)	PERCENTAGE OF SAMPLE BETTING	AVERAGE WEEKLY STAKES	AVERAGE ANNUAL STAKES	AVERAGE PERCENTAGE OF INCOME	DISTRIBUTION OF TOTAL STAKES
	1	2	3	4	5
Under 135	32%	25*d.*	1/0/0	1%	3.3%
135–250	49%	35*d.*	2/0/5	1%	29.4%
250–380	60%	35*d.*	2/12/6	.81% ⎫	44.1%
380–500	55%	43*d.*	2/19/1	.90% ⎬	
500 and above	36%	54*d.*	2/8/7	—	23.2%
					100.0%

A survey was conducted for the royal commission, which covered betting on football pools in relation to income. Using some of this information, a rough estimate of total stakes by income range can be made. In Table 68 below, column 1 shows the percentage of men in the sample who participated in football pools, and column 2 their usual weekly stake. If we multiply columns 1 and 2, and then mul-

15. *Report of the Royal Commission on Betting, Lotteries, and Gaming, 1949–51,* Cmd. 8190 (1951), p. 19.

16. The estimates are found by multiplying the 20% pool duty receipts by five, and the 10% totalizator duty by ten.

tiply by 30 (the average number of weeks in the year for which pools run), an estimate can be made of the average annual stakes per man in that income group. This is shown in column 3. Column 4 shows this amount as an approximate percentage of the average annual income of persons in each range. If these percentages are then turned into pounds by multiplying by the aggregate disposable income of each group, the percentage of total stakes arising in each income group may be found (in column 5).

It seems likely that about the same type of person who bet on football pools also bet on dog races,[17] so that the distribution of stakes shown in column 5 above will be used for both. Although bookmaker's licenses are not based on stakes, presumably bookies pass the tax on to their clientele in their odds, so that betters pay the tax in direct proportion to their wagers. This assumption is not entirely satisfactory, but it represents the best possible guess. In column 15 of Table 70 the estimated distribution of betting taxes is shown, the amount of the tax increasing directly with disposable income, but declining as a percentage of that income.

Purchase Tax

The purchase tax is an ad valorem excise duty on certain classes of nonessential consumer articles. For most of 1948–49 there were three schedules, the lower of $33\frac{1}{3}$, a middle classification taxed at $66\frac{2}{3}$, and an upper group of luxury items taxed at 100%.[18] Before the 30th of June there had been five rates from $33\frac{1}{3}$ to 125%. Expenditure on goods subject to purchase tax in 1948–49 probably amounted to about £1,320 million, about 80% of this representing goods taxed at the lowest rate(s), 13% at the middle rates, and 7% at the highest rate.[19]

17. Probably fewer people bet on dogs, but their total stakes are larger. The relative proportion of stakes to disposable income is assumed to be the same for each income group on both betting on dog racing and football pools.

18. It is not really proper to classify purchase tax items as grades of luxury goods, for as with the luxury tax in the U. S., many relatively essential items were included. For example, heating appliances and many toilet requisites were taxed at 100%, while luxury foods, books, and cooking appliances were free of tax. Most automobiles were subject to $\frac{1}{3}$ tax, while umbrellas, nonleather bags, and domestic textile articles were liable at $66\frac{2}{3}$%. The purchase tax has also taxed many a manufacturer's ingenuity. Women's bags, if closed at the top were taxed at 100%; if they were left open they were free of tax. Various shaped dishes that might conceivably be used as decorations faced a tax of $66\frac{2}{3}$% unless they were oven-proofed and therefore tax free as kitchen ware.

19. The tax is based on the wholesale price. Therefore taking the tax revenue from items taxed at $\frac{1}{3}$ and multiplying by three gives an estimate of the wholesale price. Adding the wholesale price and the tax, plus an estimated $\frac{1}{3}$ retail markup, gives roughly the total amount spent on such items. On this basis £1,040 was spent on items taxed at $\frac{1}{3}$, £187 million on items at $\frac{2}{3}$, and £95 million on items at 100%.

There are 35 different schedules of articles subject to purchase tax, but these can be grouped under five general headings corresponding to expenditure classifications in Table 67. This is shown below.

EXPENDITURE CLASSIFICATION	TAX	GROUPING UNDER FINANCE ACT
No. 6 Durable household goods	87.1	Items 6–19 inclusive
No. 7 Other " "	22.7	" 23–25, 30, 31
No. 8 Clothing	82.4	Items 1–6
No. 10 Private motoring	20.9	" 35
No. 16 Other goods	78.0	All other items
Total	£291.1	

The duty on classifications 6, 7, 10, and 16 have been allotted to income groups in relation to the spending on those items by persons in each group. Since most expenditures in these four classifications were on goods subject to tax (there was little that one could purchase under these headings which was free of tax), this allocation appears reasonable. On clothing, however, a large share of expenditure came under the tax-free utility program. The total amount spent on taxed and untaxed items can be estimated in the same manner in which total expenditure on purchase-taxed items was figured above. Clothing taxed at one-third produced tax revenue amounting to £153.9 million and that at two-thirds produced £28.5 million. Assuming a one-third retail markup, this accounts for £287.5 million and £95.1 million expenditure respectively. Thus of the £853.0 million total expenditure on clothing, £382.6 million was on taxable items and £470.4 million represented utility clothing.

Utility articles were available in every essential type of clothing, so

INCOME RANGE (IN POUNDS)	ESTIMATED PERCENTAGE OF CLOTHING EXPENDITURE ON TAXED ARTICLES	AMOUNT SPENT ON TAXED ARTICLES	DISTRIBUTION OF CLOTHING EXPENDITURE SUBJECT TO PURCHASE TAX
Under 135	15%	6.0 million	1.6%
135–250	25%	44.5	11.5%
250–500	35%	115.0	30.0%
500–1,000	55%	86.4	22.6%
1,000–3,000	80%	90.4	23.8%
3,000 and above	90%	40.3	10.5%
		£382.6 million	100.0%

that it can be assumed that persons in the lowest income group paid very little purchase tax. The exact proportions of taxed and utility clothing purchased by each income group must be estimated rather arbitrarily. The manner in which it has been done is shown below. It is assumed that the proportions spent on items taxed at different rates are the same for each income group.

Table 69 summarizes the five categories of articles subject to purchase tax, showing the distribution of net receipts from each type of taxed article. The totals in column 6 have been carried over to column 16 of Table 70 completing the itemization of customs and excise duties.

TABLE 69

Allocation of the Purchase Tax
(In Thousand Pounds)

INCOME RANGE (IN POUNDS)	CLOTHING 1	DURABLE HOUSEHOLD GOODS 2	OTHER HOUSEHOLD GOODS 3	MOTORING 4	OTHER GOODS 5	TOTAL 6
Under 135	1,312	2,613	545	188	3,267	7,934
135–250	9,429	14,807	3,882	1,003	14,742	43,863
250–500	24,507	28,569	6,084	2,821	25,974	88,045
500–750	12,540	11,153	3,461	5,367	11,213	43,734
750–1,000	6,095	6,180	1,805	2,680	5,245	22,005
1,000–2,000	13,640	10,988	2,994	4,894	7,420	39,936
2,000–3,000	5,874	5,125	1,430	1,541	2,954	16,924
3,000–5,000	4,604	3,905	1,290	1,178	3,200	14,177
5,000–10,000	2,665	2,302	735	769	2,105	8,576
10,000–20,000	967	1,036	342	323	954	3,622
20,000 and above	373	422	132	136	371	1,434
Foreign visitors	304	—	—	—	546	850
Totals	82,400	87,100	22,700	20,900	78,000	291,100

SUMMARY

Column 17 of Table 70 gives the total for customs and excise duties for 1948–49 and their allocation among income ranges. It is usually assumed that customs and excise taxes are regressive in effect. How far this was true can be seen if the sums of these duties are presented as percentages of disposable income for each range. In Table 71, column 2, this is shown. It is interesting to note that while the duties were generally regressive through all ranges of income, between the incomes of £750 and £5,000 they were more nearly proportional, and at one point turned slightly progressive. This was brought about entirely by the incidence of the purchase tax, for every other customs and excise tax was regressive in character. The purchase tax was quite strongly progressive up through the £3,000–5,000 range, after which it became slightly regressive. The purchase tax, although accounting for less than 20% of all customs and excise revenue, became relatively

TABLE 70

Allocation of Customs and Excise Duties
(*In Thousand Pounds*)

INCOME RANGE	ALCOHOLIC BEVERAGES	TOBACCO	TEA	COCOA AND COFFEE	SUGAR AND PRESERVED FRUIT	MATCHES AND LIGHTERS	OIL
(IN POUNDS)	1	2	3	4	5	6	7
Under 135	30,154	42,096	754	93	2,566	511	2(
135–250	118,135	196,446	3,439	457	11,760	2,396	1,1(
250–500	182,831	248,302	4,449	635	15,922	3,095	2,5)
500–750	40,634	62,969	955	151	3,577	762	3,4)
750–1,000	17,682	21,220	371	73	1,589	262	1,6(
1,000–2,000	17,249	27,189	376	75	1,642	318	2,9(
2,000–3,000	4,635	6,365	71	16	351	77	1,0)
3,000–5,000	3,463	3,267	52	13	293	46	7)
5,000–10,000	1,960	1,586	28	7	125	22	4)
10,000–20,000	742	502	7	2	38	6	2)
20,000 and above	251	136	2	1	9	2	)
Foreign visitors	—	—	—	—	—	—	)
	417,736	610,078	10,504	1,523	37,972	7,497	14,4(

more important in the higher income groups, minimizing the regressive character of other duties for incomes above £750.

Column 3 of Table 71 shows customs and excise duties per income recipient. Combined customs and excise duties rose from £32 annually for families in the lowest income group to £870 for those in the highest, the average being £65½.

The percentages in column 2 are interesting also in comparison with Barna's figures for 1937, for he found indirect taxes to be most steeply regressive in the £1,000–5,000 range. In 1937 indirect taxes as percentages of disposable income ranged from 12½% for incomes of £125 to 3½% for incomes over £20,000. From the above figures for 1948–49 it appears that indirect taxes have increased both absolutely and relative to disposable income and that there has been a partial redistribution of the burden. This latter effect, however, has only resulted from the imposition of the purchase tax, which fell most heavily on the middle and upper income ranges. If one excluded the purchase tax from the comparison, other customs and excise duties would be found to be regressive in all ranges, varying from approxi-

TABLE 70 (*continued*)

INTERNMENT	SILK	IMPORT ACTS FOOD	IMPORT ACTS OTHER GOODS	OTTAWA DUTIES	BEEF AND VEAL	LIQUOR AND CLUB LICENSE	BETTING	PURCHASE TAX	TOTAL
8	9	10	11	12	13	14	15	16	17
3,872	137	948	869	307	153	383	771	7,934	91,753
2,325	622	4,676	3,914	1,526	703	1,503	6,867	43,863	409,841
7,141	1,144	6,555	6,896	2,139	889	1,963	10,302	88,045	592,820
4,847	389	1,611	2,986	514	184	605	2,437	42,734	168,788
2,358	212	684	1,483	237	65	169	1,137	23,005	72,238
3,130	260	755	1,850	248	59	274	998	37,936	95,324
1,045	118	204	804	65	14	80	334	17,424	32,620
771	84	146	861	41	6	78	260	15,677	25,780
507	46	65	552	27	4	40	164	8,576	14,182
371	19	19	244	7	2	12	66	3,762	5,818
58	8	6	103	2	1	4	26	1,294	1,980
992	16	47	155	15	5	15	—	850	2,121
7,217	3,055	15,716	20,717	5,128	2,085	5,126	23,362	291,100	1,513,265

mately 17½% of income for the lowest group to only 4½% for the highest income range.

TABLE 71

Customs and Excise Duties per Capita, and as a Percentage of Disposable Income, by Income Range

INCOME RANGE (IN POUNDS)	CUSTOMS AND EXCISE DUTIES (IN MILLION POUNDS)	AS PERCENTAGE OF DISPOSABLE INCOME	PER TAX FAMILY (IN POUNDS)
Under 135	91.75	19.7	32
135–250	409.84	19.9	46
250–500	592.82	19.1	70
500–750	168.79	17.2	102
750–1,000	72.24	15.9	124
1,000–2,000	95.32	16.1	179
2,000–3,000	32.62	16.1	294
3,000–5,000	25.78	15.1	406
5,000–10,000	14.18	13.9	470
10,000–20,000	5.82	13.8	695
20,000 and above	1.98	13.0	870
Foreign visitors	2.12	—	—
Total	1,513.26	18.5 (average)	65½ (average)

CHAPTER 15

The Allocation of Other Indirect Taxes

IN ADDITION to the customs and excise duties allocated in the previous chapter, there were minor indirect taxes of £79 million which can be allocated to persons as consumers and £91 million which may be classed as taxes on business in general. To complete the allocation of all taxes, an attempt will be made in this chapter to allocate as much of these amounts as is possible.

MINOR INDIRECT TAXES

Minor taxes, as listed below, totaled £120 million in 1948–49. Of this amount, £79 million is estimated to be attributable to persons; most of the remaining amount fell on business in general and is discussed in the second half of this chapter.

TABLE 72

Minor Indirect Taxes
(In Million Pounds)

	TOTAL TAX	ALLOCABLE TO PRIVATE PERSONS
Stamp duties	56.6	48.1
Motor vehicle duties	48.5	23.9
Post Office surplus *	12.7	5.1
Net profit on home broadcasting	2.3	2.3
	120.1	79.4

* Surplus, not including profit on home broadcasting, but inclusive of overseas broadcasting expenditures. See below, p. 195.

Net receipts from these minor indirect taxes did not quite double in the 1938–48 decade, and in 1948–49 were about 15% greater than 1946. Since 1946 they have represented about 3.4% of all tax revenues, compared with 8.2% in the years immediately preceding the war. The relative distribution among income ranges has changed only slightly (per capita), and this slight change is due largely to the shortage, and consequently high price, of automobiles which has restricted their ownership in the lower-middle income groups.

Stamp Duties

The classification of stamp duties shown in Table 73 is summarized as falling on individuals, business, government, and foreigners.

TABLE 73

Classification of Stamp Duties, Great Britain, 1948–49
(In Million Pounds)

Stamp duties directly attributable to individuals
  1. Transfers to real property

Land and houses	14.42	
Other property	.99	
Leases	.80	
Mortgages	1.39	17.60

  2. Stocks, shares, debentures, and duties on private companies

Transfers of real property	4.23	
Stocks, shares, and debentures	19.17	
Company Share Capital duty	1.77	
Less: duty on foreigners	— .50	
duty on insurance companies	— .75	23.92

  3. Checks and receipts

Checks	3.72	
Receipts	1.73	5.45

4. Other: duty paid by insurance companies	1.16
Total attributable to persons	48.13
Stamp duties on production in general	7.76
Stamp duties on foreigners	.50
Stamp duties on government	.24
Total	56.63

Most of the stamp duties attributable to private persons fell on the transfers of, or legal matters concerning, property. In the allocation of these duties the Inland Revenue classification of property in estates falling in can be used to determine the relative holdings of shares, insurance, land and houses, mortgages, and other property by estate groups. These holdings have been translated into relative holdings by income range following the method used in the allocation of private capital in Chapter 11.[1] Using this method, we may allocate £42 million stamp duties on property (items 1, 2, and 4 in Table 73) as shown in column 1 of Table 74.

In addition, there was £5.45 million duty on checks and receipts,

1. See p. 147.

192

falling directly on individuals. The practice of using checks in the payment of bills has been assumed to be a function of income up to incomes of about £1,000, being a constant rate per income recipient for incomes above that level. On this basis the average duty on checks and receipts has been estimated to have ranged from 2s. 2d. for persons in the lowest income group to 13s. 6d. for incomes above £1,000. The allocation of stamp duties on checks and receipts is shown in column 2 of Table 74.

TABLE 74

Distribution of Stamp Duties on Private Individuals, Great Britain, 1948–49
(In Million Pounds)

INCOME RANGE (IN POUNDS)	ON PROPERTY	CHECKS AND RECEIPTS	TOTAL
	1	2	3
Under 135	.91	.33	1.24
135–250	4.04	1.44	5.48
250–500	6.26	2.16	8.42
500–750	2.68	.69	3.37
750–1,000	3.23	.32	3.55
1,000–2,000	6.76	.36	7.12
2,000–3,000	3.50	.08	3.58
3,000–5,000	4.38	.05	4.43
5,000–10,000	4.29	.02	4.31
10,000–20,000	2.99	—	2.99
20,000 and above	3.64	—	3.64
	42.68	5.45	48.13

Total stamp duties allocable to private persons are shown in column 3 of Table 74. These duties are nearly proportional to pretax incomes, but moderately progressive in relation to actual disposable incomes. Of the remaining £8.5 million, £7.8 million is estimated to have fallen on business in general, £.5 million on foreigners, and £.2 million on government. These will be dealt with in the latter part of this chapter.

Motor Vehicle Duties

In 1948–49 there were 1,931,000 private cars and 537,000 motorcycles with current licenses in Great Britain.[2] Tax receipts from licensing amounted to £48.5 million in 1948–49, 40% more than in the years

2. The number of vehicles and taxation receipts in this section are from the Ministry of Transport Return No. 144.

immediately preceding the war. The number of current licenses and net tax receipts from each type of vehicle are shown below in Table 75.

TABLE 75

Vehicle Licenses and Net Tax Receipts from Licenses,
Great Britain, 1948–49

TYPE OF LICENSES	No. OF LICENSES (IN THOUSANDS)	NET TAX RECEIPTS (IN THOUSAND POUNDS)
Cycles (with motors)	537.2	996
Hackneys	129.3	5,144
Agricultural engines	240.0	60
Tractors	3.9	141
Goods vans	756.2	18,732
Private cars	1,931.3	21,434
Trade licenses	42.0	509
Total vehicle licenses	3,725.1	47,016
Driving licenses	—	1,505
Total tax receipts		48,521

Automobile licenses averaged about £11 each in 1948–49 and motorcycles just under £2 each. In allocating license fees it will simplify matters to work with vehicle units, i.e. one automobile or six motorcycles to a unit. The number of vehicle units in each income group can be roughly estimated, partly from expenditures on motoring by income group and partly from general observation.[3] In the allocation in Table 74 it has been assumed that each tax-family unit whose income was greater than £2,000 possessed one vehicle unit (those with no vehicles being compensated for by others with more than one), and that the percentage of ownership for lower-income groups was 85% for £1,000–2,000; 45% for £500–1,000; 35% for £250–500; 10% for £135–250; and 2% for under £135. Multiplying these percentages by the number of tax families in each income group gives an estimate of the number of units for each group, and then these unit numbers can be reconverted into an index of ownership by income group. This index is shown in column 1 of Table 76.

Vehicle licenses in Britain in 1948–49 were dependent upon horsepower, cylinder capacity, or time of purchase. Cars purchased since 1947 were licensed at the flat rate of £10 each, while the licenses on older cars varied with size (power-rated). Only about 10% of all licenses came under the flat rate, so that an adjustment has been made for variations in licensing fees in estimating the amounts in

3. See p. 174.

column 2 of Table 76.[4] The amount allocated in Table 76 is equal to the sum of motorcycle and automobile licenses, plus 90% of drivers' licenses. The remaining £24.65 will be handled later in this chapter as a general tax on business.

TABLE 76

Estimated Distribution of Vehicle Units and Licensing Fees

Income Range (In Pounds)	Index of Vehicle Units (Percentage)	License Fees (In Million Pounds)
Under 135	.04	.01
135–250	.29	.08
250–500	12.87	3.08
500–750	31.52	7.55
750–1,000	15.52	3.71
1,000–2,000	25.66	6.08
2,000–3,000	6.77	1.62
3,000–5,000	4.32	1.03
5,000–10,000	2.17	.51
10,000–20,000	.63	.15
20,000 and above	.21	.05
	100.00	23.86

Post Office Surplus

Postal charges are not a tax, but the surplus of the Post Office arising from its postal, telephone, and telegraph services is best considered as an indirect tax (or perhaps more aptly, as a negative subsidy). Wireless services of the BBC are actually part of the General Post Office, but since there was a separate duty on wireless and television, the home services (but not the overseas services) will be considered separately below.

The Post Office surplus was £11 million in 1938, £27 million in 1946, and £15 million in 1948–49. After deducting the surplus on home broadcasting, the Post Office surplus for 1948–49 was £12.7 million. Only about 40% of this amount is directly attributable to private persons, and the remaining amount must be considered a tax on business in general. Postwar budget studies are not detailed enough to give a distribution of General Post Office services by income

4. The adjustment has actually been included in the index in column 1. Before turning the number of vehicle units estimated for each range into a percentage index, a variable multiplier has been applied to the number of units for each income group. These multipliers, to compensate for varying average licensing fees, were as follows: .75 for under £500; .9 for £500–1,000; 1 for £1,000–2,000; 1.1 for £2,000–3,000; 1.2 for £3,000–5,000; 1.3 for £5,000–10,000; and 1.4 and 1.5 for the two next highest groups.

range; hence the distribution for prewar years has been the basis of the present estimate.[5]

In 1937 it was estimated that the private share of the surplus (£4.6 million) represented a per capita tax ranging from 1s. 1½d. for the lowest income group to 9s. 7d. for the highest. Applying this scale of charges to 1948–49 data would give a total tax of £9.3 million. This is much too high, the desired total being about £5 million (i.e. about 40% of the total surplus). The scale therefore has been reduced so that it ranges between 7d. for the lowest incomes to 5s. 1d. for the highest. The resulting allocation is shown in column 3 of Table 77 below.

TABLE 77

Distribution of Minor Indirect Taxes, 1948–49
(In Million Pounds)

INCOME RANGE (IN POUNDS)	STAMP DUTY	MOTOR VEHICLE DUTY	POST OFFICE SURPLUS	BBC SURPLUS	TOTAL
	1	2	3	4	5
Under 135	1.24	.01	.13	.09	1.47
135–250	5.48	.08	.75	.56	6.87
250–500	8.42	3.08	2.38	1.13	15.01
500–750	3.37	7.55	.93	.29	12.14
750–1,000	3.55	3.71	.36	.11	7.73
1,000–2,000	7.12	6.08	.36	.11	13.67
2,000–3,000	3.58	1.62	.08	.03	5.31
3,000–5,000	4.43	1.03	.04	.01	5.51
5,000–10,000	4.31	.51	.01	.01	4.84
10,000–20,000	2.99	.15	.01	—	3.15
20,000 and above	3.64	.05	—	—	3.69
	48.13	23.86	5.05	2.34	79.39

Wireless Services

Wireless services can be treated separately, but similarly to the Post Office surplus. Although there was a duty on the ownership of wireless equipment, the receipts went to the BBC rather than into the general treasury. Thus, the home services account can be considered as a separate self-supporting unit, and the net surplus or deficit can be treated as a tax or subsidy. The overseas services are assumed to be a part of the General Post Office; only the home services are considered here.

5. See Barna, p. 165.

According to the licensing revenue for 1948–49 there were slightly over 11½ million radios and almost 125,000 television receivers in use in Great Britain. Little is known about the distribution of ownership (and rentals), but one should be able to hazard a fairly reliable guess. In the allocation shown in column 4 of Table 77 two assumptions have been made concerning the possession of radios and television receivers. For radios, it has been estimated that each tax family with income exceeding £2,000 had one set; that 90% of those in the £500–2,000 range owned sets; 65% in the £250–500 group; and 30% and 20% respectively for the two lowest groups. For television, 1% of tax families in the £250–500 range have been assumed to possess sets, 5% in the £500–2,000 range, and 10% of all higher income families. In estimating shares of the BBC surplus, the total duty for radio and television combined has been worked out on the basis of these assumptions, and then the amount for each group has been multiplied by 18.2% (since the surplus represented 18.2% of all license fees). The estimated distribution of shares in the BBC surplus is shown in Table 77.

MISCELLANEOUS INDIRECT TAXES

In this and previous chapters all taxes have been dealt with at least in part; there remains, however, that part of tax revenues which could not be directly allotted to specific income groups. These are taxes which fell on business in general or on specific nonconsumer goods industries. These may be itemized as follows:

TABLE 78

Miscellaneous Indirect Taxes

(MILLION POUNDS)

Customs and excise duties	
Key industries duty	.88
Import act duties	5.22
Excise licenses	.32
Monopoly value duty	.81
Oils duty	42.84
	50.07
Stamp duties	8.50
Motor vehicle duty	24.64
Post Office surplus	7.61
Corporation tax	.10
Total	90.92

Following the assumption used in the allocation of other indirect taxes (that such taxes raise the prices of products—or services—by the amount of the tax) the above amounts could all be allocated if one could follow the basic services and materials through final consumer products. Input-output tables provide information on interindustry relationships, but an attempt to follow the divergent paths of a single type of unfinished article or raw material through interindustry channels until it reaches consumers in various forms shows the impossibility of a too literal use of the tax-raises-price assumption. Taking any single input in a multi-industry classification, if it is traced through hundreds of interindustry exchanges, figures become so infinitesimal that it is impossible to follow it further. Such an effort would unduly stretch the reasonableness of the assumption.

In the allocation of these remaining indirect taxes (and later in the allocation of indirect benefits) a compromise course has been adopted. Taxes will be partially allocated to persons, government, and foreigners only in the first or second instance in which the taxed article enters into the cost of a finished consumer product. For example, a tax which increases the cost of fertilizers to farmers is assumed to raise the prices of agricultural products by the amount of the tax. Therefore this tax will be allocated to persons, government, and foreigners in proportion to their share in the consumption of agricultural products. A good part of agricultural end products, however, are not directly consumed, but go as inputs to other industries. In this secondary use of the original taxed article by other industries it is again assumed that the tax is wholly reflected in the prices of the products of these secondary users. Thus, that part of agricultural products which is used in the manufacture of alcoholic beverages is assumed to affect the final price of the products of this industry, and this share of the tax is again divided between persons, government, and foreigners. Whatever part of the product of this secondary industry again goes to other industries as an input is assumed to be unallocable.

In theoretical terms the assumption merely is that a tax on inputs directly affects the prices of outputs as long as the taxed input represents a fairly substantial part of all inputs. When the input plays only a negligible part in the cost of any product, the tax on the input is assumed to be absorbed within the industry—i.e. rather than being passed on to consumers of the product the added cost is borne by labor and capital. To draw some line between substantial and negligible effects, a tax on an input of industry A is assumed to affect the prices of A's products directly, and to the extent that at least 2% of A's products become inputs to industries B, C, and D, the tax is assumed to be reflected in the prices of the products of these secondary users.[6]

Only one study on interindustry input-output relations for Great Britain has been completed in recent years, that of Tibor Barna, "The Interdependence of the British Economy." [7] The figures relate to 1935, and therefore adjustments have been necessary in certain industries to reflect the larger defense program and the increased proportion of some exported products. Fortunately, these adjustments only slightly affect industries in which taxed articles are primarily used, and therefore any inaccuracy in the adjustments will have relatively small effects on the final distribution of these indirect taxes.

TABLE 79

Allocation of Taxes on Electrical Engineering Inputs
(In Thousand Pounds)

	PERCENT-AGE OF PRODUCT	CONSUMED BY :	TOTAL AMOUNT	PERSONS	GOVERN-MENT	EX-PORT	UNAL-LOCABLE
1.	20	Persons	58	58			
2.	1	Government	3		3		
3.	12	Export	35			35	
		INPUT TO INDUSTRY					
4.	9	Gas, electricity, water	26	10	1		15
5.	6	Building	17		3		14
6.	5	Mechanical engineering	14		1	3	10
7.	2	Shipbuilding	5		2	1	2
8.	2	Motors	5	1		2	2
9.	43	Unallocable	126				
	100	Totals	289	69	10	41	169

An example of the method by which these taxes have been allocated is reproduced in Table 79. Under the Key Industries Duty Act a number of articles, mostly partially manufactured goods, were liable to duty. Quite a few of these, for example meters, electrical instruments, valves, magnetos, arc lamps, etc. can be grouped together as inputs for the electrical engineering industry. The taxes on these articles amounted to £289,000 in 1948–49. In this example, reference to the input-output table shows that approximately 20% of the electrical engineering industry's products were directly consumed by

6. The assumed dividing line between substantial and negligible inputs is not completely satisfactory. It probably would have been preferable if substantial inputs were defined as those which represented at least 2% of the receiving industry's total inputs, rather than those which constituted at least 2% of the selling industry's outputs. However, the amounts were relatively small, and this appeared to be a simpler rule. Over the spread of industries the net error should be negligible.

7. *JRSS, 115* (1952), 29–77.

persons, 1% by government, and 12% went to export. These figures are shown in lines 1 to 3 of Table 79, the appropriate amounts being placed in the corresponding columns. Another 24% of the product of this industry went as identifiable inputs (i.e. accounting for at least 2% of the output of the electrical engineering industry) to secondary industries. These are listed on lines 4 to 8, the percentage in the first column and corresponding values in the amount column. By referring to the input-output table for each of these five industries the percentage of total output consumed by persons, government and foreigners can be found and these percentages multiplied by the total-amount figures. Thus, 38% of the output of the gas, electricity, and water industry group was consumed by persons, and 38% of this industry group's share of the tax on electrical engineering items, or £10,000, is placed in the "Persons" column. Similarly, £1,000 went to government, and the remaining product (£15,000) of this industry group was consumed in small quantities by other industries and is

TABLE 80

Allocation of Key Industry Duty, by Type
of Personal Expenditure
(In Thousand Pounds)

INCOME RANGE (IN POUNDS)	DURABLE HOUSE-HOLD	OTHER HOUSE-HOLD	FOOD	DRINK AND TOBACCO	CLOTH-ING	FUEL	OTHER GOODS	TOTAL
Under 135	3	1	1			1	2	8
135–250	20	10	7	2	2	3	11	55
250–500	37	17	8	3	3	5	19	92
500–750	15	9	2	1	1	1	9	38
750–1,000	8	5	1		1	1	3	19
1,000–2,000	15	9	1		1	1	5	32
2,000–3,000	6	3	1				2	12
3,000–5,000	5	4					3	12
5,000–10,000	3	2					2	7
10,000–20,000	2	1					1	4
20,000 and above	1	1						2
Persons	115	62	21	6	8	12	57	281
Government								22
Export								157
Unallocable								421
Total key industry duty								881

put down as unallocable. This has been done for the other four major secondary industries, and the columns totaled. Of the tax on electrical engineering articles, £69,000 is estimated to have fallen on persons, £10,000 on government, £41,000 on foreigners, and £169,000 remains unallocable. This same process has been used for all groups of dutiable imports under the Key Industries Duty Act.

When the duty on all articles has been allotted, it is estimated that £281,000 fell directly on persons, £22,000 on government, £157,000 on exports, and £421,000 was unallocable. The amount falling on persons can be allocated among income ranges by grouping the articles in relation to the distribution of personal expenditure in Table 67. In the example in Table 79 above, of the £69,000 falling on persons £10,000 would be allocated in relation to expenditure on utilities, £1,000 to expenditure on motoring, and £58,000 divided between durable and other household goods. Table 80 shows the allocation of all key industry duty estimated in this manner.

The same method has been used in allocating duties under the import act. Dutiable articles (not already accounted for in Chapter 14) were mainly raw materials, semimanufactured goods, and animals (pets and breeding stock). Table 81 shows the final allocation of these duties to income ranges.

Excise licenses can all be allocated to income ranges, since these license duties fell on retailers and persons providing direct services. These can be classified as follows:

EXCISE LICENSES
(IN THOUSAND POUNDS)

Estate agents	21	
Auctioneers	74	
Hawkers	6	
Money lenders	21	
Pawnbrokers	13	
Total services		135
Methylated spirits retailers	13	
Plate dealers (silver)	50	
Refreshment houses	11	
Tobacco dealers and manufacturers	109	
Miscellaneous	2	
Total retailers		185
Total licenses		320

This amount is allocated among income ranges in relation to expenditure on services, tobacco, and other goods, in Table 82.

The remaining customs and excise duty, that on monopoly value, will be classed as unallocable. Monopoly value duty was charged on the premises for which excise licenses had been granted for the retailing of specific commodities (chiefly beer and spirits). Since the granting of licenses is limited, new grants immediately increase the value of property, and monopoly value duty is charged by assessing

TABLE 81

Allocation of Import Act Duties, by Type
of Personal Expenditure
(In Thousand Pounds)

Income Range (In Pounds)	Food	Drink and Tobacco	Fuel	Durable Household	Other Household	Clothing	Riding	Motoring	Other Goods	Total
Under 135	25	2		20	23	1		2	19	90
135–250	120	10	1	112	161	2	2	5	86	496
250–500	157	14	2	216	252	4	4	10	152	806
500–750	37	4	1	87	136	1	2	5	64	343
750–1,000	14	2	1	43	82	1	1	8	32	181
1,000–2,000	15	2		83	126	1	2	4	46	283
2,000–3,000	3			39	57	1	1	3	15	120
3,000–5,000	2			33	50	1	1	2	20	110
5,000–10,000	1			18	28			1	12	61
10,000–20,000				7	19				6	33
20,000 and above				2	7				3	12
Persons	374	34	5	661	941	12	13	40	455	2,535
Government										145
Export										356
Unallocable										2,181
Total import act duties										5,217

the increase in value of the property caused by the grant. This duty presumably was chiefly borne by the *rentier,* but with the passage of time part of it may be shifted to the lessee. The rentier is often a brewery, or, in urban areas, real estate trusts or banking and investment houses. Because of the difficulty in determining ownership and incidence, it is felt that this duty is better classified as unallocable.

TABLE 82

Distribution of Certain Excise Licenses
(In Thousand Pounds)

INCOME RANGE (IN POUNDS)	SERVICES	TOBACCO	OTHER GOODS	TOTAL
Under 135	8	7	3	18
135–250	31	35	14	80
250–500	49	45	25	119
500–750	19	11	11	41
750–1,000	8	4	5	17
1,000–2,000	10	4	7	21
2,000–3,000	4	2	4	10
3,000–5,000	3	1	3	7
5,000–10,000	2		2	4
10,000–20,000	1		1	2
20,000 and above			1	1
	135	109	76	320

Stamp duties falling on business concerns are equally difficult to distribute. Following the division in the first part of this chapter, £243,000 is assumed to fall on the government, £504,000 on foreigners, and the remaining amount, £7,754,000, will be left as unallocable.

Motor vehicle duties, other than those falling on private motoring (discussed above), are mainly attributable to the transport industry. Three per cent has been charged to the government for defense and various services, 1% to foreigners, and the remainder left as unallocable. The remaining portion of the Post Office surplus is of a similar nature and has been added to this unallocable portion.

The corporation tax has been distributed using the share (income) index (see Chapter 11).

Table 83 summarizes the distribution of miscellaneous indirect taxes. The largest part of these is classified as unallocable, but is more than counterbalanced by unallocable expenditures on the other

TABLE 83

Distribution of Miscellaneous Indirect Taxes, by Income Range
(In Thousand Pounds)

Income Range (In Pounds)	Key Industries Duty	Import Act	Excise Licenses	Corporation Duty	Stamp Duty	Transportation and Communication	Miscellaneous	Total
Under 135	8	90	18	1				117
135–250	55	496	80	4				635
250–500	92	806	119	10				1,027
500–750	38	343	41	9				431
750–1,000	19	181	17	5				222
1,000–2,000	32	283	21	18				354
2,000–3,000	12	120	10	10				152
3,000–5,000	12	110	7	12				141
5,000–10,000	7	61	4	12				84
10,000–20,000	4	33	2	9				48
20,000 and above	2	12	1	10				25
	281	2,535	320	100				3,236
Government	22	145			243	2,027		2,437
Export	157	356			504	675		1,692
Unallocable	421	2,181			7,754	64,880	8,424	560
	881	5,217	320	100	8,501	67,582	8,424	91,025

side of the budget.[8] Miscellaneous indirect taxes are moderately progressive through all ranges of income, on the average from about 10*d.* to £12 per tax family.

SUMMARY, OTHER INDIRECT TAXES

Combining the allocations of indirect taxes shown in Tables 77 and 83, in Table 84 we have an indication of the estimated distribution of all indirect taxes other than customs and excise duties described in the previous chapter. Column 3 is the same as the distribution of other indirect taxes given in Table 11 of Chapter 4.

TABLE 84

Allocation of Other Indirect Taxes
(In Million Pounds)

INCOME RANGE (IN POUNDS)	MINOR INDIRECT TAXES 1	MISCELLANEOUS INDIRECT TAXES 2	TOTAL OTHER INDIRECT TAXES 3
Under 135	1.47	.12	1.59
135–250	6.87	.64	7.51
250–500	15.01	1.03	16.04
500–750	12.14	.43	12.57
750–1,000	7.73	.22	7.95
1,000–2,000	13.67	.35	14.02
2,000–3,000	5.31	.15	5.46
3,000–5,000	5.51	.14	5.65
5,000–10,000	4.84	.08	4.92
10,000–20,000	3.15	.04	3.10
20,000 and above	3.69	.03	3.72
Miscellaneous *		4.13	4.13
Unallocable		83.56	83.56
Totals	79.39	90.92	170.31

* Combined "government" and "export" shown in Table 83.

8. Unallocable taxes have been subtracted from unallocable expenditures in the estimate of redistribution. See indivisible expenditures, p. 50.

CHAPTER 16

The Allocation of Transfer Incomes

TRANSFERS were defined in Chapter 3 as income payments made by the government to persons without the performance of any reciprocal service by those persons. They include, therefore, all social security and related payments made by the state, where the receipt of such income is determined by particular circumstances other than productive contributions.[1] Transfer incomes allocated in this chapter total £665 million.

CLASSIFICATION OF TRANSFERS

Transfer payments by the state to private persons have been a very important part of the government budget in Britain for many years. Transfers by central and local governments totaled £275 million in 1938 and had increased to £713 million by 1948–49. Central government transfers alone were £249 million and £677 million for these years, accounting for 24% of all central government expenditures in 1938 and 20% in 1948–49.[2]

Transfers to the private sector were temporarily swollen during and immediately after the recent war by the payment of sums directly connected with the war effort. In 1946, for example, almost twice as much was paid to persons in transfers in the form of war gratuities, pay and allowances of demobilized members of the armed services, income tax credits from wartime tax savings, and war pensions arising out of the 1939–45 war combined as was spent on *all* transfers in 1938. By 1948, as Table 85 shows, these abnormal items had been reduced to £96 million from a height of £490 million.

1. Interest payments on the national debt have been excluded from the transfer classification, and are regarded as the rewards for the provision of a service to the government, i.e. the lending of funds. Neither the British White Papers nor the U.S. Department of Commerce consider such interest to be "productive" in their national accounting estimates, because loans to government to cover a deficit do not necessarily mean the creation of productive (i.e. income-producing) assets. From the point of view of the private investor who is faced with a variety of investment choices, however, interest is a reward for the contribution of a productive service, regardless of the ends for which borrowed funds are used.

2. These figures are for the combined account of the central government and the national insurance funds. See pp. 152–4.

As the burden of transfers related to the war decreased, however, there was a rapid expansion of the social security programs. Social security benefits amounted to £229 million in 1938, £345 million in 1946, and £540 million in 1948–49. This increase was almost entirely attributable to the new Family Allowances Act of 1945 and the two National Insurance Acts of 1946. The full effect of the legislative changes embodied in the national insurance acts, however, will not be felt for about a decade because of the contribution requirements necessary to quality fully for many of the new benefits. Persons who were fully qualified under the old social insurance schemes automatically became qualified for the new benefits on July 5, 1948, when the changeover took place, but this group included only about two-thirds of the population.[3]

In many of the published estimates of the distribution of incomes, transfers have been lumped together in the lowest income group with no effort made to allocate shares to other income groups. This, for example, was done by Clark in his 1936 study of redistribution.[4] It is also the practice of the White Paper income estimates, and has been followed by Seers in his recent posttax income estimates.[5] Before the 1939 war this was probably a fairly reliable short cut, since most of the social security programs were limited to persons with very low incomes. The most distinguishing feature of the new social security programs, however, has been that all persons are included regardless of income. For the years since 1951 it is actually more appropriate to assume an equal per capita distribution for many programs. For 1948–49, a year of transition, much is to be gained by constructing a more realistic estimate of the distribution of transfer incomes on the basis of whatever information is available. In the following sections transfers will be discussed under each of the major groupings shown in Table 85.

PENSIONS

The White Papers include in the pension classification, as indicated in Table 85, both contributory and noncontributory old age and retirement pensions, widows, orphans, and guardians benefits, national assistance, and pensioners' tobacco duty relief coupons. The revised national insurance program under the 1946 acts went into effect in July of 1948, so that the first quarter of the fiscal year came under

3. There were an estimated 24,365,000 persons entitled to benefits under national health insurance, 24,378,000 insured for contributory pensions, and 15,760,000 insured under the unemployment insurance program, as of July 4, 1948. See *Cmd.* 7955, appendices 14, 20, 23.
4. *National Income and Outlay.* See pp. 3–4, above.
5. *Cmd.* 8203, table 12, n. 4; and Seers, *Levelling of Incomes,* p. 44.

TABLE 85

Classification of Transfer Incomes *
(In Million Pounds)

	1938	1946	1948–49
Social security			
Pensions			
Contributory	47	75	244
Noncontributory	47	80	27
Widows and guardians	—	—	16
National assistance	—	51	37
Old age tobacco coupons	—	—	9
Total pensions	94	206	333
Health			
Sickness	22	32	54
Maternity	—	—	6
Industrial injuries	—	—	6
Total health	22	32	66
Unemployment			
Unemployment benefits	55	26	20
Outdoor relief	23	15	2
National assistance	35	4	—
Total unemployment	113	45	22
Miscellaneous			
Family allowances	—	19	60
Milk and welfare foods	—	28	35
School meals	—	15	24
Total miscellaneous	—	62	119
Total social security	229	345	540
Other transfers			
War gratuities and pay credits	—	229	—
Armed forces leave pay	—	162	21
War pensions and grants	38	82	86
Postwar tax credits	—	54	19
Training allowances	—	9	10
Scholarships and allowances	2	11	24
University arts and sciences	3	7	13
Miscellaneous	3	2	1
Total, other transfers	46	556	174
Total transfers	275	901	714

* See *Cmd.* 7933, table 31. Only £665 million will be allocated in this chapter. Local authority transfers are excluded in this study, and they accounted for £36.4 million of the 1948–49 amounts (outdoor relief £2 million, school meals £24 million, scholarships £9.4 million, and miscellaneous other transfers £1 million). Grants to universities, arts, and sciences of £12.5 million were included in Ch. 5 as an indivisible benefit.

208 *Redistribution of Income*

the old programs and the remaining three quarters under the new. In Table 86 the cost of the pension programs in 1948–49 by type of benefit is shown, plus the number of persons actually receiving benefits under the various programs during the fiscal year.

TABLE 86

Total Cost of Pensions, 1948–49
(In Thousand Pounds)

PROGRAM	NUMBER OF PENSIONERS	OLD PROGRAMS: APRIL 5, 1948 TO JULY 5, 1948	NEW PROGRAMS: JULY 5, 1948 TO APRIL 4, 1949
Contributory retirement and old age pensions	4,050,000 *	67,370	176,448
Noncontributory old age pensions	453,500 *	7,175	20,210
Supplementary pensions	512,476 †	3,090	—
Widows' benefits ‡	452,440 *	—	15,700
Guardians' benefits	39,421 *	—	450
National assistance	1,011,034 *	—	33,530
Old age tobacco coupons	1,590,000 *	1,970	6,780
Totals		79,605	253,118
Combined cost		332,723	

* December 31, 1948.
† June 30, 1948.
‡ Not including widows' allowances and pensions under the retirement and old age contributory pension scheme.

The contributory pension program began in Britain in 1926, and was compulsory for all employed persons between the ages of 16 and 70 engaged in manual labor who had incomes not exceeding £250 (not exceeding £420 after 1942). Although the revised program under the National Insurance Act of 1946 did not go into effect until 1948, the new benefit rates of 26s. weekly were put into force in October of 1946. Throughout the 1948–49 year, therefore, the benefit rates were as follows:

(1) 26s. weekly for retired men between the ages of 65 and 70, and women between 60 and 65, or above the upper age limits irrespective of retirement; but only 16s. for married women while their husbands were living. Pensions in the first five years subject to reduction if earnings of more than 20s. weekly were made.

(2) 26s. weekly for widows, subject to reduction if weekly earnings exceeded 30s.

Noncontributory pensions during the 1948–49 year were paid

at the same rates as contributory pensions. These pensions were subject to reduction, however, if earnings exceeded 10*s*. weekly, ceasing if weekly earnings reached 34*s*. 4*d*. After July 5, 1948, these noncontributory pensions were administered by the national assistance board, and it is planned to eliminate them in 1961, by which time all persons will be fully covered by contributory pensions.

The new national insurance act also added a widowed mother's allowance of 33*s*. 6*d*. while a child was of school age, and a guardian's allowance of 12*s*. weekly.

National assistance allowances (for unemployment assistance) were determined by need. The general scale rates before July 5, 1948, were 31*s*. for a married couple, 18*s*. for a single householder, 15*s*. 6*d*. for other single persons over 21, and from 7*s*. 6*d*. to 12*s*. 6*d*. for children. Supplementary pension rates were 2*s*. higher for each person over 21. Eligibility for national assistance depended upon the board's computation of each applicant's resources and requirements.

The old age pensioners' tobacco duty relief coupon scheme began in October, 1947, and continued through 1948–49. These coupons permitted pensioners to buy tobacco without paying excise duty and were worth 2*s*. until September, 1948, and 2*s*. 4*d*. after that date. An estimated 1.5 million persons benefited by the value of one coupon a week.

In allocating old age and retirement pension benefits it has been assumed that the number of elderly persons (over 65) as a percentage of total persons in each income group varied inversely with size of income over the three lowest income groups. The distribution of elderly persons in income groups above £500 is not important, because only those who had incomes before retirement of less than £420 were insured (and new registrants will not be eligible for contributory pension benefits until 1958). In the allocation of pension benefits in Table 86 it has been assumed that 25% of all persons in the lowest income group were eligible for either contributory or noncontributory pensions,[6] 21% in the £135–250 range, and about 10% in the £250–500 group. Of the estimated 860,000 pensioners in the lowest income group about 500,000 were receiving noncontributory pensions.[7] Benefits for the remaining 360,000 pensioners in the lowest income group and for the estimated 2,800,000 in the £135–250 group have been assumed to have averaged 26*s*. each. Some persons eligible for retirement were still employed, but others were receiving

6. These are persons classified in Table 45 of Chapter 11 as recipients of national assistance or "others." See p. 130.

7. See p. 208.

supplements for the support of dependents, presumably enough to maintain the average of the standard benefit. The remaining amount paid in pensions has been allotted to the £250–500 group. This allocation of contributory pensions is shown in column 1 of Table 87.

Widows' pensions have been allocated in the same proportion to the three lowest income groups as indicated in column 2 of Table 87. Guardians' benefits have been spread more widely over the income groups, since there were no eligibility rules other than caring for an orphan. The estimated distribution in column 3 is in proportion to the number of children in each income group, the two lowest income groups having first been reduced by 25% (since guardianship is probably, within limits, a function of income).

National assistance benefits, after July 5, 1948, averaged about £2 weekly for a single householder and £3 15s. for married couples. Special rates were in effect for blind and tubercular persons. The payment of national assistance and noncontributory pensions was based on the board's estimate of needs and resources, so that it can be assumed that most noncontributory and other national assistance pensions were paid to persons in the lowest income group. In column 4 of Table 87 these benefits are allocated on the assumption that 80% went to the lowest income group and 20% to the £135–250 group.

TABLE 87

Allocation of Pension Benefits
(*In Thousand Pounds*)

INCOME RANGE (IN POUNDS)	RETIRE-MENT AND OLD AGE 1	WIDOWS 2	GUARDIANS 3	NATIONAL ASSISTANCE 4	TOBACCO RELIEF 5	TOTAL 6
Under 135	30,855	3,035	16	51,200	1,798	86,904
135–250	169,115	9,195	136	12,805	4,395	195,646
250–500	43,848	3,470	231	—	2,557	50,106
500–750	—	—	48	—	—	48
750–1,000	—	—	13	—	—	13
1,000–2,000	—	—	4	—	—	4
2,000 and above	—	—	2	—	—	2
Totals	243,818	15,700	450	64,005	8,750	332,723

Tobacco duty relief for pensioners has been divided among the three lowest income groups in proportion to the over-65 population as estimated above. The allocation of this amount is indicated in column 5 of Table 87.

Combined pension benefits, in column 6 of Table 87, were greatest per capita in the lowest income group, and greatest in magnitude in the £135–500 income group. Above £500 benefits were negligible.

HEALTH BENEFITS

National health insurance has been in effect in Britain since 1912, although until the National Insurance Act of 1946 it was compulsory only for employed persons below a moderate level of income.[8] During the first quarter of the 1948–49 year benefit rates were 18s. weekly for men and 15s. for women when ill, and 8s. to 10s. 6d. weekly in case of disablement. After the new national insurance act went into effect, benefit rates were raised to 26s. In addition, a maternity benefit of £4 for each childbirth was instituted, plus another £4 benefit for attendance allowance in the first month after birth, or for employed women an allowance of 36s. weekly for 13 weeks beginning 6 weeks before birth. The amounts paid out in health and maternity benefits, and the number of persons receiving benefits is shown in Table 88.

TABLE 88

Cost of Health Programs

PROGRAM	No. OF INSURED (IN THOUSANDS)	No. RECEIVING BENEFITS (IN THOUSANDS)	COST TO JULY 5, 1948 (IN THOUSAND POUNDS)	COST JULY 5, 1948 TO APRIL 4, 1949 (IN THOUSAND POUNDS)
Sickness benefits				
Old program (NHI)	24,365 *		11,236	
New program (NI)	all persons ‡	5,648 †		43,489
Maternity benefits	" "	630 §		5,900
Industrial injuries	21,000 ‖	575 †		5,675
Totals			11,236	55,064
Combined cost			66,300	

* June 30, 1948.

† Number of claims received in the first nine months of the new schemes, not concurrent claims. Weekly claims averaged 135,000 for sickness benefits and 14,500 for industrial injuries.

‡ Although the whole population was insured, many were not entitled to full benefits. 156 weekly contributions were necessary to get full benefits, although partial benefits of limited duration were available after 26 weeks' contributions. After January, 1949, most new entrants were entitled to limited benefits. A woman could get maternity benefits, however, on her own or her husband's insurance, although the larger 13-week benefit was available to working women only on their own insurance.

§ The number of births for which mothers were eligible. This was about 80% of all confinements. Of this number 11% qualified for mothers' allowances.

‖ The number of "employed persons," as of March 31, 1948.

The National Insurance (Industrial Injuries) Act of 1946 created a new program, wider in scope but similar in nature to the old

8. National health insurance was compulsory for all employed persons with incomes below £160 from 1912 to 1920, below £250 from 1920 to 1942, and below £420 from 1942 to 1948.

workmen's compensation scheme.[9] Injury related to employment was insured against, with benefits of 45*s*. weekly (plus supplements for dependents) for the first 26 weeks, replaced in the event of longer disablement by a benefit varying in amount with the degree of disablement (45*s*. maximum). Supplements of 16*s*. for a wife and 7*s*. 6*d*. for the first child were included, as was a death benefit (amount and duration depending upon type and number of dependents). Insurance was compulsory for all employed persons. The cost of the program and the number of persons receiving benefits is shown in Table 88.

In allocating sickness and maternity benefits to income ranges the largest share must be divided among the three lowest income groups, since persons with incomes greater than £420 became eligible for limited benefits only in the last three months of the fiscal year. In column 1 of Table 89 benefits have been assumed equal per

TABLE 89

Allocation of Health Benefits
(In Thousand Pounds)

INCOME RANGE (IN POUNDS)	SICKNESS AND MATERNITY 1	INDUSTRIAL INJURIES 2	TOTAL HEALTH 3
Under 135	6,190	1,050	7,240
135–250	27,090	2,690	29,780
250–500	25,470	1,720	27,190
500–750	1,030	190	1,220
750–1,000	364	25	389
1,000–2,000	352	—	352
2,000–3,000	65	—	65
3,000–5,000	41	—	41
5,000–10,000	16	—	16
10,000–20,000	6	—	6
20,000 and above	1	—	1
Totals	60,625	5,675	66,300

capita for employed adults up to the income level of £420 (i.e. including 70% of those in the £250–500 group). Above that level benefits have again been assumed equal per capita, but only 15% as great as for persons under £420. This latter makes due allowance for the fact that new contributors were entitled to benefits for only

9. Workmen's compensation until 1948 was handled industrially under government regulation. Benefits were therefore not a government transfer until the second quarter of the 1948–49 fiscal year.

one-quarter of the year, and then only to limited benefits of short duration.

There were no contribution requirements for industrial injuries benefits, so that these must be allotted to the employed population. The incidence of injuries—especially those of a more serious nature —is probably highest in the heavy industries and among manual laborers. For this reason benefits have been allocated among the 5 lowest income groups in column 2 of Table 89 on the assumption that, starting from the lowest income group, 4%, 3%, 2%, 1%, and ½% of income recipients in each respective group received average benefits of approximately £10 each.

UNEMPLOYMENT BENEFITS

Unemployment insurance on a compulsory basis originated under the National Insurance Act of 1911, applying only to manual laborers in certain industries where employment was known to be particularly unstable. The program was extended in 1916 and again in 1920 to insure all manual and nonmanual workers with incomes not exceeding £250. In 1936 agricultural workers were included, and at the beginning of the war the income maximum was raised to £420. The number of insured persons increased to 16 million in 1939, and after dropping to about 13 million during the war, returned to the earlier figure by July, 1948.[10] During the first quarter of 1948–49 the benefit rates ranged from 17s. to 24s. weekly, depending upon sex and age, with supplements of 16s. for an adult dependent, 5s. for the first two children, and 4s. for additional children.[11]

The new unemployment scheme under the National Insurance Act of 1946 raised benefits to 26s. for both men and women, with supplements of 16s. and 7s. 6d. for an adult dependent and first child (other children now included under the family allowances program). Continuity rules required at least three days of waiting before benefits began, 180 days being the limit of standard benefits. Extended benefits were available for persons who had paid 30 unemployment contributions since January, 1944.

Supplementary unemployment benefits under the national assistance board ceased on July 5, 1948. In the first half of 1948 roughly 30,000 persons were on the board's unemployment rolls, and benefits

10. These figures are based on the old series statistics. New series figures for 1948 were 20,970,000, based on the more accurate estimate of insurance contributions rather than on the issue of unemployment insurance books. The number of insured workers in 1939 was almost equal to that for 1948 under either series.

11. Actually the old program was brought more nearly in line with the new one before July 5, 1948, extended benefits being introduced in early 1947 and the new higher rates on June 1, 1948.

of about £1 million were paid out. Benefits during the first quarter
of 1948–49 were so small that they have been included in national
assistance benefits in the pension section above.

Unemployment benefits were not subject to income tax, so that
persons unemployed for lengthy periods were most likely to have
been in the lowest income groups (income groups having been defined here in relation to taxable income). In allocating benefits, we
have assumed that all extended benefits (£4,430,000) have gone to
persons in the lowest income group, plus 60% of supplementation
grants (£2,150,000), all "under 18" unemployment benefits (£570,-
000), and 25% of the remaining standard benefits (£4,140,000—for
women unemployed more than 10 weeks and men more than 20
weeks). Of the remaining amount, two-thirds has been allotted to
the £135–250 group, and one-third to the £250–500 range. Table 90
shows this estimated distribution.

TABLE 90

Allocation of Unemployment Benefits
(In Thousand Pounds)

INCOME RANGE (IN POUNDS)	BENEFITS
Under 135	11,290
135–250	5,927
250–500	2,963
Total	20,180

MISCELLANEOUS SOCIAL SECURITY BENEFITS

Of the remaining social security transfers shown in Table 85 the
school meals program costing £24 million was conducted and paid
for by local authorities and therefore has been excluded here. Family
allowances of £60 million and the Ministry of Food's expenditure on
milk-in-schools schemes and welfare foods costing £35 million remain to be allocated.

The Family Allowances Act of 1945 provided for direct cash payments of 5s. weekly (£13 annually) to mothers for each child (except
the eldest) under the school-leaving age. The program was originally
proposed in the Beveridge Report of 1942,[12] although the originally
suggested rates were higher than those finally adopted.[13] The passage

12. *Cmd.* 6404, pars. 410–25.
13. The Family Endowment Society and other related groups had been making
similar suggestions for two generations, and the idea had become quite popular by the
recent war. It is interesting to note that one person favoring such allowances also
predicted their exact amount. "In lieu of the whole of the present system of children's

of this act was hailed in some quarters as a revolutionary move, but for the majority of taxpayers it merely supplemented the tax allowances program which had been in force since before the 1914 war.[14] Payment of family allowances was begun in August, 1946, and by the end of the 1948–49 year some 2,790,000 families were receiving allowances in respect of 4,700,000 children. Family allowances were not exempt from tax, a fact which helped to keep the number of allowances something less than 100% of the number eligible. For high income families the £13 allowance, net of taxes, amounted to only 6s. 6d., a sum which some felt hardly worth the bother of obtaining from the Post Office.

TABLE 91

Number of Children Eligible for Family Allowances,
and Estimated Number for Whom Allowances
Were Actually Being Claimed,
December 31, 1948

INCOME RANGE (IN POUNDS)	No. ELIGIBLE (IN THOUSANDS)	No. CLAIMED (IN THOUSANDS)
Under 135	82	82
135–250	1,342	1,342
250–500	2,284	2,284
500–750	483	483
750–1,000	184	184
1,000–2,000	180.5	175.5
2,000–3,000	35.2	20.1
3,000–5,000	20.2	3.4
5,000 and above	7.5	—
	4,618.4	4,574.0

In allocating family allowances to income ranges the number of allowances actually claimed on December 31, 1948, has been used. Compared with the estimated number of eligible children, it appears that about 1% of those eligible had not claimed allowances. In Table 91 it has been assumed that all eligible persons in families with incomes of less than £2,000 claimed allowances and that the percentage of eligible claimants above £2,000 actually obtaining allowances varied

allowances (as supplementary allowances under the various social security schemes) I propose a flat payment of 5s. per week per child or £13 annually both for income tax payers and for the insured population." John Maynard Keynes, *How to Pay for the War* (1940), p. 39.

14. The cost of income tax allowances was discussed in Ch. 10. For a fuller discussion of the comparative benefits of income tax allowances and family allowances, see Cartter, *Population Studies, 6,* 218–32.

inversely with the level of incomes. The estimated number of allowances claimed in Table 91 for each income group has been multiplied by £13 to obtain the amount of benefit for each group, as shown in column 1 of Table 92.

TABLE 92

Distribution of Miscellaneous Social Security Benefits
(In Thousand Pounds)

INCOME RANGE (IN POUNDS)	FAMILY ALLOWANCES	MILK AND WELFARE FOODS	TOTAL
Under 135	1,063	3,260	4,323
135–250	17,596	12,892	30,488
250–500	29,609	14,646	44,255
500–750	6,261	2,932	9,193
750–1,000	2,386	811	3,197
1,000–2,000	2,275	709	2,984
2,000–3,000	260	121	381
3,000–5,000	44	61	105
5,000–10,000	—	20	20
10,000 and above	—	—	—
	59,494	35,452	94,946

Expenditure on milk and welfare foods was more widely spread among income groups than most transfers. A large part of the expenditure on milk, although classified by the White Papers as a transfer, was a subsidy on retail milk. The remaining milk scheme was the provision of free milk in schools. Welfare foods consisted chiefly of items strong in vitamins, primarily available for expectant mothers and young children. Since many of these items were difficult to purchase elsewhere, they were used by persons in all income groups. The distribution in Table 92 assumes that per capita benefits were about twice as great in the three lowest income groups as they were in the £750–3,000 range, benefits to higher incomes becoming progressively smaller. Table 92 shows the estimated distribution of these miscellaneous social security benefits among income groups.

OTHER TRANSFERS

Armed Forces Release Leave Pay

Release leave pay of £21 million in 1948–49 was paid to the approximately 650,000 released members of the armed forces. This sum has been allocated in Table 93 to income ranges roughly in accordance with the number of wage earners in each group. The distribution has been weighted, however, in favor of the three lowest income groups, since (a) most of those demobilized in 1948–49 were young men who had entered service at the end of the war and (b) many of them did not return to work immediately, thus diminishing their total incomes for the fiscal year.

War Pensions and Service Grants

War pensions and service grants amounted to £86,177,000 in 1948–49, divided as follows:

1914 War	£35,620,000
1939 War	46,054,100
Medical service	4,502,000
Total	£86,177,000

Of this amount, £375,000 was paid in constant attendance allowances for 6,670 pensioners, £846,300 in unemployability allowances to 13,020 pensioners, £250,000 in lowered standard allowances to 10,160 pensioners, and the remainder for partial disablements.

As explained in the estimate of the under-£135 population in Chapter 11, three-fourths of those 70% (plus) disabled, one-tenth of all other partial disablements, one-half of those receiving lowered standard allowances, and all persons receiving constant attendance and unemployability allowances were estimated to have been in the lowest income group. (War pensions are not subject to tax, so that the income ranges correspond to personal income *before* such pensions.) The next highest income group is assumed to include one-third of the lowered standard allowances and partial disablement pensions in proportion to the total male population of that group. The other one-sixth of lowered standard allowances has been placed in the £250–500 range and remaining disablement pensions distributed to incomes above £250 in proportion to the male population. This estimated distribution is shown in Table 93.

Postwar Income Tax Credits

The Finance Act of 1941 provided that for the war years the extra tax paid by persons as the result of the lowering of the earned income allowance, age allowance, personal allowance, and the exemption limit should be credited to each taxpayer and repayment made after the war at a date to be determined.[15] These credits totaled £800 million for the war years 1941–46. Beginning in 1946–47 credits were released to men reaching the age of 65 and women of 60. Re-

15. *RCIR, 1942, Cmd. 6771* (1946), p. 20.

payments were £60 million and £56 million in the first two years and £18.8 million in 1948–49. If one had been married and had had an earned income of at least £1,500 in each of the five years of tax credits, a maximum of £325 might be reclaimed. Since repayment was made when a person reached normal retirement age, it should be allocated to the income group in which his retirement placed him rather than the group to which he belonged when he originally paid the extra taxes. The distribution of postwar tax credits repaid in Table 93 has therefore been reached by estimating the average tax saving for persons in each income group (where they were originally created) and then shifting these average savings down one group and multiplying by the number of males turned 65 within the year. (This number has been assumed to be proportional to the total number of over-65 males in each income group.)

TABLE 93

Allocation of Other Transfer Incomes
(In Thousand Pounds)

INCOME RANGE	ARMED FORCES LEAVE PAY	WAR PENSIONS	TAX CREDITS	TRAINING ALLOW- ANCES	SCHOLAR- SHIP AL- LOWANCES	TOTAL
(IN POUNDS)	1	2	3	4	5	6
Under 135	3,590	19,251	750	3,605	433	27,629
135–250	8,260	28,015	6,640	5,665	4,950	53,530
250–500	7,690	28,794	6,410	1,031	8,010	51,935
500–750	638	4,120	2,780	—	870	8,408
750–1,000	360	2,398	860	—	150	3,210
1,000–2,000	375	2,240	445	—	150	3,210
2,000–3,000	65	627	450	—	—	1,142
3,000–5,000	16	443	265	—	—	724
5,000–10,000	5	226	160	—	—	391
10,000–20,000	1	51	31	—	—	83
20,000 and above	—	12	9	—	—	21
Totals	21,000	86,177	18,800	10,301	14,563	150,841

Training Allowances

These consisted of allowances for traveling and lodging for transferred workers and wages and lodging allowances for trainees. Since the majority of persons benefiting from these allowances were either disabled persons, returning servicemen receiving vocational training, or displaced persons (European volunteer workers), the bulk of these benefits can be assumed to have gone to the lowest income groups. In Table 93 they have been divided among the three lowest income groups, 35%, 55%, and 10% respectively.

Scholarship and Maintenance Allowances

Of the £24 million government scholarships and allowances shown in Table 85 only £14½ million was the expenditure of the central government. Eighty per cent of this latter amount was spent under the further education and training scheme and the remaining amount for the emergency training of teachers. Most students, while in further education, can be claimed as dependents by their parents for income tax purposes and so are included as "children" in the family classification in Chapter 11. The benefits, therefore, must be allocated to their families, wherever they stand in the income scale. In Table 93 it has been assumed that 3% of these benefits went to the lowest income group, 34% to the £135–250 group, 55% to the £250–500 group, 6% to the £500–750 range, and 1% each to the two next highest income grades.[16]

SUMMARY. ALL TRANSFER INCOMES

All transfers of income to the private sector originating with the central government have now been allocated.[17] Table 94 summarizes the preceding sections, showing these transfers by type of benefit and by income range. Twenty-two per cent of all transfers are estimated to have been received by the lowest income group, and 47% and 26% by the two next highest groups. These figures indicate that a fairly substantial error would be made if one followed the usual practice of lumping all transfer incomes in the income range below £250, for less than 70% of transfers fall within this range in the estimate in Table 94. In 1937 Barna found that 84% of all social transfers went to incomes below £125 and 15% to incomes between £125 and £250.[18]

16. There were about 15,000 persons in full-time further education and approximately 150,000 taking part-time classes under the further education program. If the benefits to the latter were only about 10% as great per person as for full-time students, then average benefits were £200 for full-time and £20 for part-time. In terms of full-time units, the allocation of these benefits in Table 93 is the same as it would be if one assumed that as a percentage of the number of children in each income group students receiving allowances were .6% for the lowest income group, .7% for £135–500, .4% for £500–750, and .2% for £750–2,000. It is impossible to estimate the number of persons in each group actually receiving allowances, for probably more persons in the lower income groups were receiving small allowances for part-time courses, and more persons in the middle income groups were receiving large allowances for full-time education. The smaller percentage of persons receiving allowances in the middle income groups is likely, since most scholarships were based on parents' incomes.

17. With the exception of £12.5 million grants to universities, arts, and sciences which has been dealt with in Ch. 5 as an indivisible benefit. See also p. 207 n., above.

18. Barna, *Redistribution*, p. 79.

Even if we double these incomes to make them more comparable in real terms with 1948–49, it appears that transfers are more widely distributed than a decade ago. This would still be true, although to a slightly lesser extent, if one considered only the distribution of social security transfers. The postwar government policy of making most social security benefits available to all persons regardless of income has been primarily responsible for this shift. As all new insured persons fulfill the contribution requirements, this shift in the relative distribution of transfer incomes will be even more noticeable. It should be remembered, however, that many of these transfers were not exempt from tax (e.g. family allowances, old age and retirement pensions, and most nonsocial security transfers), so that the equalization effect is partially counteracted as regards posttax incomes.

TABLE 94

Estimated Distribution of All Transfer Incomes (*In Thousand Pounds*)

INCOME RANGE (IN POUNDS)	PENSIONS	HEALTH	UNEMPLOYMENT	MISCELLANEOUS	OTHER	TOTAL
	1	2	3	4	5	6
Under 135	86,904	7,240	11,290	4,323	27,629	137,386
135–250	195,646	29,780	5,927	30,488	53,530	315,371
250–500	50,106	27,190	2,963	44,255	51,935	176,449
500–750	48	1,220		9,193	8,408	18,869
750–1,000	13	389		3,197	3,768	7,367
1,000–2,000	4	352		2,984	3,210	6,550
2,000–3,000	2	65		381	1,142	1,590
3,000–5,000		41		105	724	870
5,000–10,000		16		20	391	427
10,000–20,000		6			83	89
20,000 and above		1			21	22
Totals	332,723	66,300	20,180	94,946	150,841	664,990

The distribution of transfers shown in Table 94 is the same as that in Table 13 of Chapter 5.

CHAPTER 17

The Allocation of Other Divisible Benefits

OTHER divisible expenditures were classified in Chapter 4 as consisting of all allocable services performed by the government. These expenditures, including funds spent on education, health, housing, subsidies on consumers' goods, etc. are intended to benefit specific income groups, and the benefits are fairly accurately measurable. Other divisible expenditures amounted to £1,010 million in 1948–49, and each type of expenditure program will be discussed separately in this chapter.[1]

EDUCATION

In 1948–49 about 6% of the nation's school-age children were being educated in public schools,[2] about 1% were in direct-grant (independent) schools, and the remainder were in grant-aided schools maintained by the Education Department. In allocating education benefits arising from central government expenditures for state-supported schools, it has been assumed that the type of school attended was a function of income. All children in families with incomes in excess of £1,000, plus 45% of those in the £750–1,000 income range, are assumed to have been in public schools not benefiting from government expenditures. (These are the 6% of children in the highest income families.) Children in direct-grant schools are assumed to have been in the £750–1,000 income range, and all other children are assumed to have attended local authority schools. Education benefits have been allocated on the basis of these assumptions, as shown in column 1 of Table 96.

HOUSING

Housing expenditures under the Ministry of Health were primarily grants to local authorities for the erection and subsidization of local housing and the financing of temporary housing under the Min-

1. For an itemization of these expenditures, see the detailed breakdown in Ch. 11, pp. 152–4.
2. Public schools in Britain correspond to American private (i.e. privately financed) schools.

istry of Works. Local authority and temporary housing were low income projects, and it is unlikely that families with incomes above about £500 benefited from these housing programs. In allocating benefits it has been assumed that one-half of all married couples in the lowest income group, one-quarter of all married couples in the £135–250 range, and one-tenth of the couples in the £250–500 range were living in local authority housing or temporary housing projects. Thus 16% of the housing expenditures have been allocated to the lowest income group, 49% and 35% to the next two groups respectively. This allocation is shown in column 2 of Table 96, below.

MINISTRY OF HEALTH AND THE
NATIONAL HEALTH SERVICE

The new national health service took effect in July of 1948, and many of the functions of the Ministry of Health were absorbed at that time. Those which became part of, or which were supplemental to, the new program will be allocated on the same basis as the national health service. That part of the Ministry of Health expenditure which dealt with general health and sanitary conditions, grants to various development areas and organizations, etc. has been left as an indivisible expenditure.[3]

The allocation of health expenditures is difficult, for one must choose between alternative methods of distribution. For example, one might attempt to allocate expenditures (a) on the basis of actual use of the program in its first nine months, or (b) on the basis of the supposed ideal of an equal per capita benefit. The first would heavily weight benefits in the low and middle income groups, for there was a much greater backlog of needed attention in the groups which previously could not afford expensive medical attention.[4] There was also less hesitancy in using the new program by those who were accustomed to the old health insurance program.

The second alternative is more nearly the ultimate aim of the national health insurance, i.e. equal service for all persons in need regardless of income. However, all persons had not registered and made use of the program, nor is it likely that all persons will do so in the future.

3. See p. 152.
4. There was not any great backlog of attention for diagnosed diseases, because of health insurance and charity hospitals. There was, however, an unpredicted backlog of persons needing such things as glasses, dental attention, and certain corrective treatment. It will be interesting to see if, in future years, the national health service provides a measurable benefit through preventive medicine. A decade or so of health statistics should throw some light on the trend of sickness and disease rates under a national medical program.

Neither of these alternative methods seemed perfectly satisfactory; so a compromise course has been chosen, based on an index weighted both by estimated participation in the health program and frequency of use.

By December of 1948 about 90% of the nation's population was registered with local doctors under the new health service.[5] In weighting the health index in Table 95 it will be assumed that registration was inversely related to income and that all persons in income groups below £1,000 had registered,[6] 90% in the £1,000–5,000 range, 75% in the £5,000–10,000 group, and 50% and 25% in the two highest income groups respectively.

No information is available concerning the extent to which persons in different income ranges actually availed themselves of the health services (i.e. number of calls, prescriptions filled, etc.). One's first guess would be that the lowest income groups made most frequent use of the program. For persons with incomes of less than £420, however, the national health service was little change from the old health insurance program, where one also went to the doctor of his choosing, had access to hospital facilities, and had necessary prescriptions filled. Perhaps the greatest gainers were persons in the middle income groups who had not been eligible for health insurance [7] and whose pride previously prevented them from making full use of charity and voluntary health agencies. The 1948–49 health report, in commenting on the increased number of patients in doctor's surgeries after July, 1948, remarked that "the increase was . . . most marked in areas where much practice was formerly private," i.e. where patients came from middle and upper income families.[8]

Without information on the frequency of use of the program, the best one can do is to allow for the differences in use by age groups. Dividing the population into three age groups, children (under 15 years), adults (15 to 65), and the elderly (over 65), we may refer to health statistics for clues on medical needs. For example, the average death rate per 1,000 persons for 1948 was 2.27 for children, 4.14 for adults, and 51.78 for the elderly. Of more than half a million cases of infectious diseases reported in 1948, 90.65% were children. In a sample inquiry conducted by the Ministry of Health it was found that the annual number of medical consultations per 100 persons (exclud-

5. *Cmd.* 7910, p. 262.
6. At least half of these persons were automatically registered, since they had been compulsorily insured under the old national health insurance program.
7. Voluntary contributors were accepted into the old insurance program, but the number of such contributors was quite small, including only a few persons whose incomes were slightly above £420.
8. *Cmd.* 7910, p. 123.

ing hospital in-patients and dental calls) was 300 for adults and 488 for elderly persons. The annual number of days of incapacity due to illness (excluding pregnancy) for this same sample was 718 per 100 persons for adults, and 1418 for the elderly. From such data it appears that elderly persons require more attention than the average adult 15 to 65 and that children require the most attention of the three age groups. In estimating the frequency of use, therefore, the following two assumptions have been made : (*a*) The over-65 age group requires three times as much medical attention per person as does the average 15 to 65 adult; (*b*) children under 15 require seven times as much attention as the average adult. (Benefits arising from pregnancy and childbirth are allotted to the child rather than to the mother; the number of childbirths is assumed to be reflected in the number of children in each income group.)

On the basis of the registration and age-use assumptions an index can be created to use in allocating health benefits. This is shown in Table 95.

TABLE 95

Index of the Relative Benefits from the National Health Service, by Income Group

INCOME RANGE (IN POUNDS)	No. OF PERSONS (IN THOUSANDS)			AGE-USE WEIGHTED	AGE-USE AND REGISTRATION WEIGHTED	INDEX
	CHILDREN	ADULTS	ELDERLY			
Under 135	370	2,365	1,063	8,144	8,144	6.32%
135–250	3,496	10,955	2,244	42,230	42,230	32.78
250–500	5,699	13,818	1,371	57,201	57,201	44.41
500–750	1,110	2,813	220	11,903	11,903	9.24
750–1,000	411	950	135	4,223	4,223	3.28
1,000–2,000	402	880	132	4,090	3,681	2.86
2,000–3,000	77.8	154.9	58	885	796	.62
3,000–5,000	44.2	78.6	30	478	430	.33
5,000–10,000	13.6	48.1	17	194	194	.14
10,000–20,000	2.5	13.0	4	42	21	.02
20,000 and above	.9	3.2	1	12	3	.003
						100%

Expenditures in the first nine months of the national health service, ending March 31, 1949, were £275.9 million. Various receipts and recoveries totaling £22 million reduced the net cost to £253.8 million for 1948–49. This was met partially by a £27 million contribution from the national insurance fund, the Exchequer cost being £226.8 million.[9]

The national health service account for 1948–49 was as follows:

SERVICE	EXPENDITURE	RECEIPTS	NET COST
Central council	£11,000		£11,000
Hospital, specialist, and ancillary services	145,077,500	£12,259,000	132,818,500
Local health services	10,233,000		10,233,000
General medical, dental, pharmaceutical, and ophthalmic services	90,391,500	463,500	89,928,000
Other services	30,191,542	9,343,900	20,847,642
Totals	£275,904,542	£22,066,400	253,838,142
Exchequer grants			226,838,142
National insurance fund contribution			27,000,000
			£253,838,142

To this amount the hospital expenditure and part of the general expenditure of the Ministry of Health may be added, making the total divisible expenditures on health for 1948–49 £270 million. These amounts are allocated in columns 3 and 4 of Table 96 on the basis of the index presented above.

ADMINISTRATION EXPENDITURE, MINISTRY OF LABOUR

These administration costs have been allocated to the three lowest income groups in proportion to benefits received from the various Ministry of Labour programs.[10] Therefore, roughly one-sixth went to the lowest income group, and one-half and one-third to the two next highest groups, as given in column 5 of Table 96.

EMPLOYMENT AND TRANSFERENCE

Employment and transference expenditures by the Ministry of Labour consisted of lodging and maintenance allowances, household

9. In the budget accounts the Exchequer contribution is estimated at £208.3 million, after the inclusion of transfers of £18.5 million from local superannuation funds. While the receipt of contributions and the payment of superannuation benefits may legitimately be considered as income and expenditure of the national health service, the transfer of previously accumulated superannuation funds from local to central government accounts is not considered here as income to the national health service.

10. Benefits are measured at factor cost; thus, administration expenses are considered to be part of the direct cost, and therefore direct benefits, of social security programs. General government administrative expenditures are, on the other hand, considered to be indivisible benefits.

removals, fares, and grants to national service hostels. One-third has been allocated to the lowest income group and two-thirds to the £135–250 group in column 6 of Table 96.

ADMINISTRATION, NATIONAL INSURANCE

Administration expenses of the Ministry of National Insurance are allocated in column 7 of Table 96 in proportion to all national insurance contributions.[11]

ADMINISTRATION, NATIONAL ASSISTANCE

National assistance administration expenditures are shown in column 8 of Table 96, being proportional to national assistance benefits.

UTILITY CLOTHING REBATES AND ASSISTANCE TO COTTON MANUFACTURING

Under the utility clothing scheme certain materials received subsidies to bring them within the utility price range. These can be allotted by reversing the method used in Chapter 14.[12] By doing this the percentage of utility clothing purchased by income ranges beginning with the lowest group is estimated at 7.2%, 27.2%, 43.9%, 15.3%, 4.7%, .9%, .3%, and nil for groups above £3,000. These amounts are shown in column 9 of Table 96.

SUBSIDY ON UTILITY FURNITURE

The benefits arising from the price subsidy on the manufacture of utility furniture are estimated in column 10; they are assumed proportional to personal expenditures on durable household goods.[13]

MINISTRY OF AGRICULTURE

Subsidies and other payments to farmers are distributed by use of the industry input-output method described in Chapter 15.[14] This division, given in column 11, allots roughly 88% to persons, 1% to government, and 3% to exports, the remainder being unallocable.

ROADS

The expenditure on roads should, perhaps, be divided among private motorists, general transport, and all persons as a communal benefit. The latter two are unallocable, so that only the portion benefiting private motorists (which is assumed to be 25% of total ex-

11. These have been allocated on the basis of *contributions* rather than *benefits*, because a large share of the administrative costs benefited new contributors who were not yet, in 1948–49, fully eligible for benefits.
12. See p. 186.
13. See Table 67, p. 174.
14. See p. 197.

penditures) has been included here. This amount is distributed in column 12 in proportion to private expenditures on motoring.[15]

Administration, Ministry of Pensions

Administration expenses connected with war pensions have been allocated in proportion to war pensions and allowances in column 13.

Fuel Operations

The Ministry of Fuel and Power incurred losses on the production and sale of open cast coal amounting to almost £3 million. This amount is allocated in column 14, using the industry input-output method.[16] About a third of the total is allocated to income groups, the remainder being export benefits or unallocable.

Trading Losses and Assistance to Industry; Ministry of Supply

In the raw material trading and manufacturing accounts of the Ministry of Supply, profits were made in trading in aluminum and nonferrous metals, but the losses on iron and steel and iron-and-steel scrap were sufficient to make the net trading loss almost £12 million.[17] Subsidies were also paid to the iron and steel industry amounting to roughly £8 million to help meet abnormal freight on iron ore, and losses on high cost steel and on iron and steel produced in agency factories for nongovernmental sales were £876 thousand. Another £235 thousand was paid in subsidies to British watch-making firms. These amounts—subsidies, trading losses, and agency factory losses in steel combined—have been distributed by the input-output method described in Chapter 15.[18] They are shown in columns 15 and 16 of Table 96.

Net Trading Expenditure, Ministry of Food

Food subsidies under the Ministry of Food amounted to £391 million in 1948–49.[19] Only £302 million had been budgeted, but the government's decision to absorb the increasing production cost of food items and keep prices stable during the year increased trading losses by almost £100 million. Most items were subsidized at the consumer level rather than "at the farm," and these subsidies will be directly allocated to consumers of the products. The benefits can be

15. See Table 67 above, p. 174.
16. See pp. 197–9.
17. See *Trading Accounts and Balance Sheets, 1948–49,* H.C. 14 (1950).
18. See p. 197.
19. For a detailed account of these expenditures see *H.C.* 14, pp. 74–109.

divided among rationed and unrationed foods, and those going to agriculture in general, as shown below.

Subsidy Item	Rationed Food	Un-rationed Food	Agricul-ture
	(In Thousand Pounds)		
Feed			24,229
Bacon and ham	16,964		
Cereals		124,088	5,000
Eggs	28,183		
Milk	44,294		
Dairy products, miscellaneous	59,797		
Oils and fats	7,413		
Potatoes and carrots		11,619	
Sugar	20,326		
Meat	57,521		
Tea	18,534		
Miscellaneous foods		—19,954	
Total trading losses	253,032	115,753	29,229
Less: miscellaneous levies and receipts	—312	—6,409	
Net trading loss	252,720	109,344	29,229
Combined total		391,293	

TABLE 96

Allocation of Other Divisible Benefits, 1948–49
(In Thousand Pounds)

Income Range (In Pounds)	Edu-cation	Ministry of Health Hous-ing	Health	National Health Service	Admin-istration, Ministry of Labour	Employment and Transference	Admin-istration, Ministry of National Insurance	Adm-istrat Min of Nat Assist
	1	2	3	4	5	6	7	8
Under 135	5,832	11,136	1,024	16,053	335	2,070	217	3,5
135–250	55,614	34,103	5,317	83,219	1,000	4,135	1,139	8
250–500	90,233	24,360	7,197	112,676	665	—	1,115	
500–750	17,833	—	1,490	23,470	—	—	217	—
750–1,000	2,058	—	530	8,331	—	—	78	—
1,000–2,000	—	—	460	7,264	—	—	60	—
2,000–3,000	—	—	101	1,575	—	—	12	—
3,000–5,000	—	—	50	838	—	—	5	—
5,000–10,000	—	—	24	355	—	—	2	—
10,000–20,000	—	—	3	50	—	—	1	—
20,000 and above	—	—	—	7	—	—	—	—
Personal benefits	171,570	69,599	16,197	253,838	2,000	6,205	2,846	4,4
Government	—	—	—	—	—	—	—	—
Exports	—	—	—	—	—	—	—	—
Unallocable	—	—	—	—	—	—	—	—
Total	171,570	69,599	16,196	253,838	2,000	6,205	2,846	4,4

Subsidies have been allocated to income groups in proportion to their expenditures on rationed and unrationed foods.[20] Subsidies benefiting agriculture in general, plus the sugar industry deficiency payment of £3.44 million, have been allocated by the industry input-output method. The results are presented in column 17 of Table 96.

ADMINISTRATION, FAMILY ALLOWANCES

The costs of administering the Family Allowances program were £1.24 million in 1948–49, and this amount has been allocated to income groups in proportion to the cash benefits from family allowances discussed in the preceding chapter.

SUMMARY, OTHER DIVISIBLE BENEFITS

All divisible benefits arising from government expenditures on goods and services have been allocated, and these are summarized in Table 96. Of the total £1,010 million, £977 million has been estimated to have benefited persons directly, £2 million to have benefited government, £7 million to exports, and the remaining £23 million has been classified as unallocable. This last amount was added to indivisible expenditures in the listing in Chapter 5.[21] The figures in column 19 of Table 96 are the same as those of Table 14 in Chapter 5.

Other divisible benefits have been estimated as averaging about £44 per tax family. The size of benefits per family varied directly with size of income up to an income level of about £500 and were nearly constant per family above that level.

20. See Table 67, p. 174.
21. See p. 50.

TABLE 96 (*continued*)

Board of Trade Subsidies	Furniture	Ministry of Agriculture, Payments	Roads	Administration, Ministry of Pensions	Fuel Operations	Ministry of Supply — Watches	Iron and Steel	Ministry of Food, Subsidies	Administration, Family Allowances	Total by Income Group
	10	11	12	13	14	15	16	17	18	19
44	1	3,170	62	854	61	8	39	25,705	22	70,321
86	4	14,529	336	236	218	34	219	126,765	366	329,617
32	8	19,741	938	276	353	62	388	164,370	617	424,901
08	4	4,531	759	184	112	27	229	35,225	130	85,519
01	2	1,896	916	107.	43	10	117	14,390	48	28,617
23	2	1,919	1,598	101	59	17	198	14,025	47	25,773
6	2	495	547	27	18	7	81	3,207	5	6,083
•	1	355	385	20	15	6	73	2,128	—	3,876
•	1	239	255	11	7	3	43	972	—	1,912
•	—	66	119	2	3	2	18	338	—	602
•	—	21	40	1	1	1	6	121	—	198
50	25	46,962	6,955	3,819	890	177	1,411	387,246	1,235	977,419
•	—	549	—	—	76	3	1,518	252	—	2,398
•	—	1,514	—	—	528	12	4,293	760	—	7,107
•	—	4,871	—	—	1,381	43	13,595	3,035	—	22,925
50	25	53,896	6,955	3,819	2,875	235	20,817	391,293	1,235	1,009,849

BIBLIOGRAPHY

Books

Barna, Tibor. *The Redistribution of Incomes through Public Finance in 1937*. Oxford, the Clarendon Press, 1945.

Beveridge, William H. *Full Employment in a Free Society*. London, George Allen and Unwin, 1944.

—— *Voluntary Action*. London, George Allen and Unwin, 1948.

Bowley, Arthur L. *The Change in the Distribution of the National Income, 1880–1913*. Oxford, the Clarendon Press, 1920.

—— ed. *Studies in the National Income*. Cambridge, Cambridge University Press, 1942.

—— *Wages and Income in the United Kingdom since 1860*. Cambridge, Cambridge University Press, 1937.

Brady, Robert A. *Crisis in Britain*. Berkeley, University of California Press, 1950.

Bray, F. Sewell. *The Measurement of Profit*. London, Oxford University Press, 1949.

—— *Social Accounts and the Business Enterprise Sector of the National Economy*. University of Cambridge Department of Applied Economics, Monograph No. 2. Cambridge, Cambridge University Press, 1949.

Butler, David E. *The British General Election of 1951*. London, Macmillan, 1952.

Campion, H. *Public and Private Property in Great Britain*. London, Oxford University Press, 1939.

Campion, H. and Daniels, G. W. *The Distribution of the National Capital*. Manchester, Manchester University Press, 1936.

Clark, Charles E. *Social Insurance in Britain*. Cambridge, Cambridge University Press, 1950.

Clark, Colin. *National Income and Outlay*. London, Macmillan, 1937.

Crawford, William S. and Broadley, H. *The People's Food*. London, William Heinemann, 1938.

Dalton, Hugh. *The Inequality of Incomes*. London, George Routledge and Sons, 1929.

De Jouvenal, Bertrand. *The Ethics of Redistribution*. Cambridge, Cambridge University Press, 1951.

—— *Problems of Socialist England,* tr. J. F. Huntington. London, the Batchworth Press, 1949.

Harrod, Roy. *And So It Goes On*. London, Rupert Hart-Davis, 1951.

———— *Are These Hardships Necessary?* London, Rupert Hart-Davis, 1947.

Hawtrey, Ralph G. *Economic Rebirth.* London, Longmans Green, 1946.

Hicks, J. R. and Hicks, U. K. *The Incidence of Local Rates in Great Britain.* NIESR, Occasional Papers, *8.* Cambridge, Cambridge University Press, 1945.

Hicks, J. R., Hicks, U. K., and Leser, C. E. V. *The Problem of Valuation for Rating. NIESR,* Occasional Papers, *7.* Cambridge, Cambridge University Press, 1944.

Hutchison, Keith. *The Decline and Fall of British Capitalism.* New York, Charles Scribner's Sons, 1950.

Keynes, John Maynard. *How to Pay for the War.* London, Macmillan, 1940.

Kuznets, Simon. *Shares of Upper Income Groups in Income and Savings.* New York, National Bureau of Economic Research, 1953.

Lewis, Roy and Maude, Angus. *The English Middle Classes.* London, the Phoenix House, 1949.

McCallum, Ronald B. *The British General Election of 1945.* London, Oxford University Press, 1947.

McGonigle, G. C. M. and Kirby, J. *Poverty and Public Health.* London, Victor Gollancz, 1936.

Madge, Charles. *War-time Pattern of Saving and Spending.* NIESR, Occasional Papers, *4.* Cambridge, Cambridge University Press, 1943.

Newcomer, Mable. "Estimate of the Tax Burden on Different Income Classes." *Studies in Current Tax Problems.* New York, the Twentieth Century Fund, 1937. Pp. 1–52.

Nicholas, Herbert G. *The British General Election of 1950.* London, Macmillan, 1951.

Orr, J. B. *Food, Health and Income.* London, Macmillan, 1936.

Orr, J. B. and Lubbock, D. *Feeding the People in Wartime.* London, Macmillan, 1940.

Radice, Edward A. *Savings in Great Britain.* London, Oxford University Press, 1939.

Rathbone, Eleanor. *Family Allowances.* London, George Allen and Unwin, 1949.

Reddaway, W. B. *The Economics of a Declining Population.* London, George Allen and Unwin, 1946.

Rignano, Eugenio. *The Social Significance of Death Duties,* tr. Dr. Shultz. London, Noel Douglas, n.d.

Rowntree, Seebohm. *Poverty and Progress.* London, Longmans, Green, 1941.

Rowntree, Seebohm and Lavers, G. R. *Poverty and the Welfare State.* London, Longmans, Green, 1951.

Seers, Dudley. *The Levelling of Incomes since 1938.* Oxford, Basil Blackwell, 1951.

Shirras, G. Findlay and Rostas, L. *The Burden of British Taxation.* NIESR, Economic and Social Studies, *2.* Cambridge, Cambridge University Press, 1942.

Stamp, Josiah. *British Incomes and Property.* London, P. S. King, 1927.
———— *The National Capital.* London, P. S. King, 1937.

Thompson, D. *Equality.* Current Problems Series, No. 29. Cambridge, Cambridge University Press, 1949.

Wedgwood, Josiah. *The Economics of Inheritance.* London, G. Routledge, 1929.

Wickwar, Hardy and Wickwar, Margaret. *The Social Services.* London, Bodley Head, 1949.

Williams, Francis. *Socialist Britain.* New York, Viking Press, 1949.

Williamson, R. V. and Greene, L. S., eds. *Five Years of British Labour, 1945–50.* Reprinted from the *Journal of Politics, 12* (1950).

Wilson, Thomas. *Modern Capitalism and Economic Progress.* London, Macmillan, 1950.

Worswick, G. D. N. and Ady, P. H., eds. *The British Economy, 1945–50.* London, the Clarendon Press, 1952.

Wright, David McCord. "Income Redistribution Reconsidered." *Income, Employment and Public Policy.* New York, W. W. Norton, 1948. Pt. II, ch. 1.

Articles and Pamphlets

Barna, Tibor. "The Burden of Death Duties in Terms of an Annual Tax." *RES, 9* (1941), 28–39.
———— "Indirect Taxes, Subsidies and the Cost of Living." *RES, 10* (1942), 53–61.
———— "The Interdependence of the British Economy." *JRSS, 115* (1952), 29–77.

Bowley, Marion. "Local Rates and Housing Subsidies." *RES, 8* (1940), 33–43.

Cartter, Allan M. "Income Tax Allowances and the Family in Great Britain." *Population Studies, 6* (1953), 218–32.
———— *Memorandum on British Income Tax Allowances and Family Allowances.* Royal Commission on Taxation, Document No. 63. 1951.
———— "A New Method of Relating British Capital Ownership and Estate Duty Liability to Income Groups." *Eca, 20* (1953), 247–58.

Dalton, Hugh. "The Measurement of the Inequality of Incomes." *EJ, 30* (1920), 348–61.

Edelberg, G. Victor. "Flexibility of the Yield of Taxation." *JRSS, 103* (1940), 153–79.

Fijalkowski-Bereday, G. Z. "The Equalizing Effects of the Death Duties." *OxEP,* n.s., *2* (1950), 176–96.

Fisher, Allan G. B. "Alternative Techniques for Promoting Equality in a Capitalist Society." *AER Supplement, 40* (1950), 356–68.

Fisher, Irving. "Income in Theory and Income Taxation in Practice."
  Eca, 5 (1937), 1–55.
Galbraith, Kenneth. "Europe's Great Last Chance." *Harper's Magazine,*
  198 (1949), 41–8.
Jones, D. Caradog. "Pre-war and Post-war Taxation." *JRSS, 90* (1927),
  685–718.
Kaldor, Nicholas. "The Income Burden of Capital Taxes." *RES, 9*
  (1942), 138–57.
Kuznets, Simon. *Shares of Upper Income Groups in Income and Savings.*
  NBER Occasional Papers, No. 35. 1950.
Langley, Kathleen. "The Distribution of Capital in Private Hands in
  1936–38 and 1946–47." *BOxIS, 12* (1950), 339–59; *13* (1951), 33–54.
Lydall, H. F. "A Pilot Survey of Incomes and Savings." *BOxIS, 13*
  (1951), 257–91.
Macy, C. Ward. "Social Security Taxes in the War Finance Program."
  JPE, 51 (1943), 135–47.
Mallet, Bernard. "A Method of Estimating Capital Wealth from Estate
  Duty Statistics." *JRSS, 71* (1908), 65–84.
Metzler, Lloyd A. "Effects of Income Redistribution." *REStat, 25*
  (1943), 49–57.
Musgrave, Richard A. and others. "The Distribution of Tax Payments by
  Income Groups: A Case Study for 1948." *NTJ, 4* (1951), 1–53.
Nicholson, J. L. "Variations in Working Class Family Expenditure."
  JRSS, 112 (1949), 359–411.
Peacock, Alan T. and Berry, D. "A Note on the Theory of Income Re-
  distribution." *Eca, 18* (1951), 83–90.
Pettengill, Robert B. "Tax Burdens among Income Groups." *AER, 30*
  (1940), 60–71.
"Poverty Ten Years after Beveridge." *Planning, 19* (1952), 21–40.
Lord Samuel. "The Taxation of the Various Classes of the People." *JRSS,*
  82 (1919), 143–82.
Sandral, D. M. "The Burden of Taxation on the Various Classes of the
  Community." *JRSS, 94* (1931), 83–94.
Schulz, T. "Family Expenditures in 1949," *BOxIS, 13* (1951), 128–40.
——— "Working Class Household Expenditure in 1948." *BOxIS, 12*
  (1950), 81–97.
Stauffacher, Charles. "The Effect of Governmental Expenditures and
  Tax Withdrawals upon Income Distribution, 1930–1939." *Public Policy,*
  2 (1941), 232–61.
Tarasov, Helen. "Who Does Pay the Taxes?" *Social Research Supple-
  ment, 4* (1942), 1–48.
——— *Who Pays Taxes?* TNEC, Monograph No. 3. 1941.
Weaver, Findlay. "Taxation and Redistribution in the United Kingdom."
  REStat, 32 (1950), 201–13.
Yntema, Dwight B. "Measures of the Inequality in the Personal Distribu-
  tion of Wealth or Income." *JASA, 28* (1933), 423–33.

Publications of Her Majesty's Stationery Office

EXPENDITURES

Civil Estimates for 1948–49, H. C. 68, 1–10 (1948) ; *for 1949–50, H. C.* 77, 1–10 (1949).
Report of the Ministry of Health, 1948–49, Cmd. 7910 (1950) ; *1949–50, Cmd.* 8342–3 (1951).
Report of the Ministry of Labour and National Service, 1948–49, Cmd. 8017 (1950).
Report of the Ministry of National Insurance, 1944–49, Cmd. 7955 (1950).
Report of the Ministry of Pensions, 1948–49, H. C. 260 (1949).
Report of the National Assistance Board, 1948–49, Cmd. 7767 (1949).

FINANCE

Finance Accounts of the United Kingdom for the Financial Year 1948–49, H. C. 189 (1949).
Finance Act of 1948: 11 and 12 Geo. VI, ch. 15, H. C. (1948).
Financial Statement, 1948–49, H. C. 105 (1948) ; *1949–50, H. C.* 124 (1949).
Public Income and Expenditure, 1949–50, H. C. 151 (1949).

GOVERNMENT PERIODICALS

Labour and Industry in Britain, Central Statistical Office.
Ministry of Labour Gazette, Ministry of Labour.
Monthly Digest of Statistics, Central Statistical Office.
Registrar General's Returns of Births, Deaths, and Marriages, Registrar General.

NATIONAL INCOME ESTIMATES

An Analysis of the Sources of War Finance and an Estimate of the National Income and Expenditure in 1938, 1940, and 1941, Cmd. 6347 (1942).
Economic Survey for 1947, Cmd. 7046 (1947) ; *for 1948, Cmd.* 7344 (1948) ; *for 1949, Cmd.* 7647 (1949) ; *for 1950, Cmd.* 7915 (1950) ; *for 1951, Cmd.* 8195 (1951).
National Income and Expenditure, 1946–48, Cmd. 7649 (1949) ; *National Income and Expenditure of the United Kingdom, 1946 to 1949, Cmd.* 7933 (1950) ; *1946 to 1950, Cmd.* 8203 (1951).

TAXATION

Report of the Commissioners of Customs and Excise, 1949, Cmd. 7834 (1949) ; *1950, Cmd.* 8120 (1951).
Report of the Commissioners of Inland Revenue, 1938, Cmd. 5865 (1939) ; *1939, Cmd.* 6099 (1940) ; *1940, Cmd.* 6769 (1946) ; *1941,*

Cmd. 6770 (1946); *1942, Cmd.* 6771 (1946); *1943, Cmd.* 6772 (1946); *1944, Cmd.* 6773 (1946); *1945, Cmd.* 6774 (1946); *1946, Cmd.* 7067 (1947); *1947, Cmd.* 7362 (1948); *1948, Cmd.* 7738 (1949); *1949, Cmd.* 8052 (1950); *1950, Cmd.* 8103 (1951).

MISCELLANEOUS

Annual Abstract of Statistics, No. 86, 1938–48, Central Statistical Office (1949); *No. 87, 1938–49* (1950); *No. 88, 1938–50* (1952).

The British Broadcasting Corporation; Annual Report and Accounts for the Year 1948–49, Cmd. 7779 (1949).

Central Health Services Council; Report for Year Ended Dec. 31, 1949, H. C. 84 (1950).

Co-operative Societies, Statistical Summary, 1939–49, Registry of Friendly Societies (1950).

Education in 1949, Cmd. 7957 (1950).

Employment Policy, Cmd. 6527 (1944).

Food Consumption Levels in the United Kingdom, Cmd. 7842 (1949).

Friendly Societies, Statistical Summary, 1939–49, Registry of Friendly Societies (1951).

Government Proposals for an Industrial Injuries Insurance Scheme, Cmd. 6551 (1944).

Government Proposals for Social Insurance Generally and for Family Allowances, Cmd. 6550 (1944).

Health Services in Britain, British Information Services (1948).

Housing Summary, Cmd. 8025 (1950).

Industrial Assurance, Statistical Summary, 1939–49, Office of Industrial Assurance Commissioner (1950).

Industrial Productivity, Cmd. 7991 (1950).

Interim Index of Retail Prices, Ministry of Labour and National Service (1950).

Mechanically Propelled Road Vehicles, Great Britain, Ministry of Transport, Return No. 144 (1948).

Memoranda Presented to the Royal Commission, Royal Commission on Population Papers, 5 (1950).

National Debt, 1938–39 to 1949–50, Cmd. 8058 (1950).

Overseas Food Corporation; Reports and Accounts for 1948–49, H. C. 252 (1949).

Report of the Committee on National Debt and Taxation (Colwyn Committee), *Cmd.* 2800 (1927).

Report of the Committee on the Taxation of Trading Profits, Cmd. 8189 (1951).

Report of the Economics Committee, Royal Committee on Population Papers, 3 (1950).

Report of the Inter-departmental Committee on Social and Economic Research, Cmd. 7537 (1948).

Report of the Royal Commission on Betting, Lotteries, and Gaming, 1949–51, Cmd. 8190 (1951).

Report of the Royal Commission on Population, Cmd. 7695 (1949).

Social Insurance and Allied Services (report by Sir William Beveridge) *Cmd.* 6404 (1942).

Social Services in Britain, British Information Services (1948).

Statement of Government Policy Relating to the Establishment of a National Health Service, Cmd. 6502 (1944).

Tables Relating to Employment and Unemployment in Great Britain, Ministry of Labour and National Service (1948).

Trading Accounts and Balance Sheets, 1948–49, H. C. 14 (1950).

United Kingdom Balance of Payments, 1946–50, Cmd. 8065 (1950).

Index

(Italicized numbers indicate pages with tables)

Stamp, J., 232
Stauffacher, C., 4–5, 11n., 12, 233
Stocks (*see* Share index)
Subsidies:
    classification of, 47–8;
    farm, 226–7;
    food, 227–8;
    manufacturing, 226–7
Succession duty, 42, 164
Sugar duty, *170, 179, 188*
Surtax:
    changes in, 117;
    distribution of, *39*, 158–9;
    incomes liable to, 158;
    rates and regulations, 155–6;
    receipts, *35*, 38–9, 117, 158

Tarasov, H., 3n., 233
Tax family:
    composition of, *26, 28, 81–2*;
    definition of, 24, *27*;
    and U.S. "consumer unit," 81–2
Tax revenue, *35*, 37–45;
    lag in receipts, 5, 162;
    and level of income, *70*, 84;
    in 1937, 66–71;
    by type of tax, 71–2
Taxes:
    Barna's estimates for 1937, 66–7;
    customs and excise duties, *43*, 169–89;
    direct, 37–42, 71, 155–68;
    distribution of, 37ff., 54ff.;
    incidence of, 14ff.;
    indirect, 43–4, 169–204;
    on nonpersonal income, *41*, 160–3;
    percentage of income, 57, 84, 86;
    on personal income, *39*, 155–9;
    on profits, *41*, 160–3;
    receipts from, *35*, 37–45;
    regulations, 155ff.;
    summary allocation, *44*, 54–5;
    U.S., 82–4;
    on wealth, *42*, 71, 163–8
Tea:
    duty on, 170, 178, *188;*
    rationing, 178

Thompson, D., 232
Tobacco:
    expenditure on, *175;*
    imports, 175–6;
    old age tobacco duty relief, 208–9, *210;*
    taxes on, 170, 175–6, *188*
Trade unions (*see* Societies)
Transfers:
    classification, *35*, 46–7, 152–4, 207;
    definition, 31, 46, 205;
    distribution of, *47, 52*, 205–20;
    tax exempt, 138–9;
    U.S., 82–3

Undistributed profits:
    changes in, 75, 86–7;
    comparison with U.S., 86–7;
    definition, 31;
    distribution as imputed income, 143–4;
    share index, 148–51;
    tax on, 40–1, 160–3
Unemployment (*see* Employment)
Unemployment compensation:
    allocation of benefits, *214, 220;*
    national assistance, 209, 213–4;
    provisions, 213–4

Wages, 29, *30, 133,* 157
Wealth (*see* Capital, private)
Weaver, F., 4–5, 233
Wedgewood, J., 103n., 232
White Papers on national income, 34, 39n., 130–1, 137–8, 172, 234
Wickwar, H. and M., 232
Williams, F., 78, 232
Williamson, R. V. and Greene, L. S., 232
Wilson, T., 232
Wine (*see* Alcoholic beverages)
Wireless services (*see* BBC; Radio and television)
Workmen's compensation, 212
Worswick, G. D. N. and Ady, P. H., 232
Wright, D. M., 232

Yield of capital, 104–7, 147
Yntema, D. B., 73, 233